Chicken Soup for the Soul

for the Soul®

Family Matters

Chicken Soup for the Soul: Family Matters
101 Unforgettable Stories about Our Nutty but Lovable Families
Jack Canfield, Mark Victor Hansen, Amy Newmark, Susan M. Heim.
Foreword by Bruce Jenner

The publisher gratefully acknowledges the many publishers and individuals who granted Chicken Soup for the Soul permission to reprint the cited material.

Front and back cover illustration courtesy of iStockphoto.com/skeeg (© Shannon Keegan).Back cover photo courtesy of iStockphoto.com/AntiGerasim. Interior photos courtesy of iStockphoto.com/ PictureLake (© Ken Brown)

Cover and Interior Design & Layout by Pneuma Books, LLC
For more info on Pneuma Books, visit www.pneumabooks.com

Distributed to the booktrade by Simon & Schuster. SAN: 200-2442

Publisher's Cataloging-in-Publication Data
(Prepared by The Donohue Group)

Chicken soup for the soul : family matters : 101 unforgettable stories about our
  nutty but lovable families / [compiled by] Jack Canfield, Mark Victor Hansen,
  Amy Newmark, [and] Susan M. Heim ; foreword by Bruce Jenner.

      p. ; cm.

  Summary: A collection of 101 true personal stories from regular people about their
  families and relatives.
  ISBN: 978-1-935096-55-9

  1. Families--Literary collections. 2. Families--Anecdotes. I. Canfield, Jack, 1944- II.
Hansen, Mark Victor. III. Newmark, Amy. IV. Heim, Susan M. V. Jenner, Bruce, 1949-
VI. Title: Family matters

PN6071.F2 C45 2010
810.8/02/03525   2010931575

Chicken Soup for the Soul®

Family Matters

101 Unforgettable Stories about Our Nutty but Lovable Families

Jack Canfield,
Mark Victor Hansen,
Amy Newmark and Susan M. Heim
Foreword by Bruce Jenner

Chicken Soup for the Soul Publishing, LLC
Cos Cob, CT

www.chickensoup.com

Contents

❸

~Newlyweds and Oldyweds~

❹

~Happily Ever Laughter~

❺

~Family Fun~

❻
~Relatively Strange~

❼
~Kids Will Be Kids~

❽

~On the Road~

❾

~Not So Grave~

⑩
~The Serious Side~

Foreword

Every family seems a bit dysfunctional when you get to know it well. No one seems to think his or her own family is "normal." So if we are *all* a bit abnormal, then that becomes the new normal. Every family has its unusual members — the ones who make holidays *so* interesting, who make funerals a minefield, who have to be "managed" at weddings, and so on.

Family *matters*. And there are always lots of family matters to discuss in any modern family, especially mine. In my sixty years, I have sure experienced a lot of family, and my family is the most important, most rewarding, most challenging, and most wonderful part of my life.

I have had my share of family ups and downs, including the loss of my brother at age eighteen, but I am happy about the journey I have taken. My childhood was happy and in my adult years I've been married three times and I have ten children. The most exciting thing in life and the most difficult thing in life is family. With ten children, it does get complicated! Not only do I have to deal with being a husband to a strong and accomplished woman, but I also have to deal with the massive personalities of the children. When you're dealing with this many people your life is very full. Dealing with a large family and large personalities makes the decathlon look simple.

It is amazing how different each kid is. There is a debate about genetics versus upbringing. The kids in each family were brought up the same way as each other and yet they are all so different. I believe that it's genetics that really determine who we are, with a little sprinkling of "upbringing" on top.

With my first wife, Chrystie Crownover, I had my first son and my first daughter. Burt, who is thirty-two, has grown up to be one of those kids who is going to do it on his own. I respect him for that. He is not afraid to work but only if it is for himself. He only lasted three months in the one office job that he had, selling telecommunications services over the phone. At least he learned not to take rejection personally, which is great because this hardworking kid has now combined his love of auto racing and his knowledge of the Internet in a new business that he has been working on for years. In the meantime, being an entrepreneur, he pays the bills with his dog training and boarding business. His sister, my beautiful and very smart daughter Casey, is thirty, and is married to a great guy she first met at Boston College. They gave me my very first grandchild, Francesca Marino, who is a year old now.

With my second wife, Linda Thompson, I had two more sons. Brandon is twenty-nine and has the most talent in the family. When he was a teenager he banged himself up on a Motocross bike so he decided to learn the guitar while he was recuperating. It turned out he was really good. When he quit college in his junior year to pursue his passion, music, I was okay with that. I believe that you have achieved success when you can't tell the difference between work and play. Brandon is one of those kids who doesn't tell you anything as he goes along. Even though I am a pilot, he didn't tell me that he was getting his pilot's license until he already had it. He did the same thing with his music. One day he casually mentioned to me that he was performing his first live gig at the Malibu Inn. I didn't even know he had a band. It was one of those great nights as a father. Brandon got up there and sang and played his own songs and he was phenomenally good.

Now Brandon and his girlfriend, Leah Felder, whose dad Don was the lead guitarist for the Eagles, are engaged, and are recording their first album for Warner Bros. Brandon grew up with a recording studio in his house. His stepfather was producer David Foster, an icon in the music world. Brandon and his brother Brody, who is twenty-seven, appeared with their mother in an early family reality show called *The Princes of Malibu*, which featured them living with their stepfather. The show didn't last long but it is funny that my two sons were in a reality show about family long before *Keeping Up with the Kardashians*. It must be in our genes. That early TV exposure launched Brody's career on MTV and he is now on the reality show *The Hills*, and is also well known for dating beautiful women!

Now with my new bride of twenty years, Kris, I have an even bigger family and I have had to learn a new set of rules—how to be a stepdad. Being a stepdad is very difficult. You're living with the stepchildren more than with your biological children, but you're not their real dad and they don't let you forget it. Although I got along very well with Kris's first husband, Robert Kardashian, my oldest stepchild Kourtney had a hard time accepting me as her stepfather in the beginning. She wore black for the first year of our marriage! Kourtney, who is now thirty-one, was just entering adolescence at that time, which helps explain it, although she continues to be tough and stubborn about what she wants. As time went on, Kourtney and I developed a very good relationship and it has improved even more now that she is a mother. We welcomed a new grandchild into the Kardashian side of the family almost a year ago, Mason, who is the son of Kourtney and Scott Disick.

These three Kardashian girls are very smart businesswomen like their mother, and I look forward to them all out-earning me. Kimberly, who is twenty-nine, is the most motivated of the three. She never stops working. She was a little younger when I became her stepfather and she and I have always had a good relationship. Khloe is the youngest, at twenty-six, and she was so young when I joined the family that we always got along really well.

That leaves one more Kardashian to discuss, Rob, who is twenty-three, and who we finally got out of the house recently, although he moved in with Khloe and her husband, Lamar Odom. That kid has lived a very cushy life with a doting mother and three older sisters. But he is very smart, and majored in business, and I expect him to do very well with our business partner who is teaching him the ropes as they develop the family's PerfectSkin line of personal care products. Rob was devastated by the sudden loss of his father to cancer in 2003, at only age fifty-nine, so he is still overcoming that. And he is quite a perfectionist—he lines up his shirts by color—so we'll see who he ends up with.

This brings me to my little angels, Kendall, who is turning fifteen, and Kylie who is thirteen. Kris and I had children with people we didn't even want to be married to anymore, so it made sense to have kids together. These girls are really growing up in the public eye, between the TV show and their other activities. Kendall is already modeling for the Wilhelmina agency, and Kylie is waiting for her turn, but I told her she has to wait until she's fourteen, which doesn't make her happy. I've learned not to take her displeasure personally—I'm a professional father when it comes to young women and their hormones. But Kylie has a closer personality to Kourtney than anyone else because of her tough independence, so she will be fun to watch.

They are all fun to watch. And I know many of you enjoy watching them too. Kris and I have been starring on the ultimate family TV show, *Keeping Up with the Kardashians*, on E! for the last four years, along with all six of Kris's children and guest appearances from my older children. Many of you have been watching the ups and downs of our very colorful lives. By the way, it is all true. We really do act that way!

I think I am viewed as the stable guy in this mix of families and ex-wives and children. The Jenner/Kardashian household certainly swirls around me every episode, with so many bizarre events that you can see why that old adage "truth is stranger than fiction" is so wise.

Being in the show does not affect how the family operates. We really are who you see. We love each other, fight with each other, and stick up for each other. The bottom line is we all love and respect each other. We are a tight family and we have been through a lot together—divorces, the controversy over the OJ Simpson trial when Robert Kardashian undertook OJ's defense. His attitude was that *someone* had to represent him, no matter what he thought of his guilt or innocence, and Robert had been his friend in college. Robert's death was a terrible blow to the family. And then there is all the media furor. The show has actually made the family tighter. It's not really a show about three crazy girls running around and having high-profile lives, but about a real family... a tight family. You see that at the end of every episode—the show always ends with the family making up and enjoying each other once again.

Everyone makes mistakes as they grow up. As a parent you just have to keep an open mind, lead by example, and give kids room to grow up. Kim, for instance, snuck off to Las Vegas when she was just nineteen and married some guy and then didn't tell anyone. Kourtney figured it out after a while and went online and found the marriage record in the Las Vegas court. That marriage lasted a couple of years and ended badly. And just to show you that kids do listen to us, back then I told Kim that it was okay to get this first marriage out of the way while she was young and she told me I was an idiot. Then Khloe, who we thought was the least likely to get married, met Lamar and married him in two weeks, and I overheard Kim telling Khloe that it was good to get the first one out of the way while young! By the way, Khloe's marriage seems to be working well, so we're happy about that.

Khloe, who is so sweet, made her own mistake recently, had a couple of drinks with friends and then drove home. She was pulled over and got a DUI. It has been a year and a half of hell for her, between the media and all the consequences for this in California. It was a big mistake, but it was a good mistake: no one was hurt; there was no accident; and she learned a valuable lesson. I wasn't mad, although she would have a problem with me if she did it again.

It could have been a lot worse. Three months after I won my gold for the United States in the Olympic decathlon in 1976, my younger brother Burt was killed in an auto accident that was his fault. He was only eighteen. You never get over something like that. I still have two sisters. Pam is older than me. She was always perfect—a great student and athlete who studied seven hours a night. She married a tax attorney and they live in Florida and Wyoming, having quite a nice life. Lisa is sixteen years younger than me, so we didn't really grow up together, but she and my mom live in Idaho now so I see them there. My mom, by the way, is in her eighties, and she got remarried a few years ago to a ninety-year-old guy. So now I have a stepdad too.

Growing up, I was dyslexic and had low self-esteem. Everyone could read better than I could. So sports became my refuge, a place where I could excel and where I could bash into smart guys on the football field. My parents never encouraged me to do sports — they were just there for me. Back in those days, parents didn't routinely attend their kids' sporting events the way they do today. But I would look over at the stands during a basketball game and the only parents in the stands would be mine. My dad was a real hero. He was in the Fifth Ranger Battalion and landed on Omaha Beach. He got a Purple Heart and is buried at Arlington. He was a great example for me. I try to be a good example to my children as well. Kids watch everything their parents do.

Family is what really counts in our lives. My life is all about my family, first and foremost, so when I was asked to write the foreword for *Chicken Soup for the Soul: Family Matters*, I jumped at the chance. No matter what hurdles your family puts in front of you, no matter how tough the ups and downs, no matter how unpleasant the discourse they throw at you, raising a family and being a part of a family is a race worth running. Chicken Soup for the Soul has always been a great source of inspiration, comfort, understanding, and humor about family life, and I loved their first book on this subject, *Chicken Soup for the Soul: All in the Family*. This new volume of stories that you hold in your hands really resonates with me — the stories are so funny, so outrageous, and so real. I hope you will enjoy these great stories as much as I did. They certainly rival the ones I live every day.

~Bruce Jenner

Forebear...ance

*Nothing is so soothing to our self-esteem
as to find our bad traits in our forebears.
It seems to absolve us.*

~Van Wyck Brooks

A Guy for All Seasons

To solve any problem, here are three questions to ask yourself:
First, what could I do? Second, what could I read?
And third, who could I ask?
~John Rohn

If you've got a problem, my father's got just the guy for you. After representing alleged organized crime members in court for most of his career, my father likes to think he's connected. When he can't be the "go-to guy" himself, he will settle as the "go-to-go-to guy." Among his army of consultants, there's his Doctor Guy, his Directions Guy, his Business Guy, his Fireworks Guy, and his Upper East Side Restaurant Guy. He's a Guy-necologist.

His Interior Decorator Guy is a large Italian man named Val. Before meeting Val, my father's decorating style could be described as "post-modern bachelor." He was content to cover his walls with sports memorabilia and paintings of clowns. Now, his apartment is furnished with gaudy Italian furniture and esoteric framed artwork. These include black-and-white photos of ornate vases, and prints of ink drawings of horse sculptures and Corinthian Greek columns.

When his stepson, Sean, was kicked out of college for academic deficiency, my father contacted his Admissions Guy at a local community college not known for its academic integrity. I think its motto is "We Take Discover Card." The guy came through, and Sean was quickly matriculated. Anytime I ask about Sean, my father says, "Did I tell you how I got him into college?"

The first time I called one of my father's Guys, I was fifteen years old and looking for a summer job. I had a vision of working at the local park, passing out basketballs and scheduling tennis court reservations. A city job like that, my father told me, required some kind of inside connection. "I think I may have a guy for that," he said.

The next day, my father called me, beginning the conversation with "Write down this number." These four words always signaled that my father had found his connection. "Ask for Lou. He knows about summer jobs."

I called the number, and then nearly hung up when I heard the greeting. "Chicken and Ribs. This is Lou. How can I help you?" Chicken and Ribs was a fast food restaurant located a few blocks from my home that displayed a permanent "Help Wanted" sign in the window, since most teenagers have enough acne problems without subjecting their pores to gaseous chicken grease.

"Hi. I'm Bernie Rubinstein's son. He mentioned that you may have some information about job opportunities at the town park."

"I don't know nothing about the park, but we have a part-time opening here if you want."

This was the first of many disappointments with my father's Guys. Most were not experts at all.

When I have a relapse of my hypochondria, my father insists that I call his Doctor Guy, my Uncle Dennis. Uncle Dennis is a talented, but minimalist physician. He rarely prescribes antibiotics because everything sounds to him like nothing. When his wife, Aunt Emily, was having trouble breathing, he wasn't alarmed. A few weeks later, she nearly died of pneumonia. Knowing my uncle's history of conservative diagnoses, I'd sometimes upset my father by challenging the ability of one of his Guys.

"Your Uncle Dennis is a brilliant doctor," he'd argue. "He read *Hawaii* in one night."

At college, I got an urgent call from my father. "My friend David's daughter has a problem," he said. "She has to write an essay or something for freshman English. I told her that you're a writer, and I gave her your number." If my Bar Mitzvah made me a man, this phone call had made me a Guy.

A few hours later, David's daughter called. "Your dad said I should call you. I have to write an essay on how I could use an ordinary object in an unordinary way." Only able to think of vulgar ideas, I told her I wasn't very creative with that kind of assignment. If she wrote it, however, I'd be happy to check her spelling.

Eventually, I was my father's Theater Guy, Movie Guy, Writing Guy, and French Dessert Guy. Half the time that people called me for advice on my supposed specialty, I had no idea what they were talking about.

Sometimes, my father's Guys could have been, just as easily, my Guys. In these cases, my father still insisted on acting as the Guy liaison. A few years ago, I wanted to take a date to my cousin Mark's wedding. I asked my father what he thought, and he said that he'd take care of it. My cousin became his Wedding Invite Guy. "I got you an extra invite to the wedding," my father proudly reported.

When I was ten, my parents divorced, and my mother started seeing Jerry, one of the stars of her theater group. Jerry quickly became my father's understudy when he took over his role as man of our household. He acted as my unofficial stepfather for almost ten years. In many ways, he was as much of an influence on me as my father was. It was Jerry who taught me about movies, theater, and writing—three of the things for which I eventually became my father's Guy.

My father resented that Jerry lived in our house, in direct opposition with the alimony agreement. I was somewhat shocked, therefore, when my father called our house once and asked to speak with Jerry. He had a job for him.

Using his theatrical directing abilities, Jerry worked with my father's clients to help them act more innocent on the stand. Jerry had made the transformation from Homewrecking Guy to Acting Coach Guy. By getting divorced, my father didn't lose a wife; he gained a Guy.

~Gary Rubinstein

2

Chicken Soup for the *Soul*

The Day Dad Shot Conan

The nightmare is you spend the rest of your life being funny at parties and then people say "Why didn't you do that when you were on television?"

~Conan O'Brien

"Come quick, your dad just shot Conan!" my mother screamed into the phone.

"Conan who?" my brother asked.

"You know... Conan, the red-headed guy on the late show."

"Huh?"

"Conan O'Brien—you know..."

"What do you mean he shot him?"

"He shot at the TV with a shotgun."

"Holy cow, I'll be right there!"

• • •

My phone rang about 12:45 in the morning. It was my brother.

"Carol, we've got a problem at Mom and Dad's. Can you come over?"

"What's wrong?"

"Dad just tried to shoot Conan."

"Who's Conan?"

"The red-headed dude—Conan O'Brien."

"Conan O'Brien?"

"Yep, and he almost shot Mom in the process."

"Leroy, have you been drinking?"

"No, but I wish I had a drink right now. He didn't like the way Conan laughed, so he got out of his recliner and found a shotgun behind the kitchen door. He found some shells, loaded the gun, and shot a hole in the kitchen floor. He reloaded and headed for the den to shoot the TV. He fired the gun, but he shot a hole through the den floor instead."

"Oh, my gosh! I'll be there in about ten minutes."

As I raced to my childhood home, I knew things had gone from bad to worse. Dad's Alzheimer's was getting nearly out of control, almost to the point Mom could no longer deal with it without some help. My brothers and I had begged her for several months now to let us find someone to help her, but she had steadfastly refused. After all, Mom and Dad had been married for sixty years and she'd married him "for richer, for poorer, in sickness and in health." She wasn't about to let someone else come in and take over her duties for the man she loved. Maybe, just maybe, this shooting event would make her change her mind.

As I pulled open the screen door and stepped up onto the back porch, I heard Dad say, "You are not taking my gun, and that's that! Don't think you're too big for me to whup!"

"Dad, you don't need a gun in the house. It's dangerous. You could have killed Mom," my brother tried to reason with him.

"I wasn't even close to her. You think I can't shoot any better than that? Who do you think taught you to shoot a gun?" Dad insisted.

At that point I opened the door and let myself into the kitchen where the heated conversation was taking place. Dad turned and stared at me, but his eyes were blank. After a few seconds, he turned to my brother and said, "Why didn't you wake up the whole neighborhood?"

"What's going on?" I asked as I pulled up a chair beside him. His weathered face and deep blue eyes looked tired. His white hair was tousled. The red and black plaid flannel shirt over the dark blue Dickies looked dirty and worn—it was his favorite. Where has my father gone? I thought to myself.

"Ask your brother what's going on. He's got all the answers," he replied. This was so unlike him. The man I knew years ago would never have gotten his feathers ruffled like this and would never have talked in this hateful tone to anyone. Alzheimer's is a terrible thing for those on the outside to deal with.

"Why'd you try to shoot Conan?" I asked.

With that question, he looked me straight in the eye as a wicked grin overtook the contours of his mouth. "Because I don't like the way he laughs."

I let that sink in a minute before I replied. "Why didn't you just change the channel?"

Quickly and without having to make up an answer, he replied, "Because I shouldn't have to change my channel, that's why. He has no right to be in my living room laughing like a hyena."

I had to turn my head away to keep him from seeing me smile. Even though we were dealing with a serious matter, I found it somewhat amusing that he thought he could eliminate Conan O'Brien by shooting him through the TV. I finally got my thoughts under control and asked, "Where'd you get the shotgun, Dad?"

"Behind the kitchen door."

I looked at my brother. Supposedly all the weapons in the house had been removed months earlier. How did we miss the shotgun behind the kitchen door? My brother shrugged his shoulders and shook his head.

As I looked around the kitchen, I saw the hole in the floor from Dad's first shot. "Looks like you missed, Dad," I said.

He was silent.

I walked into the den to survey the damage to the floor in front of the TV. I noticed the position of his and mom's recliners, hers perilously close to the second hole in the floor. Dear God, this could have been a disaster, I thought to myself, while Conan O'Brien continued to laugh in the background.

More than a dozen years have passed since Dad's attempted shooting of Conan O'Brien. After a thorough search, all the guns and ammunition were removed from the house — again. The floors were repaired. Eventually, though, Dad and Mom had to be removed from the house, too, as his Alzheimer's condition worsened. We moved them to an assisted living facility where Mom continued to care for him until his death two years later.

Late at night sometimes as I flip through the channels in search of something worthwhile to watch, the laughter of talk show hosts finds its way into my den. The older I get, the more annoyed I've become with this form of canned laughter for entertainment.

As I change the channel, I think, "Sorry you missed, Dad!"

~Carol Huff

Generationally Challenged

It's hard for me to get used to these changing times. I can remember when the
air was clean and sex was dirty.
~George Burns

Another trip to visit my parents, another milestone as I notice their even slower walking and the increasing focus on their meals. With each visit, their delight to see me is progressively underlined by their awe at the adult I have become.

There is something new on this visit, though; I have brought my laptop computer. Every AOL robotic chant "You've got mail" brings them rushing in. They stand mute, their faces disapproving, as though the computer defies God in some mysterious way.

I am chatting with a friend at a café when my cell phone rings. My mother interrupts to report that the power in the entire building is off.

"Call the electric company," I say.

"It's your computer."

"What about my computer?"

"You know," she says. I used to hear her voice not through my ears but through my skin. Now it is breathless, flustered. "The computer has burned up the switches."

"Mom, my computer will go up in smoke before it burns the switches for the entire building."

"So how come we have no electricity?"

The next day, as I am nursing a late morning cup of coffee in the kitchen, my mother pulls out the chair across from me. The resolved squeeze of her lips tells me something serious is about to be discussed. Maybe her living will.

"We got a wake-up call this morning," she says. "At five o'clock."

I look at her, waiting.

"The phone rang funny. Ding... ding... ding...." When I seem to have turned into a dimwit, she explains, "It's your modem."

I sip my coffee, my eyes registering the faint remains of the cheekbones of her youth, the cheekbones I inherited, and which one day, too, will be no more.

"I don't understand," I say.

"We didn't order a wake-up call." Her tone means it is all self-explanatory.

"What does this have to do with my modem?" I ask.

"Isn't it connected to the phone line? It made the phone ring!"

Slowly, I put down my cup. I count slowly. One, two, three. "My modem doesn't make your phone ring. It only dials out for data."

"So why would our phone ring at five o'clock in the morning?"

"I'll disconnect the modem whenever it's not in use. Okay?"

But the solution rattles my father. He picks up the end of the phone cord — his phone cord — its plug loose on the desk. Fumbling for the context in which to frame his question, he examines the small, clear plastic tip, turning it around for a better view.

"This wasn't meant to be plugged in and out," he finally says. "It will break."

"All over America, every day, plugs are being plugged and unplugged," I say. "These plastic thingies are sturdy little creatures."

"It will break." Gently, he lays it down and turns to leave. But the room — with his books, with his lemon-scented after-shave — is still filled with his presence.

I follow him out and touch his shoulder. "Tell you what; I'll stop in the hardware store and buy my own cord."

The next evening, while I'm out visiting a friend, my cell phone rings. On the crystal display I identify the number of my parents' joint cell phone, the one that is for "emergencies."

My mother is agitated. "We told you," she says. "Now our home phone is dead."

"At least you won't get any wake-up call at five o'clock in the morning," I say.

"You really have to do something about your computer. Since you arrived it has given us nothing but trouble."

"Okay, Mom." I sigh. "I'm sorry. I'll put it away."

For the next several years, when visiting, I stay with friends whose building electricity, phone service—and wellbeing—remain unaffected by my laptop.

This year, when I arrive at my parents' apartment, they lead me to the study. There, on a polished oak stand, a new computer greets me, its large monitor gleaming through a clear vinyl protective cover.

"What happened?" I asked.

My mother replies in the no-nonsense, purposeful tone I haven't heard in years. "Oh, on the way back from another funeral we stopped at the computer store. They gave us a good deal."

"I'll e-mail to the grandchildren," my father interjects. The creases on his cheeks bunch up with pride. "And it will cost nothing. Your sister's son will show me how."

My nephew is nine years old. I could ask how the electric power and phone lines will withstand the extra traffic, but something swells up in me. In my head I hear the drum beat of time receding. Unexpectedly, unknowingly, my parents have made it turn around, go someplace else. I don't remember ever being so proud of them.

"I want to improve my bridge game." There is a new spark in my mother's eyes as she points to a stack of software packages. She fumbles behind the computer and plugs it into the electric socket. "Just install these games and show me how they work."

But as I lift the monitor cover and turn on the power switch, I can't read the screen. My eyes are misty.

~Talia Carner

Try It, You Won't Like It

It isn't so much what's on the table that matters, as what's on the chairs.
~W.S. Gilbert

My kids act like I'm trying to poison them if they see anything in the kitchen that contains high fructose corn syrup. So I read labels, and buy only organic products when I know they are coming to visit. My sister's nutritionist has an ever-changing list of food prohibitions for her—right now it is bread, dairy, and chicken. Chicken? My stepdaughter doesn't like meat... except bacon. Her boyfriend doesn't eat animals... except ones that swim. My stepson doesn't eat strawberries, his dog must have organic pumpkin once a day, and his girlfriend can't eat dairy or gluten. One of my kids hates raisins. They both loved raisins until I hired a really weird nanny when they were little. She didn't like raisins and she convinced the kids they didn't like them either. A dislike of raisins eliminates a lot of things that are usually served to small children—very inconvenient. Now one of them eats raisins again, too late for me.

My father-in-law must have white bread and plain lettuce at every dinner. So I have to make sure we have a head of iceberg lettuce and some plain white rolls when he comes. My sister-in-law and niece don't eat dairy or gluten. After trying many stores, they have found the best salmon at one particular seafood shop in our town, but I never remember which one, so I always worry I am serving salmon from the wrong place. And what if my salmon was in the same truck as the salmon that ended up at the wrong store? Do they separate families?

Sometimes, *I* would like to separate from my family, especially when I am hosting a large family event and have to juggle the conflicting and ever-changing needs of so many people. I frankly think this is all ridiculous. There are lots of foods I hate — olives, cherries, avocados, sushi — but I just keep my mouth shut. That's right — I don't eat the offending items and I don't say anything. Once I had a hard time keeping my cool during a business lunch as I sat in a very authentic Japanese sushi restaurant in midtown Manhattan watching Japanese businessmen scarf down slithery slimy sushi. I kept drinking Cokes to soothe my stomach, as I was nauseated just from looking at the sushi. And this is the Iron Stomach that did not get sick in India, Turkey, Bolivia, or the Amazon.

But my entire family's list of dislikes added together is nothing compared to those of my father. He has never tried any kind of soda or any alcoholic beverage, but he knows he doesn't like them. Can you imagine he has never had even a sip of wine? And he didn't drink beer in college or in the Air Force? He has never tried a bit of Indian food, Chinese food, Japanese food, Thai food, Mediterranean food, or any ethnic food whatsoever. He is eighty-one years old, but he has never in his life tried pizza or pasta or rice. He knows he doesn't like them. His face goes pale at the sight of salad dressing, even oil and vinegar. He orders plain steak at restaurants and if they bring it to the table with a little butter sauce on top, he looks stricken and sends it back. The amazing thing is that his sister has the exact same taste in foods. She has never tried any of the foods that he has never tried. They were raised back in the 1930s, when many Upper East Side New York families had cooks, but they have never tried ninety percent of the foods that the rest of us eat. What did the cook actually cook?

When Dad traveled to China for a week, despite the fact that his group was being feted all over the country as visiting dignitaries, practically with state dinners, he brought an entire suitcase filled with Sara Lee coffeecakes to subsist on. Basically, he doesn't like any dish in which different types of food are touching each other. I have joked that I should serve him his dinner on one of those compartment plates, like we use for little kids, so that each food is walled in, safely protected from the other foods.

The most stressful family event for me is Christmas Eve. We have been hosting Christmas Eve at our house for the last ten years or so, and we usually have more than twenty people, seated at three tables in three different rooms. It is chaotic, but lots of fun. Promptness is not my family's forte, and multi-tasking in the kitchen is not fun on a holiday, so I plan a menu that does not require precise timing. That usually means stews, beef and peppers, or pasta sauce, since I can cook them for four, five, or even six hours without worrying.

Every Christmas Eve I have to go through the list of food issues and prepare accordingly. I need iceberg lettuce for my father-in-law, a steak ready to broil for my father, something gluten free for my sister-in-law, niece, and stepson's girlfriend. Bread without raisins for one of my children, I forget which one. No strawberries in the dessert. Something besides chicken for my sister. Something that swims for my stepdaughter's boyfriend. The list goes on....

But despite the extra planning for the finicky tastes of my family, we have a great time and the "afterglow" from Christmas Eve lasts throughout the season. With my parents getting older, I am just thankful to see them around the table. And last Christmas Eve, in an act of great paternal love and sacrifice, Dad announced that he would not require a separate steak, but would eat my beef stew, even though the beef and the carrots and the onions and the potatoes were touching each other and he had never tried beef stew before in his life. I think my mother convinced him that since he liked the four items that were in the stew, he should give me a break from broiling the steak-for-one while trying to feed twenty other people. I watched him that night and saw that he did manage to get some of it down, which I really appreciated. I didn't tell him that I had poured a little red wine in the pot!

~Emma Dyson

The Optimist

Safety never takes a holiday.
~Author Unknown

Most parents stress safety to their kids, but my dad was a maniac about it. He was convinced disaster had us in its crosshairs. By the time we were six, he'd told us that pinworms, ringworm, and tapeworms devour children who aren't careful. During a thunderstorm, he'd describe how lightning blasts the roof off houses. At supper, we heard tales of deadly flu, TB, rickets, hemorrhoids, cancer, blindness, and accidents that would leave us amputated, blind, deaf, and drooling.

Dad had been badly wounded as a soldier, his father had died in an accident, and Grandma had cancer, so I understand as an adult today that he was even more terrorized than we were because he loved us. But as a child, I ran out the door to avoid a loose slate falling from the roof that would decapitate me, and I ran past alleys in case a rabid dog lurked there. He lectured us about puncturing our eardrums when cleaning our ears, about becoming "impacted" if we didn't eat spinach, and about being hit in the head while playing baseball and becoming brain dead.

So by age twelve, I wished he cared a little less. The holidays, especially, seemed to bring him to an even higher state of alert, if that were possible. One Christmas, Dad brought home the usual scrawny New Jersey pine tree. Dad, Mom, Grandma, my little brother Stevie and I decorated it with all blue bulbs, balls and tinsel until the holes were filled in, and it sparkled and filled the house with warmth and joy.

"It looks so pretty!" Mom said.

Dad nodded. "But we have to make sure it's watered every day and the lights don't stay on too long."

"I know," Mom sighed. "I'm not one of the children."

"Why can't we leave it on all day, Dad?" I said. Geez, I thought, we get something beautiful like this, and five minutes later he wants to turn it off.

"You want to know why? I'll tell you why. Come here." He pulled me to the tree, and I knew I shouldn't have asked. "Here. Touch this bulb." As I reached out my finger, he barked, "Carefully!" I tapped my forefinger on the hot bulb. "Aha!" he crowed. "Think of it! All that heat—a hundred bulbs pressed against ten thousand dry pine needles. One needle's just a little too dry or one bulb just a tad hotter. The heat builds up. Hour after hour. Hotter and hotter. The needles start to smoke. Then—poof!" He clapped his hands so I jumped out of my skin. Dad's face shone with horrified exhilaration. "Poof! The whole tree goes up. Tree resin is like gasoline. One giant ball of fire. Flames licking the ceiling. The whole house will be gone in minutes."

"Shouldn't we turn it off?" I asked.

"Not yet. I'll keep an eye on it." Then he whispered to me, "When I'm not home, you just remind your mother to water it to keep it moist. Can you do that for me?"

"Suppose it catches fire when we're not looking?"

Dad was pleased that I saw the danger. "You're right! You're 100% right! That's why we're going to have a family fire drill! Right now. We need an emergency escape plan. We never should have put it off. Our lives are at stake! Stairway here. Hmm. The windows. Porches." His mind clicked as he surveyed room after room. Finally, he nodded. "Come on, Stevie. Dot, too. We'll go upstairs to our bedrooms and pretend there's a big fire down here."

I was excited. This was interesting stuff. I loved escapes. One thing about Dad's stories: They were horrible, but there was always a way out.

Mom sighed. "I have supper to start."

"No, no, come on. We have to think this out before the emergency happens. Suppose the stove catches on fire when you're cooking dinner?"

"I'd turn it off?" Mom suggested. But he was already shooing us upstairs.

"Now," Dad said, "when I yell 'Fire!' we'll see if you boys can open your bedroom window and get ready to crawl out on the porch roof, okay?"

I said, "Why don't we just run downstairs?"

Dad stared at me like I was an idiot. "Because the hallway will be a sheet of flames! The stairs will be crackling like the pit of hell, and when you step on them, they'll collapse and you'll fall into the basement. Burning wood will cover you and sizzle you like a pork rind. That's why!"

When I could breathe again, I gasped, "How will you and Mom get out?"

Dad held up a forefinger. "We go out the window to the porch from our bedroom. See? Then we'll meet out there and all climb down the wrought iron porch posts."

Climb down the porch posts? Wow! This was great! Just like commandos or burglars. At the word "Fire," I'd be out there like a weasel. Mom was not happy. She didn't figure to be a good climber, but Dad didn't notice because he was pondering something. "That's the four of us. Now we have to figure out how to evacuate your grandma."

As he mulled this over, I could see his problem. Her bedroom was on the other side of the house—no porch roof there. And she had that bad leg. I pictured her trying to stump away from the flames, moaning and throwing up her hands. I could tell everybody else was thinking the same thing. Stevie began to cry. "Gramma's gonna burn up!" he wailed.

Dad, ever resourceful, said, "Why, there's only one answer. We'll carry her out!" He clapped my shoulder. "You and me, son. The men will do it!"

Right, I thought. We'll dash through the flames of hell in the hallway, lift fat Grandma from bed screaming and fainting, stagger back through the flames to my bedroom, then shove her out the window onto the snowy roof and make her and Mom climb down the ironwork. Whew! This was an unexpected turn for Christmas. I didn't ever remember Dad doing anything so daring. I was ready to give it a try, though I was pretty certain if Mom didn't object to the rehearsal, Grandma sure would. She'd whack me with her cane if I ever tried to shove her onto the porch roof.

"Okay," I said, "let's go!" I unlatched my window, shoved it up, and started to crawl out.

"What are you doing?" Dad grabbed me by my belt and yanked me back inside.

"Sorry. I forgot to wait for your signal."

"Are you crazy?" he said. "There's ice out there. You'll slip and break your neck!"

~Garrett Bauman

The Cooking Lesson

Recipe: A series of step-by-step instructions for preparing ingredients
you forgot to buy, in utensils you don't own,
to make a dish the dog wouldn't eat.
~Author Unknown

I t was time to learn the family secret. The particulars had never been recorded on paper or even shared verbally. The silence needed to be broken, and I gathered up my courage to confront my mother.

I was nineteen years old and engaged to be married. The eldest of three daughters, I would be the first to leave the nest. However, I was not about to leave without the top-secret information. So I sat my mother down, took a deep breath, and blurted, "I want the recipe for your spaghetti sauce."

There, the words were out. Still, the worst was yet to come. I dreaded her response, because I knew what she would say.

"There is no recipe. It's in my head."

We set a date for the information transfer: Thursday night. While this event did not approach the level of national security, it was certainly important in my world. Ready-made sauce was not good enough for the love of my life. He was special, and that meant he deserved special meals—homemade meals—with such ingredients as my mother's world-renowned spaghetti sauce. This was an event worthy of clearing my calendar and bearding the lioness in her den.

I wished it were a matter of simply watching Mom while she

cooked. Mom is a fantastic chef, but she did not like interlopers in her kitchen. She preferred to be left alone, and we girls knew better than to bother her while she was cooking up her culinary achievements. Even Dad steered clear when she was at work. My plan to sit in the kitchen and carefully document each step as she prepared her sauce meant that I would be entering uncharted and dangerous waters.

Thursday arrived accompanied by rising anticipation. I rushed home from work, quickly changed my clothes, and sat at the kitchen table with pad and pen. "Don't worry, Mom. I'll stay out of your way. You won't even know I'm here."

Mom gave me a look that said, "I already know you're here." She set an empty pot on the stove and began chopping an onion. I watched her and asked my first question. "How big is that onion?"

"What do you mean, 'How big?' It's an onion."

Her back was to me, but I was sure she rolled her eyes.

"I know it's an onion, but is it a small, medium, or large onion?"

She sighed. "Let's just say it's a medium one."

I wrote that down: one medium onion, finely diced.

Then she reached for the garlic, broke off a couple of cloves, and crushed them.

"How many cloves was that?"

"Two… unless of course they're large, then you only need one."

I wrote that down as well.

Mom poured some olive oil into the pot, and then added the onion and garlic.

"Wait! How much oil did you use?"

"I don't know. Enough for the pot."

I ignored the growing annoyance in her voice. "Well, how much is that?"

"It depends on the size of the pot. Just enough to coat the bottom. Use your judgment."

I didn't want to use my judgment. I wanted a recipe.

Mom emptied a can of pureed tomatoes into the blender. Then she added the blended mixture to the onions.

I grabbed the empty can and noted the size. "But why did you bother to blend tomatoes that are already pureed?"

"Because this is the way I make it. Are you here to tell me how to prepare my sauce, or to learn?"

Next, she poured one can each of tomato soup, tomato sauce, and tomato paste into the blender. I wrote down the size of each empty can when she finished.

While I wrote, Mom took a bunch of parsley and began chopping. Scooping up a handful of the chopped parsley, she moved toward the blender.

"Wait!" I jumped up and reached for her wrist. "How much parsley is that before you add it to the tomatoes?"

"A handful."

"But, Mom, how much is a handful? Your hands are smaller than mine!"

I grabbed a large measuring cup and had her empty the parsley into it, noting the amount. After blending the parsley and tomatoes, she added the mixture to the pot. I could see she was beginning to get a little rattled, but thankfully we seemed to be near the end.

"Mom, I forgot to ask. How long were the onions cooking before you added the other things?"

"Once the oil begins to bubble, simmer for about five minutes."

Then she sprinkled some oregano into the palm of her hand and walked over to the stove, only to be intercepted by me once again. I carefully emptied the contents of her hand into a measuring spoon. "Aha. Just about one teaspoon." I dashed back to my pad and wrote it down.

"That's it. Simmer the whole thing for about an hour."

"Uh… Mom? That's the second time you said 'simmer.' Exactly what does that mean?"

She counted to ten before she answered. "It means cook over a low flame."

The sauce was simmering, and so was Mom.

I waited a few moments before venturing to ask my final question. "Are we done?"

"Yes, we're done. Now it just cooks—simmers—for an hour. There's nothing more for you to write down, so please get out of my kitchen before you drive me completely crazy!"

An hour later, we all sat down to dinner. My sister was the first to speak up. "Mom? This sauce doesn't taste like you usually make. Did you do something different?"

"Of course not. It has the same ingredients I always... wait a minute." Mom grimaced and shot me one of her patented looks. "I forgot the sugar... and the salt and pepper."

The rest of the family laughed as I shrunk down in my seat.

I learned an important lesson that day. We've now been married more than thirty years, and my very special husband has always been served a very special spaghetti sauce.

Ragu.

~Ava Pennington

7

Chicken Soup for the Soul

Answer the Phone

An amazing invention—but who would ever want to use one?
~Rutherford B. Hayes

In this day and age, it's hard to believe a person doesn't own an answering machine; my mother is that person. She has never really grasped the concept of the answering machine. When she calls and leaves a message, it goes as follows: "Hello, anybody there? (This is followed by a short pause.) Hello! It's me (which is followed by a second short pause). Anybody? Alright! Don't pick up the phone! Well, if you're really not there, give me a call when you get in. Remember, I can always change my will."

To my mother, leaving a message is equivalent to a game of hide-and-seek when the kid looking chants, "Come out, come out, wherever you are." She's under the impression we're all hiding from her, and she's got to smoke us out.

Sometimes, her messages are longer than our conversations. The following is an example of a typical conversation with my mother.

Mother: "Hi. How are you?"
Me: "I'm fine."
Mother: "Still breathing?"
Me: "Yes, still breathing."
Mother: "Good, then you have nothing to complain about."
Me: "No, I can't complain."
Mother: "How's the family?"
Me: "Everybody's fine."

Mother: "Good. So, nobody can complain, can they? Good talking to you. Talk to you soon. Oh, one thing before I go. You may want to get that damn answering machine of yours fixed. The last time I called and started talking, nobody picked up. Find out what the problem is."

Me: "I'll look into it."

Should my mother have company, our two-minute conversation will be cut down to one as I'll be resigned to chat with whoever's visiting at the time.

Mother: "Your aunt's here. Want to talk to her? Of course, you do. Hold on. She answers her phone when I call, unlike some people."

Just as I'm about to say, "Had I really wanted to talk to so-and-so I would call them," my aunt gets on the line.

Aunt Ann: "Hello, Cindy, how are you?"

Me: "I'm fine."

Aunt Ann: "Still breathing?" (She's my mother's sister.)

Me: "Yes, I'm still breathing."

Aunt Ann: "Good, then you can't com... hold on a second, Cindy, your mother's yelling at me. Oh, your mother says I have to hang up now as this is the second time she's called today. The first time she got the machine, and nobody picked up. Oh, Cindy, that's not good. You really should find out what the problem is and get it fixed."

Me: "I'll look into it. Bye."

As I bang my head against the wall, I think—one phone call—double the aggravation.

~Cindy D'Ambroso-Argiento

Cotton Balls

*The trouble with always trying to preserve the health of the body is that it is
so difficult to do without destroying the health of the mind.*
~G.K. Chesterton

y mother calls from Florida every day. Today she asks,
"Are you okay? Are the kids okay? Where are they?"

I make the mistake of telling her the kids are playing outside. Now she calls every five minutes. "Are they back yet?"

"No, Mom, they're still outside."

"Can you see them?"

"No, but they're fine."

"You can't see them? They're in the woods? With the bears?"

"Yeah."

We hang up. I am trying to read, but it's hard to concentrate
when I'm constantly interrupted. The phone rings. I sigh and put the
book away.

"Are they back YET?"

"I can see them, Mom. Sophie is by the pond. Max is on the
swing."

"The pond? She'll fall in! Go get her."

"Mom, she's fine."

My kids are ten and twelve. Not likely to fall in ponds, get lost
in the woods, or eaten by bears. But she worries. She worries about
us, but even more, she worries about herself.

"I ate a banana!"

"That's great, Mom. Hold on."

Now I am trying to help my daughter with her math homework while holding the phone and stirring a pan of veggies.

"I can't remember how to do that long division, Sophie. You'll have to ask Daddy when he gets home.... Hold on, Mom. Max, no computer until you finish your spelling. What was that, Mom?"

"I said I ate a banana!" Her voice is high, like it gets when she is anxious.

"Yeah," I say, "a banana. And the problem with that is..."

"I'm allergic to bananas!"

I want to say, "Then why did you eat it?" But I bite my tongue and say, "Are you okay?"

"I don't know. My stomach hurts."

Her stomach hurt for a week after that, but I am pretty sure she isn't really allergic. She just scared herself into believing she was.

The next week, it was a peach. "I ate a peach!"

"Are you allergic?"

"No, but the peach was on the counter, and I had just washed dishes. I think some dish soap got on the peach. Do you think it will hurt me?"

"Dish soap on the peach?" Now she's caught us in the middle of a rip-roaring game of *Monopoly*. I'm beating the pants off the kids, and I want to keep it that way, but I just landed on Kentucky Avenue and Max has a hotel on it.

"Hold on, Mom."

"Ha! Pay up!" my kid says. I don't want to, but I hand him the money.

"You're not listening to me!" my mom yells. "I ate a bottle of dish soap! I'm going to die!"

"You ate the whole bottle? Sophie, your turn."

"You're not taking me seriously! I'm going to call Poison Control."

"Okay, call me back."

Poison Control tells her she'll be fine. That's what they always tell her. She calls every day. It's often a dish soap kind of thing, but sometimes it's that she got some face cream on the side of her mouth and may have licked it. Many times, it's the chicken. She calls Poison Control because after she eats chicken, she thinks she might remember having seen a slight blue tinge on the tip of the wing. "When in doubt, throw it out," is their motto, or so she tells me, which means more than half her groceries end up in the trash.

The phone rings while my family is eating dinner.

"The cotton ball is missing!" my mom cries.

I had just dropped a beautiful chunk of butter on a steamy mound of mashed potatoes. With a sigh, I leave my plate of food and my family, and take the phone into the living room.

"Cotton ball?" I say as I plop onto the couch.

"It's gone!" Her voice is near hysterics. I pet the kitty, who rolls over for a tummy rub.

"It was a new bottle of medicine," she says. "You know how they have the cotton in them?"

"Yeah?" I haven't heard this one yet.

"The cotton is missing!" I can tell she is pacing her kitchen, going back to the bottle of medicine again and again, looking for the cotton.

I change the phone to my other ear. "Okay, so maybe this bottle never had the cotton in it."

"It had the cotton!" she practically yells at me.

"But if it's not there…"

"It's not there because I ATE IT!"

My family hears her yell through the phone. My husband raises his eyebrows, while my daughter points to my mashed potatoes and rubs her tummy. "Yum," she mouths. I shake my head.

"You really ate a cotton ball?" I ask.

"It's not in the bottle, is it? So, yeah, I must have eaten it!"

I take a deep breath and wonder what it must be like to worry so much. I also wonder what it must be like to have a normal mother, or at least one who doesn't think she eats cotton balls.

"I gotta go," she says. We hang up. I go back to my potatoes, which are cold. The butter is congealed, but I eat them anyway. The phone rings.

"Hi, Mom, what did Poison Control say?"

"They said that if I ate a cotton ball, I'd know it."

"And do you think that's true?" I ask.

"I don't know. Maybe."

She once asked Poison Control if she was their craziest client. They told her no, that there was a man who called every day, convinced that his dog was trying to poison him. We had a good laugh about that.

"I better go," she says. "My stomach feels funny."

So does mine, but I finish my cold dinner knowing the phone will ring again in a few minutes. And who knows what it will be this time?

~Lava Mueller

Mr. Fix-It

Prepare and prevent, don't repair and repent.
~Author Unknown

My father took pride in his home repair skills. "I never pay someone to fix something that I can fix myself," he'd boast. Never mind that Mr. Fix-It's repairs usually resulted in fire, flooding, or any number of biblical disasters. No wonder my mother taped the phone number of every repairman in town to our refrigerator.

Undeterred by any challenge, as long as he had ample spackle, wood putty, or electrical tape, he'd routinely lumber down to his workshop every Friday afternoon.

Shoving *Best of the Ventures* into his eight-track machine, he'd stuff tools into his waistband, consult one of his *Popular Mechanics* magazines from Shop-Rite ("One volume free for every twenty dollars worth of groceries!"), and proceed to spend the entire weekend on a thirty-minute project.

Meanwhile, Mom would consult the front of the refrigerator for the inevitable call to a repairman.

So, I was alarmed when I returned from summer camp to a warning from my sister not to use the bathroom. I winced as a week's worth of refusal to use outdoor latrines knotted my insides.

"Whaddya mean, we can't use the bathroom?"

"Oh, you can use it alright."

"Then, what…?" I wondered, casting a wary glance around me.

Hmm, didn't see any scorch marks. Ever since he set the hallway on fire after dropping his cigarette into a bucket of turpentine, Dad was extremely careful with flammables.

Neither did I see any wacky paint schemes. He was still living down the grief he got when, after painting our house bright yellow and black, we became known as the bumblebee family.

No, nothing looked any more amiss than usual.

So, what could it be? Racking my brain for an explanation, my eyes drifted to my feet, and I suddenly remembered. A couple of weeks ago, my father had backed his truck into our driveway a few hours earlier than normal. Hoping he'd brought something home from McDonald's, we rushed outside. He threw us a wave as he leapt from the cab and dropped the tailgate.

"Look what I got," he said.

Piled in the bed of his truck were three large rolls of different-colored shag carpet. He grabbed the gold one and tossed it to the ground.

"You know that new Holiday Inn they're building?"

We silently stared as gold was joined by blue and green.

"Well, they're just throwing this stuff away."

Even at thirteen, I didn't believe that he had just found them in the garbage. Like wood paneling, lava lamps and aluminum Christmas trees, shag carpet was trés chic in the sixties. I couldn't imagine anyone getting rid of one roll, let alone three.

Even though Mom looked suspicious, she didn't protest. I think she just wanted some of the glitz that only a Holiday Inn could bring.

That night, my father schemed about how he was going to use his newfound fortune. Sketching floor plans on the back of a pizza box, he paced the living room, tape measure in hand. Finally, he hauled the green roll in through the front door. Grabbing his pizza box, he disappeared to the cellar. Minutes later, he reemerged with a carpet knife, yardstick, hammer, and plastic jar of little black tacks.

He sat on the wooden floor and pulled the roll toward him. Quickly consulting his sketch, he flipped the rug on its side. After smoothing out a length, he set the yardstick across its fibers. I figured he was going to cut a piece to run up the staircase.

Heedless of the damage to the wood underneath, he drew the knife toward him. After a foot, he made another cut at a right angle to it. When finished, he held up a perfect square.

"Ain't that something?"

Thinking he was only making a test piece, I told him it looked great.

Grinning, he promptly nailed the test piece to the floor. Beaming happily at the little island of shag adrift in the living room, he called Mom.

"Whaddya think?"

She looked doubtful. "You're going to put more down, aren't you?"

"Betcher sweet bippy," he said, cutting another square. Then he began to whistle that innocuous little tune of his that had no name.

His transformation to Dr. Frankenstein of Interior Design was nearly complete.

He was true to his word. The lonely little square was joined by a couple hundred of its friends. In short order, what was once a hardwood floor became a sea of green.

Flushed with success, the mad doctor next decided to cloak our stairs in a shaggy swath of green. Each evening, he quickly inhaled dinner and then proceeded to wail away on our stairs like Geppetto on speed. Before we knew it, shag carpet snaked a hairy finger upstairs, stopping only at our bedrooms.

As he concluded his march to the second floor, we breathed with relief. The green carpet was gone. Maybe the master decorator was finished.

Sadly, we were wrong.

Proclaiming our sleeping quarters in desperate need of a face-lift, he selected gold for our bedrooms. For the next three nights, he roared through each of our bedrooms, methodically laying a mantle of cheesy gold adjacent to our firehouse-red beds made of particle wood.

By the time he was finished, the living room, stairs, and our bedrooms were cloaked in carpet that only the rich could afford. Surely we'd raised the value of our home by thousands, he declared.

"Yep," he grinned while scratching his back with a dinner fork, "nothing says classy like shag."

For the next few days, everything remained quiet. Thankfully, Dad worked a lot of overtime and was too tired when he stepped through the door to further violate our home. Like a neglected relative, the roll of blue carpet remained on the porch.

We thought we were safe, but no one noticed our father eyeballing the carpet. Or the time he spent in the bathroom creating more sketches on grocery bags.

Preoccupied with keeping raccoons from stealing my underwear and trying to whittle something edible, I gave little thought to our Summer of Shag while at camp. After all, once my mother forbade shagging of the kitchen, there were no rooms left to assault.

So, my sister's caution took me by surprise when I returned. Overcome by a need to see what he'd done, I pushed her aside. Steeling myself, I pushed the door open. It was as I feared. The bathtub and toilet were covered in blue shag carpet like some freak mutant strain of synthetic kudzu.

"Hey, son!" my father called from the backyard. "Can you come give me a hand?"

Oh… no.

The pool.

~Kenneth C. Lynch

"UH-DAD... YOU MIGHT WANT TO CHECK THE MEASUREMENTS AGAIN."

Dad's Five-Dollar Pants

Thrift is not an affair of the pocket, but an affair of character.
~S. W. Straus

After I gave Dad his new pants, he inspected the stitching and shoved his hand in the side pocket. "What'd you spend?"

I'd hoped to avoid the money question, and even though I dreaded it might come up, I hadn't prepared. Instead, I refocused on how skillfully my sister, Susan, had hemmed them. He asked again.

"What'd these cost you?"

I'd hoped to please him, but now I felt anxious. Experience told me that confessing the price would spoil the pleasure of my gift.

I sighed, "Thirty-seven dollars."

"You paid how much?" Dad shook his head, his pale scalp showing through thinning, white hair. Then he adjusted the prongs of the oxygen tubing in his nostrils and took a big, gasping breath as if the price had sucked the air right out of him.

I'd bought my father two pairs of navy Ben Davis Workwear pants. My sister matched the length against his old, worn slacks and hemmed the new ones, stitching in the one-inch cuff that rode at the bottom of every pant he ever wore. The design contained the qualities he valued: sturdy fabric, comfortable waist, center crease down the leg and large side pockets. It didn't matter that I paid for them. Dad never distinguished between my right as a forty-five-year-old to waste my money and his determination to never let go of his.

In Dad's view, I spend too much for everything: cars, since he never paid over $8,000 for one; meals, since there is no reason to eat fancy when a smorgasbord fills you up; sweaters—he exchanged the sixty-dollar wool sweater I bought him for Christmas for two polyester ones, a package of cotton hankies, and a pair of socks—and that's only because I paid with a credit card and he couldn't get cash.

Mom use to say that Dad had "a pathological relationship with the dollar." She often told the story about one of their first dates when, in 1949, she told him she wanted to see the lights of Yankee Stadium. She hoped Dad would take her to a baseball game. Instead, one evening, he drove her to the Bronx.

"There are the lights of Yankee Stadium," Dad said, pointing into the twilight.

Mom peered out the window and asked, "Where?" He pointed again and she got a glimpse of the stadium's bright glow.

Dad proudly called himself a cheapskate.

He budgeted using "the envelope system," whereby he placed a specific amount of money for each of our expenses into a designated envelope labeled: Rent, Food, Clothes, Electric Bill.... These included two envelopes with a weekly allowance of five dollars, one for him and one for Mom. By 1999, Mom's allowance had increased to twenty dollars.

After Mom died, Dad moved in with my family. He was seventy-four. As I unpacked his clothes, I realized that his old pants were frayed at the cuffs and the pockets torn, but he clung to these clothes like a security blanket. The longer he lived, the more he looked like a raggedy old man. I wanted to spruce him up.

Now, sitting with him in his bedroom, I didn't know how to fix the price problem with the pants. After all, this had been a lifelong dilemma for me.

Mom tried to teach me how to handle it. I remember being five years old and getting new black-and-white saddle shoes. "If Daddy asks how much your shoes cost, they cost a dollar," Mom said.

She didn't take a chance on my uttering a convincing fib. I'd proven too honest even back then. Carrying the purchases into our apartment she walked swiftly past Dad.

"Cost just a dollar," Mom announced.

Dad sat at our kitchen table rewiring a lamp. By the time he looked up from his work, Mom had sped into the bedroom and I was left standing there alone in front of my father trying to hide my feet.

Back then, many items cost only a dollar: dresses, raincoats and winter boots. Slips, socks, and hairbrushes cost fifty cents. Wool sweaters were a bargain at two dollars. The floor-length, gray wool coat I got in the eighth grade cost just five dollars.

"George," Mom said, "There was a sale on coats. Five dollars."

That was the last price hike Dad suffered. After that, everything cost five dollars.

I never understood why Dad didn't ask Mom for receipts. Once I witnessed her crumple up a receipt and toss it in the curbside garbage can. And Dad seemed satisfied with the remarkable bargains Mom found.

One day Mom handed the sales clerk several twenty-dollar bills, and directed me, "Tell your father we spent ten dollars."

"But all this didn't cost ten dollars."

"I'm not going to count pennies," she said. "Just help me keep him happy."

Mom knew about pinching pennies. Her father stoked greenhouse fires in the winter and tended plants all year long. This provided less money than her family needed. They survived the Depression eating scrambled eggs mixed with onions and potatoes, and buying their shoes secondhand and stuffing the insides with newspapers. Neither of them made a lot of money as factory workers, but Mom swore off poverty and spoke proudly about being able to buy us new shoes.

It's not that Dad never bought anything. He read *Consumer Reports*, compared features and prices, and then purchased big-ticket items: cars, lawn mowers, refrigerators, washers and dryers. If Dad had to spend money on something, he expected it to outlive him. The avocado clothes dryer he bought when I was fourteen still worked thirty-one years later. When he moved into my home, he offered to give it to me.

Holding the pants I'd bought him, Dad leaned toward me, "You couldn't find anything for five dollars?"

I never could lie. Mom's strategy didn't work for me, and I didn't want to placate Dad by fabricating a more comfortable truth. So I just said it. "Pants don't cost five dollars."

He shook his head and looked down.

How could I meet this impossible expectation?

"Mom told you everything cost five dollars so that you wouldn't argue about money."

Dad flipped the pant legs over and looked me in my eyes. "No. She didn't."

I could see it in his face. Mom never told Dad a lie that he didn't expect her to tell. He grabbed the cuff of the pants and rubbed it between his index finger and thumb. "Susan did a nice job hemming these. Too bad about the price."

I sat there, knowing we had a values conflict. I valued the truth. Dad valued the comfort of relationship on his own terms. Mom had met his expectations. There was only one way I could satisfy us both.

"Sorry. I'm just not the shopper Mom was," I said.

My father locked eyes with me. "No, you're not."

The truth ended it. Mine and his.

But would he wear the pants? I needed to know, so I asked him.

Dad patted the pants softly with his palm like I'd seen him pet our puppy.

"Sure I'll wear them. Why wouldn't I?"

~Patricia Ljutic

Against the Grain

*The best way to garden is to put on a wide-brimmed straw hat
and some old clothes. And with a hoe in one hand
and a cold drink in the other, tell somebody else where to dig.*
~Texas Bix Bender, Don't Throw in the Trowel

etirement hits some people hard. And when my father retired, no one was harder hit than my mother, my sister and I. With time hanging heavy on his hands and nothing much to do but try Mum's patience and dole out long-winded advice on Shirley's legal cases, Dad had soon picked up the not-so-subtle hints about doing something better with himself than just being Man of the House. Tiring of daytime television, he had begun to hunt in earnest for a proper hobby with which to keep himself occupied. After having taken up and discarded solitaire (too slow), stamp collecting (too expensive), bird watching (too silent), origami (too messy) and even vacuuming ("not my grandmother's vase, dear!"), Dad was nearing the end of his tether and the limit of everyone's good-natured tolerance.

An emergency family meeting was convened and it was unanimously agreed that in the interests of sanity, Dad would have to be introduced to an addictive pastime on the quick or there was danger of someone doing him bodily harm (Mum had threatened to take a rolling pin to his rear). Naturally, the challenging task of selecting his hobby fell to me.

Accordingly, the very next day found me sitting amongst piles of newspapers messily spread all over the hall floor, poring over the classifieds in the local daily, muttering to myself under my breath and searching in vain for a part-time line of work that would suit my father.

"Accounts? No, he couldn't even balance his own cheque-book without bankrupting himself out of existence. Bee-keeping? Oh dear, he'll be stung by the mere suggestion. Car hire? Nope, it sure won't lift his spirits. Dance instructor? Oh-ho, I bet he's had enough of dancing to Mum's tunes. Employment consultant? Sorry, but we're going to have to let that one go...." And so on, from A to Z, option after option was rejected. "Computer programmer? Ha! He can barely decode the television remote. Library helper? Nah, he would only go to sleep. Radio presenter... hmmm...." I wondered if Dad's rich baritone filled with gravitas would appeal to today's hip-hop crowd. Shaking my head, I moved my eye further down the list of advertisements and hit the jackpot. Gardening!

It would be perfect. We'd get Dad to plant his own garden in our overgrown backyard. That way, he would be gainfully employed *and* remain under Mum's watchful eye to keep him out of harm's way. I patted myself on the back for a job well done and mentally started preparing myself for the admiration and accolades of my oft-critical family.

"You what?" gasped Mum, when I informed her rather smugly of my brilliant idea. "Gardening? And with his knees? Your father is never going to be able to sit down at the dinner table again. Really, love, you should know better." Crushed, I was about to return to the classifieds when Dad popped his head in. "I've decided to take up gardening," he announced. He had probably overhead my conversation with Mum and was determined to take the opposite side, bad knees and all. I rolled my eyes as my mother gathered enough breath to chide him. "Uh uh," he held up one hand. "My mind is made up," he said firmly. "In fact my dear, just wait till you're eating your own cabbages and courgettes," the optimist assured us over his shoulder as he walked away with a jaunty step, whistling tunelessly. And Mum doesn't even like cabbages. Or courgettes.

"Don't worry," she sniffed as she went back to sautéing her vegetables. "He'll take it up like he always does and then forget all about it in three days." I hoped Mum was right, but having noted the light of battle in Dad's eye, I wouldn't have bet on it.

Within a week, our house resembled a construction site. He had spent considerable time and effort designing a grand layout for our humble three-square-metre plot. Now the plans were spread out on the double bed. Labourers tramped in and out with muddy boots all over Mum's clean carpets. Dad had gone out with all guns blazing and got the professionals to clear the weeds and turn the soil so that it would be pliable and ready for him to use.

Once the dust had settled, Dad declared that he was ready to begin his new hobby. Chairs were brought out to the backyard and piled high with issues of *Your Garden* and *Gardening For Dummies*. Numerous bookmarks of varied shapes and sizes stuck out from them at all angles marking different pages and diagrams. The Master Plan occupied the pride of the place, propped up reverently beside a pair of thick gloves.

Dad looked up at the sky, took in the sun and beamed. "Perfect balmy weather." He rolled up his shirtsleeves and lowered himself to the ground. The rest of us crowded in around him. He began by hunting for his glasses. Shirt pockets, trouser pockets, inches of the floor around him, everything was patted and peered at. No glasses. He bellowed out for Mum, who calmly plucked them from where they were hanging down his chest and plonked them firmly on his nose. Satisfied that he could see clearly, he then looked around for a trowel to dig a few small holes according to his masterful layout design. He took several minutes to decide which one to use from the impressive array of trowels set out for the purpose.

At this point, several voices started clamouring for attention all at once. "I don't think this plan is quite right," said Shirley, holding the plan upside down and squinting into the untidy scribbles. "No, no, it is perfect, as long as you measure the exact dimensions with this ruler," insisted I and thrust one under Dad's nose. "Be sure you dig deep enough," reminded Mum.

My father ignored everybody. "Someone get me an edger." We stood rooted to the spot, looking uncertainly at each other. What in the name of heavens was that? Meanwhile, Dad had returned to poking holes in the ground at evenly spaced out distances. Mum resignedly started hunting around for something that looked like an "edger" while Dad began to get exasperated with the waiting. "Where's the spade?" Shirley pointed it out lying on the ground behind him. He picked it up, then looked at the trowel he was still clutching in his other hand and seemed puzzled. "Now, why am I holding that?" He dumped both beside him and glanced around for something else. "Bring me the watering can," he directed. Groaning under the weight of the colossal watering can, I lugged it leaking water all the way from the tap. He proceeded to tear open a packet of seeds and spill them around, with more going out of the holes than into them. Mum was getting harried still searching for the elusive edger. "What on earth happened to my trowel?" Dad asked grumpily.

Over the next couple of hours, Dad was completely immersed in his garden — and up to his knees in dirt. He hunched down regularly, leaned on his spade often and dug in with gusto several times. Now and again he grunted and consulted with the various bits of information lying around. Sometimes he stopped to sigh deeply and stare at a passing snail or two. Other times he held up his thumb in the air and closed one eye, gauging something mysterious known only to novice gardeners.

We grew restive. "Do you need more help, dear?" Mum asked. "No!" Dad barked shortly and stamped over a third of what he had dug up. We shrugged and gladly escaped into the civilised world of living rooms and air conditioning. Presently, there was an agonising yell and I rushed out to find Dad holding his stubbed toe and prancing about on the other foot. After due ministrations had been completed, he returned to his work, wary of anything pointy-ended and gingerly stepping over any loose twig or leaf, wincing exaggeratedly with every step.

Another hour and three-quarters later it was done. Our backyard "garden" had consumed six trowels, one spade, two picks, an assortment of other implements, five kilograms of top soil, several hundred pounds in professional fees and a soggy handkerchief to wipe the sweaty brow of my father. For this, all it had to show was thirty holes dug into the ground from end to end, mounds of soil heaped in all corners, two hedges damaged and an assortment of fledgling saplings shooting haphazardly out of the uneven ground. The edger was never found.

Dad was discovered bathed, changed and relaxed on the outside patio with a refreshing drink in his hand, massaging a strained knee and a pride that seemed as much hurt as his toe was bruised. He said sheepishly, "Well, that was fun. But I've decided gardening isn't quite for me." There was a collective sigh of relief. We all sent up a small prayer of thanks for the poor plants that would be spared from further agony. "I've decided to take up painting."

And as visions of paint-splattered walls and floors and a rain-bow-coloured father wielding a paintbrush like a mortal weapon rose in front of our eyes, we didn't know whether to grin or groan.

~Devyani Borade

Truck Stop Teeth

Shopping tip: You can get shoes for 85 cents at the bowling alley.
~Author Unknown

"Nothing good could possibly come from buying dentures at a truck stop," I tried reasoning with my mother after she unveiled her latest unique version of a blue light special. "This is not day-old bread or Christmas wrapping paper in January. These are your teeth," I reminded her.

"Yeah," my sister added, "you kind of messed up your first set. Don't screw these up, too!"

The news of the truck stop teeth didn't come from the back of a tabloid magazine or from a flyer tucked under the windshield wiper as one might expect. Rather, it mysteriously came from the women my mother worked with at the high school cafeteria. They were better known to us simply as "The Girls." These hard-working women ranged in age from forty to seventy, and what was newsworthy to "The Girls" usually fell into two categories. The first was their daytime soaps, which they checked on religiously from a small portable TV in the kitchen prep area of the cafeteria. The second and not necessarily lesser newsworthy category was bargains: clearance sales, two-for-one sales, end-of-the-year sales, fire sales, and now, apparently, denture sales at the truck stop off Exit 24. "The Girls" were not ones to spend carelessly, and if there was a deal out there, they knew about it before anyone else. My mother fit in well.

Of all the lessons she could have taught me as a child, I think the one my mother stressed the most was: "If it's not on sale, you're paying too much." Truck stop teeth were a somewhat logical result of that belief. Growing up with that belief system, my mother would drag me to the back of the department store hunting for red signs with percent symbols on them. In the shadows, well out of sight of mannequins showing off the latest fashions, there lived the ragtag apparel, and they were the objects of my mother's desire. They were the slightly worn, the slightly defective, and the slightly past their prime. Draped carelessly on plastic hangers, they prayed for an owner before fate or a new clothing line treated them like Rudolph's misfit toys and shipped them to some faraway island, like a Goodwill Store.

"So what if 'Yankees' looks a little lopsided?" my mother asked once, referring to an over-sized baseball jersey on which the lettering started at the collarbone and ended around the third rib. "That's the style!"

My mother always seemed to know what the style was, and as it happened, whatever the condition the clothing was in, that was generally the style. "You're starting to fill out nicely. It will fit you beautifully in the spring!"

Nothing was unsalvageable. Pants that were too long could easily be hemmed. Sweaters with pulls could be mended. Small holes could be overlooked. Like a botanist examining the rings on a sequoia tree, my mother loved to unveil the original cost of an item by peeling back the layers of sale stickers. The more stickers, the bigger the audible gasp, and the quicker the faded, misshapen, or buttonless item found its way into our shopping cart.

It wasn't until around middle school that I began to feel differently about my mother's gift for thrift. When my friends came over and had to use napkins with logos from the local donut shop to wipe the PBJ from the corners of their mouths, it was a little embarrassing. It was also tricky to explain why their sandwiches were served on Happy New Year paper plates in the middle of April.

But through the years, I began to accept my mother's quest for the perfect bargain as something that was more about the thrill of the hunt than a result of real necessity. I believe it gave her something to boast about and probably made her feel like she was pulling something over on someone, even though it was sometimes at her children's expense. But this latest find was a little more serious than stuffing your purse full of rolls at the Old Country Buffet. This was a little unsettling and required an intervention of sorts.

"The Girls said he makes the dentures himself," my mother explained. "They're the same ones you find at the dentist's office, but he's the real artist behind them."

"I like his style," I said, playing the good cop. "He's like those artists in Paris who sell their paintings along the river. He's just cutting out the middle man!"

"Did you ever consider that maybe he's not really making them? That maybe someone else made them a long time ago?" my sister asked eerily. "Your mouth probably won't be the first they've been in, you know?"

"That's right," I piled on. "If he's wearing work boots covered in mud, you'd better get out of there."

"You kids are sick," my mother countered. "They're not from a graveyard. The Girls said they come with a guarantee."

"Do you think you'll have to floss before you eat your first meal?" I asked, somewhat seriously. "And what if you end up with cheap wooden teeth and look like George Washington when you smile?"

Maybe it was the thought of getting splinters on her tongue. Or maybe it was my six-year-old daughter running into the room, singing, "My grandma's got truck stop teeth," to the tune of "My Bonnie Lies over the Ocean." But for possibly the first time in her life, my mother gave up the hot deal in the back of the store and went to the bright lights of the front, looking for a dentist who was actually listed in the phone book and didn't give consultations where you can smell gasoline and hot dogs at the same time.

Of course, it wasn't the end to my mother's bargain hunting days. Like Indiana Jones continually putting on that well-worn Stetson, my mother still searches for the ultimate bargains. She has given up on me and my sister by now, but our children are fertile fodder for her shopping exploits. Just the other day, she brought over a bag of clothes for my daughter. Among the heavily stickered items of various sizes was a little purple training bra with butterflies. My daughter is eight now, still a little too young for that particular item. But, hey, it was cute and at eighty percent off, can you really go wrong?

~John MacDonald

Chapter 2

Family Matters

Relatively Embarrassing

*If you're going to be able to look back on something and laugh about it,
you might as well laugh about it now.*

~Marie Osmond

A Fist Full of Dollars

Most grandmas have a touch of the scallywag.
~Helen Thomson

My friend, Zelda, was about to have her forty-fifth birthday party. She was a kindergarten teacher, and I volunteered a couple of years in her classroom. Her coworkers and friends decided to throw her a party.

I was excited when I got the invitation. I had never been to a birthday party that was described as "Girls' Night Out." At the bottom of the invitation was written, "Lots of fun and games. Bring five one-dollar bills." I thought that was strange, but I was ready for the fun. Then I remembered that my eighty-two-year-old grandmother-in-law was coming to our home for the weekend. We were going to pick plums and peaches, and she was going to show me how to make preserves and jams.

Grandma is the perfect picture of her title. She's from Spain, but lived in San Francisco from her teen years. She's almost five feet tall and roly-poly, hair held in place with a hairnet, feet supported by orthopedic shoes. She always wore a dress with a full apron to protect it from whatever she was creating in the kitchen. It was Grandma's favorite place to be, next to sitting at her kitchen table enjoying watching all of us devour her delicious meals.

I called the lady hosting Zelda's birthday party to see if I could bring Grandma with me. She had been to other outings with this particular bunch of girls, so she wasn't a stranger. I was told, "Of course.

Bring Grandma, and make sure she brings her own five one-dollar bills." I gave Grandma the good news, and she was excited as I was. We put a birthday gift together consisting of gift certificates for two for dinner and a movie and dessert afterward.

The big day finally came. We had our wrapped gift and tucked our dollar bills in our pockets. As we entered the house for the party, we were given party hats to wear and noise makers. Grandma and I made our way to the corner of an L-shaped sofa. Soon, Zelda the party girl came, and she got a very nice cardboard crown designating her as the birthday princess. After greeting all her guests, she sat down next to Grandma. The host announced the beginning of the games and asked everyone to display their five one-dollar bills. Grandma and I were ready to win every game possible.

Soon, music started to play, and a young man came into the room from one of the back rooms. He was wearing a very nice suit and tie, and looked quite nice. His walk started keeping tune to the music, and the girls started getting louder, shouting at him. Slowly, he began to take off his clothes! I looked at Grandma, and her eyes were glued to this young man. The birthday girl began waving one of her dollar bills, and the boy danced over to her with much of his clothing gone except a dental-floss-sized pair of briefs.

I noticed that Grandma started bouncing to the rhythm of the music as the boy got closer. As Zelda deposited her dollar in his costume, Grandma was blowing on her party favor, making it unfurl to where the tip was touching the boy's bare stomach. She giggled so hard I could have sworn someone slipped alcohol in the birthday punch. We were drinking the same, yet our reactions were not similar. I don't know which was more embarrassing: seeing the young man's almost-nude body or watching Grandma with the net still in her hair, "letting her hair down." I was sure her support stockings were probably going to end up on the floor from all the dancing she was doing while sitting on the sofa. It wasn't long before she began grabbing for my dollar bills, and then anybody else's she could reach. She had everybody in stitches.

The young man stuck so close to Grandma, almost dancing in

her lap, that Zelda switched hats with her, which she never knew. The host provided Grandma with more dollar bills. I was a little nervous trying to think how I was going to explain the birthday party to her grandson at home and her son in the next town.

As Grandma deposited her last dollar bill, her hand disappeared into the depths of the skimpy costume, and she burst out laughing. Zelda told her she couldn't leave her hand in there, to which Grandma replied, "I'm looking for change."

~Gail Eynon

My Wingman

The rate at which a person can mature is directly proportional to the embarrassment he can tolerate.
~Douglas Engelbart

I was sixteen when Grampa lost the use of his legs and moved in with my family right before Christmas. At age sixteen, it's tough enough to maintain a civil relationship with your immediate family, let alone someone two generations away.

I did have fond memories of Grampa's infinite gifts of footballs, though. Every Christmas, without fail, he'd bring me a football and blankets. Having raised my mother in a drafty cabin during tough times in northern New Hampshire, he was compelled to bring us blankets every year. We had blankets coming out the ying-yang in our house. They were packed into closets, and stashed in the basement and garage, mostly in unopened plastic packaging. Heck, I had a couch in my room I'd constructed from stacks of still-packaged blankets with a blanket draped over them. It was quite comfortable. But by the time Grampa moved in, his growing dementia combined with my adolescent angst shot our relationship all to heck. It started with the telephone.

Today's kids ought to be grateful that nearly all of them have cell phones. Back when there was just one landline in the house, that phone was the subject of endless controversy. Even worse, although it was 1994 and cordless phones were common, I somehow ended up with a black rotary dial telephone in my room.

That phone must have weighed thirty pounds. The receiver alone could double as a weapon since it was so heavy. In my adolescent daydreams, whenever I imagined someone breaking into my room, that heavy receiver was the first thing I grabbed to pummel the intruder into submission. I nearly knocked myself out with the thing a few times just by bringing it up to my ear too quickly when answering it.

One day, I was awaiting a phone call from a girl—a rare enough occasion for me in those days, believe me—so I quickly answered the phone when it rang. I had just heard the girl's voice on the line when the cordless telephone downstairs clicked on. Then I heard my Grampa's scratchy voice, sounding like his throat was made from tree bark.

"Hello?" He was out of breath. He was always out of breath. I didn't understand this too well, since he sat in a wheelchair and did not move much.

I said, "Grampa, I got it. It's for me."

He replied, "Huh?"

"I've got it, Grampa. You can hang up."

"What?"

At that point, I covered the receiver with my hand and screamed, "Grampa, I've got it! Hang up the friggin' phone!"

"Huh?"

I told the girl to hang on a second. I ran downstairs, plucked the phone from Grampa's hand, and placed it on the charger. But I knew where it would end up. Every time I left the room, he'd scoot over to the charger, grab that cordless phone, and deposit it in his T-shirt pocket where he could answer it easily.

The thing was, no one called Grampa. Ever. In fact, it was quite possible that no one had ever called Grampa, period. He wasn't exactly a social butterfly. But let me tell you, he was all over that phone when it rang, like he was waiting on a call from the president. I went through that nearly every time anyone called me. Once word got around, it became a custom at my school for students I didn't even know to call my house, just to get Grampa on the line. It was not the kind of attention I was looking for.

Somehow, even with Grampa running interference on the phone lines, I managed to convince a girl to accompany me to the movies one Saturday night. Even better, my parents were at my aunt's house for the night. All I had to do was somehow manage to get my date into the living room and cozy up on the couch — without seeing Grampa.

The house was dark when we pulled up. It was 9:30, and Grampa was always in bed by eight. I led my date up the steps, but she stopped me.

"Listen, it's getting pretty late."

"Really? You can't just stay twenty minutes?"

She smiled. "Well, maybe twenty."

I opened the front door wide and stepped aside, allowing her to pass me. Her hair smelled exhilaratingly like coconut shampoo.

When she reached the top of the stairs, she stopped. "Um…" is all she said.

"What?"

I couldn't see around her, so I squeezed in next to her to see what she was concerned about. There, upon his throne in all his glory, sat Grampa. Our downstairs bathroom sat directly across from the front door, and Grampa had chosen to use the toilet with the bathroom door wide open. So when my date reached the top stair, she looked up and instantly made eye contact with Grampa, naked from the waist down on the toilet. Grampa, not a small man by any means, made no apologies, just held her gaze unwaveringly.

She looked at me and said, "Yeah, I should probably be going!"

I think that must have set a world record for the fastest killing of the mood, ever.

~Ron Kaiser, Jr.

Strawberry Fields

Doubtless God could have made a better berry (than the strawberry),
but doubtless God never did.
~William Allen Butler

I t was summer, and my kids and I had been invited to yet another cookout. Guests were asked to bring an appetizer of some kind. I wanted to try something a little different from the usual pasta salad or chips and dip. A friend of mine suggested a recipe for Chocolate Amaretto Strawberries. I thought this sounded like a great summer treat for the adults. I bought a bunch of large strawberries and cored out the middles. Then I dipped them in chocolate, filled them with amaretto liquor, and topped each with a dollop of whipped cream. Too easy!

The strawberries were an enormous hit at the cookout. However, I guess I made too many, or perhaps made them too strong, because some guests were feeling a bit tipsy after eating only three. But no one seemed to mind! I had about ten large strawberries remaining, so I brought them home and placed them in the refrigerator.

The following morning, my dad arrived to watch my three kids while I went to work. If the weather was nice on the days he came over, he would also mow my lawn with the riding mower. I have approximately an acre of land, most of it situated in the backyard. Some of land is a bit marshy toward the back, so the grass grows faster, resembling a field if you let it grow more than a week.

That afternoon, I was working at my desk when I received a

phone call. It was my dad imitating Robin Williams from the movie *Mrs. Doubtfire*.

He yelled into the phone, "HEEELLLLOOOOO!"

I was a little confused by his tone, so I asked, laughing, "What's going on? Are the kids doing okay?"

He happily replied, "Of course! I just called to ask where those strawberries came from. They were delicious!"

I went blank for a second. I had completely forgotten they were in the fridge.

Finally, I stammered, "Uh, Dad, how many strawberries did you eat?"

He said, "Well, I don't know, but there's only two left. They were really good!"

I panicked when I realized what my next question would be.

"Dad! You didn't give any to the kids, did you?"

He started to laugh again. "Are you kidding me? No, those are all mine! I told you they were delicious!"

Relieved he didn't accidentally give any to the kids, I began to explain, "Dad, those strawberries are filled with amaretto. Couldn't you tell by the taste?"

He laughed even harder. Oh, yes, I could tell this guy was feeling pretty good. He had an occasional drink now and then, but nothing like this.

"I thought they tasted sweet. Where did you get them?"

I described how I had made them and forgotten they were in the fridge. He then interrupted me and said bluntly, "Well, I'm heading outside. I want to go mow the lawn."

Oh, no. "Wait! Dad! You can't possibly drive the mower now."

But the more I insisted, the more he brushed me off.

"What? I'm fine! The kids are playing next door, so I'm mowing the lawn."

Then he hung up the phone! I grabbed my pocketbook and headed for the next train home. I didn't even realize what I said out loud as I was leaving, "Got to go... Dad's toast... watching kids...

using mower…" I don't quite remember what I said, but people at work got quite a kick out of it.

When I pulled into the driveway almost two hours later, I noticed my front lawn was freshly cut and neatly done. I walked around back and took count of all three kids on the swing set. So far, so good. I noticed the backyard grass was also cut. It was neatly done to a point, but farther back there were large grassy patches all over the place. It looked as if he had done "crazy eights" with my mower!

I went up the back steps into the house and looked around the living room, kitchen and dining room. Dad was nowhere to be found. I walked down the hall and looked in the kids' bedrooms. When I entered my son's room, I found Dad fast asleep on his bed. I walked over to the bed and nudged his shoulder to wake him up. He opened his eyes, yawned and said, "Geez, after cutting the grass, I got so tired. I just wanted to nap." This was totally the alcohol talking since this man never sits still, let alone takes a nap.

"So, Dad, you mowed the lawn?"

He looked at me in confusion. "What? It's all done."

I brought him out back to show him the patches of grass.

"Are you sure you got all of it?" I laughed.

He then let out a loud belly laugh. "Boy, those strawberries were pretty good!"

The story of that day got around quickly to other members in my family. It is now a family tradition that amaretto strawberries are served at any and all family gatherings. As soon as someone walks in with them, someone is sure to yell out, "Dad, your strawberries are here. Get the mower ready!"

~Michele Christian

The BOEPAD Club

Winter is nature's way of saying, "Up yours."
~Robert Byrne

There I stood, silent and alone on top of the hill, taking it all in.

The moonlight bounced off the snow, lighting up the basin before me as if it were daytime. But it wasn't. Not even close. It was late Christmas Eve. And instead of sleeping, my family was out in the Idaho cold, risking our lives in the name of "fun."

The snow crunched under me as I hopped from one foot to the next. I wasn't cold. I was full of fear. The kind of fear that makes you feel like you might throw up.

Our favorite sledding run stretched for what seemed like miles down the basin. We called it The Basin of Excruciating Pain and Death, and it seemed determined to live up to its name. It had bested every member of my family except me, but I knew my time was coming. BOEPAD wouldn't rest until all of us had fallen.

My dad, my sisters, and my husband, Mike, all stood at the base of the hill holding their sleds. Battered, beaten, and quite literally bruised, my family encouraged me.

"It's not bad," said Dad. He was lying. He had twisted his ankle on his first run of the night.

"Don't be scared," said Mike, leaning on his sled, favoring his good knee. He had injured the other one riding his favorite sled, a skinny orange one he called "Dreamsicle."

"C'mon, Jessie, just do it!" called my sisters. Gwen, the baby, had just run into the pine tree that stood in the middle of our run. ("A mere obstacle," my dad had said.) Bethany had hit her head so hard after going off a jump that we were convinced she had suffered a concussion.

And yet, despite their injuries, they stood there encouraging me, goading me. They all belonged to the BOEPAD Club, a club I was scared to join. I did feel a little left out, though. And this was where I could earn my stripes.

"It's fun," they said in a kind of unison that made my skin crawl. I knew BOEPAD had brainwashed them.

My stomach was sinking. I had been lucky on my other runs, but I knew my luck was running out, and fast. My gut told me that this run, on a little blue disk, was going to be my undoing. I was convinced I could feel the basin breathing, waiting to bring me down.

"I'm coming up!" yelled Gwen, fed up with my stalling. "We'll go down together."

Despite her crash into the pine tree, she showed no fear. I couldn't understand it. It had to be the brainwashing. No normal person would want to sled again after hitting a tree.

"Just do it, Jessie," I said out loud, trying to motivate myself.

Gwen had reached me and was now physically pushing me onto my sled. She held it while I sat down, crossing my legs like a pretzel. The disk was barely big enough for me, and I suddenly laughed out loud at the absurdity of trying to pile two people on it, especially two adults. With the skill of a crafty veteran, she jumped into my lap just as the sled started its trip down the hill.

"If I don't make it, you can have my Christmas presents," I told her.

"Done," she said with a laugh. She didn't know I was serious.

Our ride started slowly. Gwen entwined her long legs with mine and wrapped her arms around my neck. I could feel the sled start to pick up speed. Terror seized me, exacerbated by the fact that Gwen had started clutching at my head and was completely blocking my vision. She was laughing and screaming. I was just screaming. Our flimsy plastic sled was sliding down the mountain while spinning in circles. I was disoriented, blinded by my sister's arms, and completely at the mercy of BOEPAD.

Suddenly, I felt weightless. We had hit a bump, the same bump that had orchestrated Bethany's concussion. With my sister still clumsily wrapped around me, I felt our sled slipping away. Panicking, I desperately clutched at its handles and braced myself for the landing that I knew would come.

It came with a bang, snapping our heads back with force. We were still sliding, still screaming and still clutching each other, but something was different. Something was colder. Horrified, I realized we had completely lost our sled. And the speed of our sliding was somehow pulling my pants down!

"Gwen! My pants!" I gasped, digging one hand into the snow in an attempt to stop while trying to unwrap her arms from around my head with the other.

"What?" she yelled, unable to hear me over the sound of the wind whipping our faces.

"My PANTS! They're DOWN!" I yelled, feeling frantic. My behind was cold and hurting more every second.

She unwrapped an arm from around my face. She could see the tears in my eyes, partly from the pain and partly from the embarrassment of realizing that I was sledding down the hill in front of everyone with my pants falling off.

Gwen tumbled off me, sending us both into an awkward sprawl. With our sled nowhere in sight and my pants askew, Gwen and I lay motionless on the snow, gasping for breath. Fearing the worst, our family ran to us. I desperately tried to pull up my pants, but my hands wouldn't cooperate.

"Jessie, look at your butt!" Bethany cried in dismay when they finally reached us.

Alarmed, I jumped up and rapidly turned in circles like a dog chasing its tail, trying to see what she was talking about. My backside stung, and even without a good view I could see little red cuts running up and down my behind. The sleds offered protection from the encrusted snow, and my bare skin had suffered without our disk. Little trails of blood were creating a bloody road map on my backside.

At the sight of my injuries, my family broke out in hysterical laughter. Gwen rolled on the ground with laughter, holding her sides. My dad attempted to be a responsible parent and asked if I was hurt, but quickly collapsed in chuckles next to Gwen without waiting for a reply. Mike laughed so hard that he had a coughing fit. And Bethany, desperate to clean up the blood, shoved huge handfuls of snow down my pants.

I was shaken and in pain, but couldn't help but join in the laughter. BOEPAD had bested me and managed to take my dignity — as well as most of the skin on my behind.

But I wasn't angry. I had lived to open my Christmas presents, and received the best present of all — I was finally a part of the BOEPAD Club.

~Jessie Miyeko Santala

17

Mom, You're Not Going to Write About This, Are You?

If you can't annoy somebody, there is little point in writing.
~Kingsley Amis

My daughter recently went to her first dance. Her anxiety over the evening wasn't that of a normal fifteen-year-old girl. What should I wear? Will my parents embarrass me when he picks me up? Will he try to kiss me good night? No, the first words out of Haley's mouth after the young man called were, "Mom, you're not going to WRITE about this, are you?" Such is the plight of a writer's offspring, especially when your mom's favorite writing topic is YOU.

While some kids might cringe to overhear their mother telling a neighbor about their latest social faux pas, my kids have to worry that their exploits will be chronicled for the world at large. To hear them tell it, every embarrassing thing they've ever done or said has been publicized in magazines, anthologies, and on the Internet.

Okay, I'll admit it's partially true. Over the years, Molly has wet her pants, Hewson mooned a church congregation, Haley picked her nose through her dance recital, and Jonah stood behind a very large man and hollered, "Don't worry, Mom, I'm not going to ask you why he's so FAT until we get in the car!" And it was all later recounted in print somewhere.

I try to remind them that the money I earn narcing on them allows me to stay at home and still offer them some of the extras in life. They are not assuaged. The long lead time on most stories only makes matters worse. I might sell an essay today, only to have it sit in a magazine's inventory for years before it actually makes it onto the page. That means the essay I wrote about Hewson playing an entire baseball game with his "cup" upside down when he was eight didn't make it into print until he was an eleven-year-old super jock.

The story about Molly's preschool streaking phase was published when she was seven. Haley's public inquiry about her grandmother's enema bag hit the magazine racks when she was in middle school (like middle school isn't excruciating enough), while Jonah's cat vs. duct tape escapade is sitting in inventory right now like a ticking bomb just waiting to devastate him one day.

In my own defense, though, sometimes the little boogers are just asking for it. Like the time we had to grease Hewson's head to get the training potty seat off. I'm going to keep that to myself? Or when Jonah swiped the surgical gloves in the pediatrician's exam room and stashed them in his underpants, not realizing she was going to check the goods during the exam and those rubber gloves would pop out of his little drawers like a jack-in-the-box. Now, how do you not write about that?

Or when Jonah said matter-of-factly to our neighbor, "Well, hey, Miss Karen, you're getting old, huh?" Or any one of their self-induced haircuts, spatial experiments involving the cat or outdoor potty adventures…

Then there was this conversation I overheard when passing my boys' room one day:

Little brother (hollering): "Mom, I need some panties!"

Big brother: "Man, you wear panties? Girls wear panties."

Little brother: "Well, what do you wear?"

Big brother: "Dude, I wear undies."

The other day, I was driving down the road with my four-year-old when he blurted out something absolutely hysterical. I laughed so hard it was a struggle to keep the car on the road. When I finally caught my breath, he said, "Well, Mom...?"

"Well, what?"

"Aren't you going to write that down?"

Am I that bad?

You hear about the preachers' kids or children of politicians who feel like they're living in a fish bowl with their every move being scrutinized. I wonder how they'd feel if their foibles were exaggerated and embellished for optimum laugh potential as well.

Still, I tell my kids it could be worse. Farrah Fawcett's son had to live with a mom who posed nude for *Playboy* at age fifty. The worst I ever did was write a story about them eating poop. Besides, as Anne LaMott so aptly put it, "If they didn't want you to write about them, maybe they should have behaved themselves in the first place."

~Mimi Greenwood Knight

18

Nana Ha Ha

Families are about love overcoming emotional torture.
~Matt Groening

ana Ha Ha lived with my family for nearly twenty years. She moved in after a car accident and subsequent head trauma left her unable to live alone. Physically, she pretty much made a full recovery. But mentally...

My mother said Nana was "a little off" even before the accident, but the crash definitely took its toll. I had dubbed her Nana Ha Ha when I was a toddler and couldn't say "Nana Hall," and the ironic suitability of this "misnomer" was revealed to me over the years she lived with us. Whatever was to blame—age, accident, personality—Nana Ha Ha was a bit loony.

She often stopped us to ask a random yet longwinded question or share some out-of-the-blue story. Growing up, my brother Jeffrey and I developed ways to avoid these encounters. Or if trapped, how to get out of them as quickly as possible. Jeffrey holds the award for The Best Getaway.

Jeffrey, my friend Kristen, and I were lounging on the couch watching TV one afternoon when we heard the telltale shuffling and throat clearing of Nana approaching. I turned to Kristen and saw a look on her face that screamed "Oh no!" We became engrossed in a commercial about the super-absorbent power of Bounty.

Nana stood right next to the couch and cleared her throat. Kristen and I stared intently at the TV and Jeffrey played dead.

Another throat clearing followed by a cough. "Not to interrupt, but…"

Kristen and I were trapped. But Jeffrey slouched on the couch, feigning sleep.

Nana started rambling about needing her wooden mixing bowl…

Jeffrey's butt inched down the couch cushions, his head resting halfway down the back cushion and his legs bent out in front of him.

Something about the ladies at church and an event…

He slithered further down the couch, easing his body slowly off the seat. His shoulders reached the edge of the seat cushions. And with a snore-snort, he slipped his body onto the floor.

Nana continued. Kristen and I nodded. Jeffrey curled up on the carpet in a fetal position.

Something about making muffins or cookies…

Letting out a soft sleepy sigh, Jeffrey rolled over. And away from the couch.

But the last time she made cookies…

Still "asleep," Jeffrey stretched and slowly rolled his body away.

She had bought blueberry muffin mix. Should she add blueberries…

Jeffrey rolled behind Nana and made a hasty roll right out the door!

If so, she would need to go to the store and she'd already been…

My brother grinned at us from the hallway. I shot him the Evil Eye before he bounded off to freedom.

Or she could use the sugar cookie mix instead…

I shot daggers at the back of Jeffrey's retreating head. Traitor.

Did we know where that wooden mixing bowl was?

"I don't know, Nana," I finally said. "Maybe you should ask Jeffrey."

In addition to ignoring social cues, Nana also seemed oblivious to some social norms. Like not walking around naked when you live with five other people, even if they are all family.

I was able to avoid most of these Naked Nana showings. But not all. One time, my friend's younger sister Heather was over to babysit my four-year-old brother James. My parents were going out. Jeffrey and I had plans with friends. Nana had a church function. I was talking to my friend's sister before I left. We heard the shower start in my grandmother's room upstairs. But then a few moments later, we heard her shuffling down the stairs and my eyes widened in horror. Utter horror.

Nana was coming down the stairs with no pants. None. Her cotton pajama top stopped at the hip. Nana's pale, wrinkly, droopy butt cheeks were in full view. Oh. My. God.

Heather had her back to Nana. Words of warning froze in my throat. And just as Nana was halfway down the stairs, Heather turned around. She got a full monty shot.

Unabashed, Nana walked right by us to the kitchen table and retrieved her address book.

"I was just about to get in the shower," she loudly informed us. Nana had obviously left her hearing aids upstairs with her pants. "And I just had to hurry down to get this before I forgot. Don't mind me."

She grabbed her address book and proceeded back up the stairs nonchalantly.

I opened and shut my mouth a few times, gaping like a fish, in attempt to speak. To formulate *some* kind of explanation for Heather. She turned to me, wide-eyed.

"I… uh… I don't even know," I finally stammered. "I'm so very sorry. Um, at least she'll be leaving soon."

We stood there, silent, for a moment and shook our heads — as if our memories were Etch A Sketches and we could clear the image. I had to let out a chuckle. How could you not laugh at the absurdity?

With a chuckle herself, Heather said, "I think I'll go find James now."

Another time Nana caught me one morning as I was coming out of the bathroom.

"I went to see Dr. Shaw yesterday. He's a cardiologist. Because of my dizzy spells — you know, I almost took a tumble in church last week when I stood up and your mother is always telling me to be more careful and with my blood pressure…," Nana rambled. "Anywho, when I went to see my doctor, he sent me to Dr. Shaw. And he wants me to wear this heart monitor for twenty-four hours. I had so much trouble sleeping last night with it on. These electrodes are stuck all over my chest. I'm wired like some kind of machine, hee hee. Do you want to see?"

"No, Nana, that's okay. I have an idea of what you're talking about," I said.

"No, really, you should see what this looks like," Nana insisted and started unbuttoning her flannel shirt.

Dread hit me. She stood in front of me, blocking the doorway. There was no way to sidestep her, unless I shouldered her out of my way. As much as I wanted to avoid this show-and-tell, I couldn't do that. So I pleaded.

"No, Nana. Really. It's okay. You don't have to show me."

No luck.

Nana opened her shirt, revealing not only the heart monitor electrodes and attaching wires, but her bare breasts as well. The wires got in the way of wearing a bra, she informed me.

"All these wires attach here, do you see?" she asked, pointing to the small box strapped around her waist that held the monitor. "And these stickies hold the electrodes in place. See? They are rather itchy."

Unfortunately, I did see. All too much.

"I go back tomorrow to have this taken off and Dr. Shaw will get the results," Nana said as she buttoned up her shirt.

She shifted slightly to the left and I saw my escape.

"Oh. That's good, Nana," I said and bolted out of the bathroom.

Quite the education. And I must admit, although begrudgingly, it was helpful to know a bit about heart monitors when a cardiologist had me wear one to check a slow heartbeat (as a runner, I was just super fit). I also learned how to look like I'm politely listening to a boring story. That came in handy innumerable times as a reporter, and even at some social functions.

Plus, you have to admire a woman who was so comfortable in her own skin that she didn't let anything inhibit her. Even clothing.

~Kristiana Glavin

Who Wears Pink Shorts?

Humiliation — The harder you try, the dumber you look.
~Larry Kersten

Why did my sister, of all people, insist that we go, of all places, to the water park? She knew my skin had not seen the light of day since I gave birth to my last child eight years ago. Why now? Why there?

Images of me in a bathing suit sent shivers up and down my spine. People would recognize me! Of course, they might not recognize me in a bathing suit. My own children wouldn't. If I covered my head with a paper bag, my husband would be hard-pressed to pick me out in a bathing suit line-up.

"I haven't been in a bathing suit in years!" I replied.

Karen shrugged. "Neither have I, but I bought one this year. Besides," she explained, "the kids really want to go. We don't go on vacation often, and I think the water park would be a lot of fun."

Because Karen took the plunge, I followed her example. I checked out every angle three times and wasn't happy with any of them. When I finally stepped from the bathroom, I was also wearing a pair of pink denim shorts. Being half-covered made a big difference. My son was pleased, my two daughters were impressed, and my sister was encouraging. What more could I ask for?

As soon as we stepped from the car, several people recognized me. I introduced them to my sister and her family, and I prayed I would have the nerve to take my T-shirt off once we got into the park. Having been a local newspaper reporter for the past eight years, everyone in the area knew me. What they didn't know is that I was cringing under my T-shirt and shorts.

We spent the entire day at the park. I honestly can't recall when I have had as much fun. So when my son grabbed my hand and insisted I go on the water slide with him, I had no reservations. We climbed the steps and waited in line, watching everyone zoom down the slide, anxious for our turn.

The older children zipped down like pros, shrieking in delight. Karen went down like a bullet. My son jumped on the slide and sailed down effortlessly. Then it was my turn. I quickly positioned myself on the slide, raised my now-sunburned arms in the air over my head, and called down, "Here I come!" My heart beat rapidly as I zipped downward.

But then something happened. About twenty feet down the slide, I jerked to a halt.

Behind me, the attendant picked up her bullhorn and shouted loudly, "Ma'am, you cannot stop on the slide."

Confused, I turned to her. "I didn't." I surveyed the miniscule amount of water rushing around my hips and innocently glanced back over my shoulder. "Did somebody shut off the water?" I asked.

"Ma'am, you must go down!" she said.

"I'm trying… Something's wrong," I replied, as I inch-wormed down another couple of feet.

Across the park, I heard another bullhorn come to life as the park manager questioned his attendants, "What's the problem?"

"A lady's stuck on the water slide."

My face flamed. A lady's stuck on the water slide? Me? Oh, my God! Was this really happening? Wasn't Homer Simpson the only one who got stuck on a water slide?

Worse, through all the bullhorns and people shouting, I heard my sister laugh. My gaze zoomed downward. Karen was laughing so hard she couldn't get out of the water! I glared at her.

As I sat there, attempting to inch downward, I silently prayed that God had seen fit to keep all cameras out of the park on this particularly sunny day. I could just see myself gracing the front page of my own newspaper—a bright pink object stuck on a big yellow slide in the middle of a hill, exposed for the entire world to see. There was no dignity in this trick, and quite possibly, if she had been handy, I would have entertained thoughts of offering up my firstborn in order to get off this slide. Unfortunately, my firstborn was at the bottom of the hill drumming up sympathy for her mother.

"Puh-lease get her down! That's my mom!"

Another bullhorn sounded. "Don't worry, folks. She's going to be fine. We'll have her down in no time."

The bright red stain on my face had nothing to do with sunburn.

"Try lying down," shouted a voice from far below.

To my abject horror, half the park had gathered at the base of the hill, some in the water, some on the sidelines, and all eyes were focused on me! My children waved and called out earnestly, "Momma, please come down!"

Oh, Lord, but that was a difficult moment.

I turned away from the sea of faces and looked at the tunnel I was slowly approaching. With renewed strength, I attempted to shift over to the side of the slide and climb out. Perhaps I could salvage a teeny bit of pride? Seeing my intention, the attendants with the bullhorns shouted, "Ma'am, you must go down!"

Being stuck on a water slide is like being born. There are no choices. One way or another, you have to go down through the tunnel and drop out into the world.

Cringing, I scooted back onto the slide and lifted one leg at a time, allowing the water to slip beneath my legs. An inch at a time, I wiggled my way toward my halfway point: the tunnel. When I reached the tunnel and was at least partially concealed, I wiggled frantically.

It only took a few minutes to free myself from that horrible water slide, but with the world watching it seemed like an eternity. The replay of voices—"I don't know what's wrong—she's just stuck!"

"Who's stuck?" "That's my sister!" "Look, Momma, a lady's stuck on the slide!" — will be burned in my memory forever.

Somehow, I managed to roll from side to side, lift one butt cheek at a time, and pull, twist, and shimmy out of the tunnel. To make matters worse, when I reappeared beneath the tunnel, the crowd cheered for me. Surely there had been no lower moment in my life.

For whatever reason, the last few feet of slide offered no resistance. Satisfied that they had their mother back, my children scampered off to play, as did my nieces. My sister, still laughing so hard she couldn't breathe, was both embarrassed for me and entertained by the whole affair.

"That could only happen to you," she said, tears of laughter streaming down her face. Sputtering and choking, she imitated me. "'Did somebody shut the water off?'"

My mouth dropped open, and I pushed her. "I thought they did!"

"It was the shorts," said the attendant with the bullhorn. "They stick."

Karen thought that was funny, too. She was still laughing so hard she backed into a chair and nearly fell down, which I thought was pretty darn funny. While it is definitely one of our favorite memories, I would change one thing if I could. I'd put those damn pink shorts on my sister in a heartbeat.

~Helen Polaski

Reprinted by permission of Off the Mark
and Mark Parisi ©2005

Chicago's Great Rat Infestation

I'm queen of my own compost heap and I'm getting used to the smell.
~Ani DiFranco

My mom has always been a bit eccentric. You know the type of mom who does such strange things that you can't believe you are related? (And I say this in the nicest possible way.) Things like:

- Pasting and constantly adding to a collage of bob hairstyles torn from magazines on our bathroom mirror, so much so that we could no longer actually see into the mirror. (Ironically, she never styled her hair that way.)

- Using Listerine in her hair to "strengthen it." (To this day, I still can't use it as a mouthwash.)

- Putting us on a no-sugar diet by substituting applesauce for sugar in our birthday cakes (which, believe me, is the last thing a kid wants and the quickest way to get kids not to come to your next birthday party).

Then, she seemed to level out to more normal things, yet still-unusual-in-their-own-way things. First, it was water aerobics. (I didn't even know she knew on-land aerobics. Or knew how to swim. Or owned a bathing suit.) Then it was chair yoga. (Excuse me?) And then it was making an organic compost heap in our backyard garden in Chicago… complete with used coffee grounds, eggshells, and urine. Yes, you read that correctly. The morning I caught my mother urinating in the garden was the morning I knew these "hobbies" of hers had to be stopped.

I asked if she could please use a disposable cup (emphasis on the "disposable") from then on for her compost heap. I mean, what if a friend of mine came over and caught my mom in the garden? Or a neighbor saw her squatting? After a little convincing, Mom finally obliged and swore that the "garden incident" wouldn't happen again. I swear, at thirteen, sometimes I felt like the one who was doing the parenting.

All seemed to be going well—until the day my friend, Mike, and I came in after school to do homework. I filled a couple of cups with water. One was a mug, and one was a red Solo cup (you know, the ones that everybody uses at parties). As Mike was about to drink from the Solo cup, my mom walked in, horror-stricken.

"I wouldn't do that if I were you," she said.

"It's only water…" Mike started to say, assuming my mother thought we were knocking back drinks in the middle of the day. But I knew what she meant.

"That's my cup," she said, starting over to us. Mike still didn't get it and was about to take a sip when my mom grabbed the cup out of his hands, spilling it everywhere.

"Sorry, I use it to garden," she said, quickly exiting the room. (I tried to think back to whether I had used that red Solo cup recently.)

A few weeks later, my mom's compost heap turned out to be working so well that it became a hit with all the neighborhood rodents: squirrels, raccoons, and rats. Yep, rats. Never before had our nice, clean neighborhood on the northwest side of Chicago had rats—until my mom brought them in like the Pied Piper. The city of

Chicago started posting rat warning signs on telephone poles in every alley. Yes, I attributed this to my mother. One hundred percent. And so did the Chicago police, who knocked on our door one day and asked that she dispose of her compost heap.

"But it's already disposed of," she said, pointing to it. "It's being absorbed by the earth."

"What the earth's not eating, the rats are," the police officer retorted. "And I didn't become a police officer to post rat warning signs, if you know what I mean. Those guys should stay in the sewers, not infest people's backyards. Do you know how much disease they spread?"

Forlornly, my mom just stared at the officer.

"Besides," the cop added, "what's the point?"

Easy for him to say… But I knew the point. And I knew my mom knew the point, too. It kept her busy. My mom looked so sad right then, as though she was back in kindergarten and her teacher had just taken away her crayons. I hated to see the tears in her eyes as she disposed of her compost heap — the inorganic way, in the garbage.

But through it all — the water aerobics, the chair yoga, the compost heap and the red cup (which sounds like a bad nursery rhyme book) — my mother is still my mother. And as eccentric as she is, I wouldn't have it any other way. The city of Chicago, on the other hand, may disagree. I swear they still think she started Chicago's Great Rat Infestation of 1990. And although there are no longer "Wanted: Rats" posters up on telephone poles in our neighborhood, the other day I saw an old one, now faded by the sun, and couldn't help but smile.

~Natalia K. Lusinski

The Evil Eye

The main problem with teenagers is that they're just like their parents were at their age.
~Author Unknown

My dad was never the kind to take us kids into jovial bear hugs on a regular basis or offer many words of adoration or encouragement. But we knew he loved us... he just had his own way of showing it.

As a teen, parental embarrassment is just part of daily life — the cars they drive, the clothes they wear, the things they say when their kid's friends are around. I don't know of anyone who hasn't been embarrassed by their parents at some point between the ages of twelve and twenty. As adults, we look back on those moments and laugh, swearing we will never do that to our kids. But I'm sure we will. Well, maybe not the exact same things: I've sworn to never drive a rusted-out station wagon with faux wood panels.

But there is one embarrassing thing that I may steal from my dad's repertoire: The Evil Eye.

I must go back almost two decades to explain.

When I was a teen, we were seasonal campers at a family campground almost an hour outside the city where we lived. Each family had their own campsite with water and electric, and you basically parked your camper there from May through October. Most "Seasonals" visited their plot of wilderness heaven every weekend during those months, with the occasional weeklong stay. There were plenty of other kids who camped seasonally each weekend, and they came to be some of my closest friends. Of course, many of them were boys.

We kids paired up with our little boyfriends or girlfriends, and we'd hold hands as we'd walk around the campground and down to the rec room that sat on the edge of the pond. We'd play pool or ping-pong, have some snacks, and play songs on the jukebox. Most weekends were pretty similar, but the couples would change. You'd see so-and-so with a different so-and-so than they were with the weekend before. You know how it is when you're a teen—a three-week relationship is, like, a really long time.

So, needless to say, my teen years were spent with quite a few different boys. But every single one of them had something in common… they'd all received The Evil Eye.

The Evil Eye was a magical sort of thing. One simple look from my dad, and the boy immediately knew not to mess with me. It was as if he could send his warnings telepathically or through invisible laser beams that shot directly from his eyes to the boys' brains.

"You will not put your hands on my daughter… You will not kiss my daughter… You will not even whisper sweet nothings into my daughter's ear."

I remember one night in particular, walking with a boy around the campground after dark. We came from one direction, and my dad from the other. The boy and my dad locked eyes for a brief second, then the boy dropped my hand like a hot potato and turned away, giving me a quick, "See ya later."

Thanks, Dad. Thanks a lot.

Yep, The Evil Eye. Best way ever to keep wandering teen boy hands away from your daughters. That, and the antique Civil War guns that my dad proudly displayed on the living room wall. Just another layer of daughter protection, but we'll save that story for another time.

~Stephanie Haefner

Throw Mama from the Wheelchair

You will do foolish things, but do them with enthusiasm.
~Colette

Whether you call them in-laws or outlaws, it is always a struggle to fit in with your new family. I had been married five short months when my mother-in-law, Janelle, invited me to Chicago with her and her two sisters. It was a "sister trip," and I was invited. How exciting! This was my first official sign of acceptance. I had made it. I was in.

The plan was to spend thirty-six hours "power shopping." No time for sightseeing or lollygagging; we were on a mission. We arrived at Midway and hurried to baggage claim. But when she picked up her suitcase, Janelle threw out her back. The sisters looked nervously at each other. There was no way Janelle would be able to keep up the pace for our shopping trip. One of her sisters decided to call the hotel and arrange to have a wheelchair waiting for us.

"It will be fine," I told Janelle. "We can push you around from store to store, and you won't miss a thing."

When we arrived at the Omni Hotel, there was a wheelchair waiting for her, but it was missing one foot rest and was completely rusted over. We pretended the chair was fine, but as we pushed her to the elevator, we heard the screeching serenade of rusty wheels. It was bad enough that Janelle had to be in the wheelchair, but now everyone would hear her before they saw her. She wasn't discouraged, however, so we began the first leg of our mission.

I volunteered to push first. After all, I was practically a nurse and far more experienced in that sort of thing than her two sisters. As we approached Michigan Avenue, the traffic light changed, prompting us to go ahead and cross the intersection. However, I began to have second thoughts. What if I didn't have enough momentum to get across all six lanes with my heavyset mother-in-law? I decided it would be best to pick up a little speed. While guiding the wheelchair into the road, the foot rest became caught on the curb. The wheelchair was at a dead stop, and my new mother-in-law was airborne!

It seemed to happen in slow motion, and there was nothing I could do but stand there watching in horror. Clad in a dressy black pantsuit, her flight was less than effortless. Her blond hair was swept back by the wind, and her arms flailed at her sides. When she finally came to rest, Janelle found herself three lanes over, in the middle of Michigan Avenue with her head a mere six inches from the bumper of a cab. Her sisters immediately began pointing and broke into hysterical laughter while the cab driver shook his head at their insensitivity.

I thought about how the traffic light would soon change, and she would be run over. I was going to have to call my husband and tell him that I killed his mother. That was not how it was supposed to go! I had just made it into the club of acceptance, and I show my gratitude by dumping my mother-in-law into the middle of a busy intersection.

Meanwhile, Janelle was trying to get up off the ground by herself because her sisters were incapacitated with laughter and I was frozen still. Then, as I had feared, the light changed. In an effort to avoid being run over myself, I instinctively backed out of the road while still clutching the wheelchair. In doing so, I was oblivious to the fact that Janelle had gimped back over to me and was attempting to sit down in the chair. Thanks to my survival instinct, I pulled the chair right out from under her and she landed, yet again, on the dirty Chicago asphalt.

Seeing Janelle in the road for the second time, her sisters quickly got their acts together and helped her back into the wheelchair. Shortly thereafter, I relinquished my wheelchair-pushing duties and began my apologies.

Thankfully, there were only minor scrapes and bruises to add to Janelle's back injury. Although I'll never live it down, I was quickly forgiven. This experience did, however, turn out to be a great litmus test regarding my new family. If your mother-in-law still loves you after you dump her in the road and leave her for dead, then she's probably a keeper.

~Lori Wescott

Chapter 3

Family Matters

Newlyweds and Oldyweds

Love is no assignment for cowards.

~Ovid

umbrella chairs

The best advice is this: Don't take advice and don't give advice.
~Author Unknown

She wanted large; I wanted small. She wanted an event to remember; I wanted intimate with only close friends. She wanted country club; I wanted backyard. She wanted a six-course meal; I wanted chocolate cake and champagne. It went on like this until she suggested umbrella chairs, and I said I wasn't coming to my own wedding. In retrospect, what my mother wanted was very generous and done with tons of love. However, what my mother wanted wasn't me. Sam and I had been living together for several years. We were just going through a formality. My mother was the one who wanted a party. We would have been happy making it formal with just a handful of our closest relatives and friends.

The "discussion" came to a head on an unusually warm Sunday in April. After several phone calls from Mom, I told her we were going out. This was before cell phones, so the ongoing stressful wedding conversation would have to wait until I got back. That's when Mom started calling the machine. I was sitting by the answering machine with Sam, listening to my mother's messages as they came through.

"It's Mom. I'm sitting in the backyard. It's about noon. Since you're insisting on doing YOUR WEDDING in the backyard, I just wanted you to know that it is already very hot out here. In August, it will be sweltering. This isn't a good idea." That was the first message.

A few minutes later, she called again. "I'm still in the backyard.

It's 12:05. We need a tent. We need a large tent with some kind of air conditioning pumped in. People will melt if they have to be out here in the heat of the summer. That's how hot it is. You'll have to have ambulances on call."

Continuing her one-sided dialogue, she left a third message. "It's Mom again. Are you sure you don't want to just do this at a country club? CALL ME BACK!"

I told Sam I wanted to elope.

The messages continued.

"It's Mom. I don't think the backyard is large enough for a tent."

"It's Mom. I don't know why you have to be so stubborn. A country club would be so nice. All you would have to do is SHOW UP. We can tell the orchestra that you don't want to do a first dance and the caterer that you don't want to make a fuss about cutting a cake."

"It's your mother. I was thinking. If I cut all my second cousins and friends I haven't seen in over two years off the list, I can get it down to 150."

"It's Mom. In August, it's also very humid. This backyard wedding idea of yours is inhumane. People will die, and then we'll be planning funerals."

"It's Mom. I've got it! This is brilliant: UMBRELLA CHAIRS!"

On that, Sam looked at me and asked, "What's an umbrella chair?"

"It's Mom, the one who carried you for almost ten months and was in horrible labor for a week before you decided to make your entrance. Umbrella chairs will solve all the problems."

I picked up the phone before she hung up. "What's an umbrella chair?"

"So you were home."

"We just walked in. What's an umbrella chair?"

"You know. Chairs with umbrellas on them to block the sun. I'll bet we can get them to match whatever color you choose for your wedding. We can even have cup holders on the chairs so people who are prone to heat stroke can have a glass of water. We can have the umbrellas removable so the guests can carry them around when they're not sitting."

"And if it rains, Mom, they won't get wet!" I added, with a definite tone of sarcasm.

Sam scribbled on a pad and put it in front of my face. "Your mother has lost it," I read. Then, "Don't fight!"

There was a long pause from my mom. Then she said, "You're making fun of me, aren't you?"

"No," I said. "But umbrella chairs are stupid. If you order umbrella chairs, I'm not coming."

"Then how will we keep everyone comfortable?" she asked, in all sincerity.

"We won't, Mom. If they're too hot, they'll eat fast, leave a present, congratulate us, and go home early. Then Sam and I can get back to our apartment and start making babies."

"Making babies?" my mother asked.

"Sure. Why else do you think we're getting married?"

At that, my mom sighed, "Babies…"

I got my small backyard wedding on one of the hottest days recorded for that day in August. People came dressed comfortably and commented on the heat, but no one complained. We handed out "Sam and Felice, August 1, 1982" spray bottles and champagne as each person arrived in case anyone needed to cool down. It was a wonderful wedding. My mother did hire a caterer because "You can't just serve chocolate cake and champagne, Felice."

And Sam and I went home… to make babies.

~Felice Prager

Reno Salutes Hal and Midge

A wedding anniversary is the celebration of
love, trust, partnership, tolerance and tenacity.
The order varies for any given year.
~Paul Sweeney

Where does the time go? One minute you're a kid arguing with your brothers about how Mom's jewelry box wound up lying broken on the floor, and the next minute you're an adult arguing with your brothers about why a nice card and dinner at the Olive Garden may not be special enough to mark Mom and Dad's 50th wedding anniversary.

Before you dismiss the Olive Garden idea as laughably insufficient, please note that my parents really enjoy eating there and usually have to pay their own way. So let's not underestimate the "wow factor" of digging into a free plate of five-cheese ziti or ordering the carafe of peach sangria without gagging at the price. (Besides, there's plenty of time for gagging after the sangria is consumed.)

My parents, Al and Marge (whose names I've changed to Hal and Midge to protect their privacy), got married in 1956. As was the custom at the time, they slipped away quietly to a justice of the peace, tied the knot, and then went about their lives as if nothing had happened. Because Midge was already two months pregnant, the secret marriage ploy soon served them well when curious family and friends inquired about her changing appearance.

"Yes, I am pregnant," Midge would admit under questioning, "but I'm also married—didn't I mention that?"

"When did this happen?"

"Remember that day I went to get new tires put on my car? Then."

Given their shaky start, a 50th wedding anniversary was an occasion that called for an extraordinary celebration, something unforgettable, something that would stay etched in all of our minds for years to come. My brothers, Bob and Jim, and sisters-in-law, Jill and Sandy, began brainstorming with my wife and I to give Mom and Dad a once-in-a-lifetime experience. Unfortunately, the Olive Garden idea was doomed from the get-go. As several more worldly members of the family pointed out during the planning phase, the restaurant didn't have slot machines, which severely limited its appeal to a couple whose chief means of shared recreation was playing slot machines.

During a series of spirited family discussions in the year leading up to the big day, a number of options were considered and discarded. Among the losing concepts were a banquet hall bash (no slots), a cruise (lame slots), a rented house on Lake Tahoe (off-site slots) and a trip to Las Vegas (way too many slots). By process of elimination, we arrived at the only logical choice for a Hal & Midge 50th Anniversary Blowout: the Peppermill Hotel and Casino in Reno, Nevada.

Reno has quite a colorful résumé. Dubbed "The Biggest Little City in the World" because of its impressive balance between mishmash development and dirt, its gaming roots go back over 100 years to the days of miners, railroad men and cowboys. When prizefighting was outlawed in most states, Reno stepped up to welcome the 1910 heavyweight championship bout between Jim Jeffries and Jack Johnson, once thought of as "The Fight of the Century."

Around that same time, Reno became known as the "divorce capital of the world," dissolving marriages for big-time celebrities such as Jack Dempsey, Mary Pickford, Cornelius Vanderbilt, and later Nicolas Cage and Lisa Marie Presley. Hang on… my wife just informed me that Nic Cage and Lisa Marie were divorced in Los Angeles. She may know something, but my sources (primarily the *National Enquirer*) report that Cage and Presley were seen throwing their wedding rings in the Truckee River in downtown Reno after their three-month McMarriage went bust.

With the stigma of Reno's divorce-happy past still lingering, the city was eager to pull out all the stops for the Hal & Midge 50th Anniversary Blowout. No sooner had we checked into the Peppermill, one of Reno's top two hotel/casino resorts, then we were all handed an exclusive VIP coupon book full of Hal & Midge discounts and perks.

"2-for-1 Entrée at the Flamingo Food Court," read one thrilling, pinch-me-I-must-be-dreaming offer. But there were more, much more:

"Up to $20 Off Island Buffet"

"Free Play on Mr. Money's Challenge Spin"

"$5 or $10 Match on Any Even Money Table Wager"

"Free Side Order of Cole Slaw at the Casino Coffee Shop with the Purchase of Any Club Sandwich or Entrée-Size Salad"

I looked at my mom and saw her eyes glistening with tears.

"Pretty generous coupons," I sputtered, choking back my own tears.

"I wouldn't know," she snapped back. "Your father's cigar smoke is killing my eyes."

Once out on the casino floor, the evidence of Reno's pride in hosting the Hal & Midge celebration was everywhere. Neon lights and mirrored walls greeted us at every turn as a sprawling, carnival-like atmosphere swept us dizzily along in a circular, trance-like pattern. As if by magic, slot machines became available whenever we felt the calling, and we all took turns plundering our stored riches and lining our pockets with our ill-gotten wealth. Hang on again… my wife just pointed out that most of us lost money during the three days, and that even a highlight like my dad winning $137 on a penny machine was nullified by a steady series of losses before and after. All I know is, I won $85 on the last night there, and if there were losses leading up to that point, you know the old saying: "What happens in Reno, stays in Vegas."

While some of us will always wonder how exhilarating an Olive Garden anniversary might have been, I'll always cherish Reno's salute to Hal & Midge. We had a blast day and night, interspersing our gambling exploits with a paddlewheel cruise of Lake Tahoe on the M.S. Dixie and a walking tour of cowboy-town-turned-tourist-tease Virginia City.

The trip's gambling theme seemed to put my parents' last fifty years in exactly the right context. After all, in the beginning, odds-makers gave the marriage five to seven years, which was an optimistic contrast to family member estimates of "till next summer" and "by midnight tonight." But no one could imagine the stubborn resilience and plucky perseverance that would carry Hal and Midge through life's turbulent times. They ricocheted through the decades raising three kids, surviving the storms and savoring the rewards of a fifty-year journey that few have the guts to tackle. As Hal & Midge, they became a brand name as familiar and cherished as Coca-Cola, Yukon Gold Condoms, Uncle Jake's Jolly Good Aftershave, and Fancy Pants Fire Ant Spray Killer.

Love, health and happiness, Mom and Dad. You just might be the last couple standing in this rambling, gambling game of marriage. You know something? It's just a hunch, but I think you crazy kids are going to make it after all.

~Alan Williamson

Reprinted by permission of Off the Mark
and Mark Parisi ©2003

25

Busted

Nature abhors a vacuum. And so do I.
~Anne Gibbons

"Okay, now I am nervous," my boyfriend Jesse said, steering his Corolla onto the street where I lived as a child. It was the first time I was taking him home to meet my parents.

"Don't be nervous. I am not worried about them meeting you," I assured him. "I am worried about what you will think when you meet them."

My innermost thoughts were a little different. "Please, God, don't let him think we are a bunch of Froot Loops."

I loved my family, but their nutty characteristics, especially those of my mother, challenged my own sanity. Even I, who had been subjected to their eccentricities for thirty years, considered taking up drinking for family get-togethers.

In the past, I had a strict rule for myself—keep any potential mate away from the family as long as possible. But this guy was special, and against my better judgment, I broke my rule and took him to my mom's autumn dinner—the one she had every year to "welcome fall." I know. How could I not see it coming?

As we pulled into my parents' driveway I breathed a sigh of relief because we had dodged the first landmine. When one of my college roommates came home with me for a visit once, my jaw dropped when we drove up to a yard full of lumpy sheets. When I explained that my mom hated losing her flowers to fall's homicidal freezes, my friend said, "Does she tuck them in and tell them a goodnight story, too?" Taking guests home during the summer wouldn't alleviate the problem. The fruit trees would be covered with aluminum pie pans to scare away the birds.

That day, I looked at the bright red front door and took a deep breath. Beyond the threshold lay a minefield of idiosyncrasies waiting to be triggered.

I cringed to think of the sticky notes lying around willy-nilly. Mom is a little forgetful, so she leaves herself notes. One time, one of my friends pointed out a sticky note on the refrigerator that simply said, "Satan 7 p.m." PBS was airing an educational documentary on dangers of the occult, and Mom didn't want to miss it, so she left herself a reminder note. You can't fault her for a lack of brevity.

Then there were Mom's decorations. She has a special place in her heart for silk flowers, artificial plants, and a host of fake woodland creatures. She could run a Hallmark store out of her house. The fireplace mantel in the living room is her special showcase, elaborately decorated each holiday. Thank goodness it wasn't February. With all the heart-shaped lights, the living room looks more like a Vegas wedding chapel. Rightfully, that would have made my boyfriend of a month run pell-mell from the house, never to be seen again.

The dinner itself would involve everyone sitting down and starting to eat, only for my mother to suddenly yell out, "Oh, I forgot the salt!" Or, "Oh, I forgot the butter!" Years ago, I began putting the salt and butter right in front of her plate before dinner, but Mom is a creature of habit and yells anyway. Then there was the worst-case scenario. She could burst out with "Oh, I forgot my Beano!"

Then my younger sister, who might drop in for dinner, could display her conversational finesse. At one Christmas gathering, she described target practice with her new gun in one breath, and then in the next declared herself legally blind.

She and my mom would probably get into a colorful "discussion." My dad, who has complained for years about his hearing loss, would sit and watch, eyes volleying between wife and daughter like he was at a tennis match. Then he would leave the room and "not hear" anyone for an hour or longer, depending on the escalation of the debate. I'm tempted to tell him that no one would blame him if he were faking. Really, it's a coping mechanism. My brother realizes we are a normal-challenged family. He wouldn't be able to make it that day.

I took another deep breath, took Jesse's hand, and we walked to the door. My dad let us in and explained that my mom was downstairs finishing a few tasks.

At first, she had her back to us, rag in hand when we stepped off the basement stairs' landing. Then she turned around. I stared in horror. She was wearing a filtration mask on the lower quadrant of her face.

"Oh, hello," Mom said, cheerful voice muffled by the mask. She said it unabashedly as if she welcomed first-time guests into her home every day wearing a face mask. Who knows, I hadn't lived there in a while, so maybe this was her new thing. She finally put the dust rag down and slid off the mask.

"I have to wear this mask while I clean," she explained. "You know how my allergies act up if I get dust up my nose." No, I didn't know. And no, I didn't want to know. But when you live in a family like mine, you find out regardless.

We made it through the introductions and the dinner, and other than the business with the mask, we made it through the night without incident. Almost… until I picked up the family calico and rubbed her head while she purred. When I put her down, there was cat hair all over my red sweater. I asked Mom if she had a lint roller I could use.

"No, but wait just a minute," she said. She disappeared for a few seconds and returned with her hand vacuum. I froze. No, she wouldn't. But, yes, she would. She flicked the on switch and came toward me. Panicked, I sprinted down the hall like she was Leatherface with a chain saw. She caught me and started running the Dustbuster over my sweater. All the while, I was flailing and wailing, "No, no! It's okay!" But the damage was done. I had been Dustbusted by my mother in front of my boyfriend. When most people I know tell stories of being "busted" by their parents, it has a whole other connotation.

It was clear that I had found the right man when, despite the fact that my mother hand-vacuumed me the first time he met her at that fall dinner, Jesse continued to date me. One day a few years later, we even said "I do" while my whole family watched, admittedly looking and faking normal effectively. And amid the shiny white wrappings on the church gift table was a present from my mother that still graces our home today: a Dustbuster.

Don't worry. I don't have any plans of "busting" my own kids. At least not the way my mother "busted" me!

~Janeen Lewis

26

Surprise, Surprise

If I were invited to a dinner party with my characters, I wouldn't show up.
~Dr. Seuss

My father is a rabbi, and of course he often officiates at weddings. One time he was asked to officiate at a surprise fiftieth anniversary party that would include a renewal of vows. The couple's daughter, Marilyn, was so excited. She had invited all of her parents' lifelong friends—her mom's mahjong group, her dad's golfing buddies, all seven of their grandchildren—and she had booked a dinner for all of them at a fancy hotel. Marilyn said that she wanted nothing but the best for her parents.

The event had begun as an elegant, fancy surprise party, but eventually grew to include a ten-piece band and a six-course expensive dinner. A photographer was even hired to make souvenir badges for each guest.

As the days went by, and the cost seemed to exponentially expand, Marilyn's husband began to question the growing expenses of the party: "I'm not so sure your parents truly need two flamingos in a rented fountain." However, Marilyn would not budge. She met again with her party planner, and the arrangements became even more and more elaborate.

The big day finally arrived and Marilyn could not have asked for a more beautiful evening as she and her husband drove up to the hotel. They hastened inside. The aroma from the kitchen was delightful. The musicians were tuning their instruments and the hall looked beautiful. As the guests began to arrive Marilyn was more excited than she thought possible.

By 8:00 p.m., all the guests had arrived for the surprise party. Marilyn had planned for her parents to get to their surprise party at 8:15 by telling them that the celebration was actually a party for their parents' good friends, Mr. and Mrs. Samuels. However, 8:15 came and went with no sign of the anniversary couple. Then 8:30 came — and also went. At 8:50, Mary was becoming extremely anxious and nervous.

"Where are my parents?" she nervously asked herself. "What if something happened to them? What would we do?"

Just then, Marilyn's cell phone rang. She grabbed it.

"Hello, hello!" she shouted.

"Marilyn, this is Mom. Please send our apologies to the Samuels, but last night we looked on the Internet for an inexpensive, last-minute cruise, and we found it. It left Galveston at 5:00 this afternoon, and we're now on our way to Key West. We'll be back next Saturday morning. You know, it's our fiftieth anniversary this Tuesday, and we wanted to celebrate it in a meaningful way. Tell everyone that we are sorry we cannot be there together with them tonight."

Marilyn was in shock. She did not even notice her cell phone dropping into the fountain with the flamingos. Her husband, however, overheard his mother-in-law's comments on the phone. He sarcastically, but calmly, stated to his wife, "Now, can we shout 'SURPRISE'?"

~Michael Jordan Segal, MSW

Here Comes the Marshmallow

We have the greatest pre-nuptial agreement in the world. It's called love.

~Gene Perret

There are few experiences that compare with accompanying your daughter to a bridal salon. Take my word; you will never be the same again. Every girl has a dream dress in mind. She has been thinking about it ever since she started playing "bride" as a child. For years, I carried around a picture of my fantasy gown in my wallet. When I found it and tried it on, I knew immediately that it was right. I saved my mother hundreds of hours of traipsing through the stores. The entire affair took less than an hour. Not so with my daughter, Elizabeth. With her, it was an entirely different story, one that seems to be the more typical experience.

Now, my friend, Marcia is going through the same trauma. Her daughter, Jane is going to be married on Valentine's Day, and she still hasn't found a dress. The shopping spree has begun and Marcia is in for a rude awakening.

"Jane was always such an easy child," Marcia said, "but since she's become engaged and set a date for a February wedding, she's in a trance. I thought we could wrap up the whole bridal gown excursion in one afternoon."

"It doesn't quite work that way," I told her.

Then I regaled her with my tales of our bridal dress capers.

"Little did I know," I said, "when my Elizabeth and I went shopping, that we were in for a series of events that would take years off my life and leave me permanently repelled by the color white."

That's because all brides-to-be are so swept away by the entire wedding adventure, they take temporary leave of their senses. Six months before Liz's wedding, we began purchasing bridal magazines that weighed more than my daughter did at birth. These tomes were dragged around as on-the-spot reference guides. While Elizabeth combed the racks of puffy white gowns, I was weighed down by these magazines, which we dragged around in a tote bag from store to store, turning the entire experience into a full-time job. But it wasn't a total loss; my daughter improved her cardiovascular system just by getting in and out of each dress and I increased the size of my pectoral muscles, carrying the dresses from the rack to the dressing room. The salesgirl was around only to zip and unzip, leaving the heavy work to me.

After I deposited the gowns with her, Liz and the salesgirl began the process of selection. My job was to sit on the sidelines making my motherly comments. Each time she emerged from the room wearing a different gown, I expressed my opinion by uttering either "hmmm," "forget it" or "it has possibilities." I soon discovered that whatever she adored, I hated. What she felt was exactly right, I knew wouldn't work. At the end of each shopping excursion, one fact was certain: her taste and mine were on opposite sides of the bridal gown spectrum.

There is nothing more comical and more exhausting than spending a day in bridal salons filled with mothers, daughters, hyperactive saleswomen and a handful of fathers who are not quite sure why they are even there. This is definitely woman's work. The main function a man serves is to keep running out to the car at one-hour intervals to throw more quarters in the parking meter.

I sat back and watched as beautiful young women, who still looked like little girls playing dress-up, pirouetted in front of a three-way mirror. The constant refrain of mothers' voices reverberated through the room: "Remember, it's you who has to love it, not me."

This is the biggest lie, second only to: "Of course, I'm still a virgin, Mother!"

Each time Liz disappeared into the dressing room, I prayed she would not emerge in one of those tulle gowns that made her look like an enormous white marshmallow. I had in mind something simple sans sequins, rosettes, and those shimmering beads that resembled a chandelier. Each time she thought she had achieved the right look, I cringed.

"What's wrong with it?" Elizabeth asked.

"Nothing, if you don't mind looking like a fairy Godmother," I said.

All she needed was the wand, and she'd have a lead role in Cinderella.

After weeks of making the bridal scene to no avail, we decided to try the smaller specialty shops. These are usually a family-owned operation where "Mom" and "Pop" stand around acting as the cheering section. Each time a girl appears in a different dress, they applaud.

One such stop was in the Bronx, nestled between a funeral parlor and a pizzeria. We had heard through the bridal grapevine that this was the place to go. The décor was subdued chartreuse and gave new meaning to the word "glitz." Its inventory included gowns that looked like wedding cakes topped with lace—the philosophy being: the bigger, the better. Elizabeth tried on a variety of gowns, any one of which would be grounds for my not having to show up at the wedding. One in particular was so ugly that when another mother asked me, "Is that your daughter?" I smiled and with a straight face said, "I never saw that girl before in my life."

I tell Marcia this story to make her feel better. But it is now the end of January, and her daughter, Jane still hasn't found a dress.

"We put 1,000 miles on the car just looking for a wedding gown," Marcia said. "Last week, Jane thought she found her dream dress at least six times, but it was never quite right. Her idea is something traditional yet elegant, understated yet romantic, subdued yet sexy. The question is, does such a dress even exist?"

I told Marcia not to fret. I would go with them and find that store in the Bronx. It turned out it was no longer there. We learned from the waitress at the luncheonette next door that it had burned down years ago. A girl was trying on a dress and her mother dropped a cigarette ash on the train. The bride-to-be nearly went up in smoke.

Jane, Marcia and I went to every bridal warehouse, specialty shop and department store from New York to Massachusetts. Marcia was at her wit's end. But, finally last week, Jane thought she had fulfilled her mother's dream: a bridal gown she found at Saks. It cost a mere $5,000 not including the veil.

"It's absolutely perfect," Jane said.

"Over my dead body," Marcia told her.

Marcia is hoping that Jane will get so disgusted that maybe, with a little bit of luck, she'll elope.

~Judith Marks-White

Second Chance

The concept of two people living together for 25 years without a serious dispute suggests a lack of spirit only to be admired in sheep.
~A. P. Herbert

It was a strange experience. Married twenty-five years, divorced two. Our ostensible reason was the empty nest syndrome when our son went away to college. Idiosyncratic words and gestures crossed the threshold from cute to dumb. Silences hung from the ceiling, cocoons of sighing air.

Anger came easily, particularly the self-righteous, enabling anger without a filter.

One night, I stormed upstairs following a number of directed remarks to sleep in the guest room. My parting words were "I'm not going to live like this." That weekend, a temporary hotel stay. A one-year apartment came next, followed by the purchase of a home for me.

We spoke to each other twice—division of property, no argument there, and also to sign the divorce agreement. Our son was not a direct part of anything, being away at college. Of course, this simplifies the story, but it was about us. He knew he was loved by both of us and would not have to make any choices.

A couple of years later, I got a letter with familiar handwriting. I was surprised, but not unpleasantly. I waited for about an hour to open it. I didn't think there were any legal or family issues to resolve. It fell from my hand once, and I nearly tore it in half when I opened it. She had apparently written the letter in installments, as there were two different colors of ink.

My uncle had passed away two weeks earlier, and our son told her. "I know how important family is to you. I'm sorry Uncle Ed died. I've found out that doing things just to please myself doesn't. Maybe we were too hasty. If you ever want to just sit down and talk about what we did and could do, we can have a beer or two and…"

Knowing she hated the taste and smell of beer, calling it "piss in a glass," I could see the sour look. While reading, I heard the sound of water falling from a large block of translucent ice, held by both of us.

I finished the letter. The second part of the letter became the conventional catch-up with the news, closing with a reminder to call if I wanted to. I reached for the telephone, sat on the couch and dialed. She used her professional voice to answer, and I giggled, "Boy, you know how to get a guy's attention. Needless to say, you have my interest. How about going to Fairchild Gardens?" This had long been a sore spot. She wanted to go there, and I resisted. I was pleased with myself for remembering that, but brought back down to Earth when she disclosed she and a girlfriend had gone down there three months earlier.

She must have sensed my disappointment, "Oh, but I'd love to go again. It's even better than I expected. How does Sunday sound? Look, I've got to get back to work. See you at noon."

Our son was home for spring break, and his total reaction to my announcement of our first date was "Cool."

When I picked her up, he admonished us to take it easy. One might say he was unimpressed with everything.

It was a perfect spring Florida day. We talked about what each of us had done over the last couple of years. Of course, our son had passed on any interesting tidbits to each of us anyway. The sunroof let us bake in the sun, and when we arrived, the breeze off the water was welcome. The Gardens looked like the paint chip counter at Home Depot.

After the Garden, we went to a Mediterranean restaurant for lunch. I had lamb shanks, while she had a gyro. I saw her looking longingly at the wine list and told her I wouldn't hold her to a beer. After we ate, she wanted to see my house.

The drive home was fairly comfortable. We spoke of our son and the immediate past and future, but did not refer to our former married life. The sun was setting when we arrived. I poured two glasses of wine, and we sat on the patio watching lights go on in the homes around the lake. Her warm hand grabbed my arm, and she pulled me to her for a kiss. I think it surprised her as much as it did me. We both sat speechless and smiling.

"Do you want to stay for dinner? I'm sure I can find something to eat." (I had nothing in the refrigerator.)

"No, thanks. I have to go home and prepare for work. Maybe next time."

"Sounds good to me."

The unspoken words hung like a Calder mobile. We both had enjoyed ourselves, but didn't want a couple of glasses of wine to rush that which must wait. I drove her home, the evening being as encouraging as the daytime. Just before leaving her house, I said, "I'll call you later."

"Okay." A friendly and chaste kiss on the cheek and a hug.

We had several more dates and began to travel together again. I had forgotten what a pleasure it was to go somewhere I hadn't been before, and how much we both enjoyed that. Mount Dora, New York City, and the Keys, even Epcot.

I found out later that she didn't date. Neither did I during the time we were apart.

The summer air was waning, fall slowly cooling the air, but not the ardor. I once again asked her to marry me. "Yes." The ceremony was the three of us and a clerk of the court, who read from a small tattered book in a government garden. We got into three cars and drove back to work.

I don't recommend getting a divorce to save a marriage, but it worked for us, an unintended consequence. We needed a separation to find a reason to be married.

~Timothy A. Setterlund

29

Chicken Soup for the Soul

What Families Do

Be kind to your mother-in-law, but pay for her board at some good hotel.
~Josh Billings

My family has a dirty little secret. It's not something we share with other people—ever. Each of my siblings married their spouses without letting them in on the secret. They just let them marry into the fold and hoped for the best when they found out. And it wasn't an especially fun discovery for them to make. Probably a bit like finding out they had leprosy or maybe just a really bad case of hemorrhoids. Either way, the newcomers to our family weren't always happy when they realized that their new mother-in-law has a tongue sharper than those knives they advertise on infomercials. (You know the ones. They can cut a Volkswagen in half in seven seconds flat.)

When I first met my husband, my siblings urged me to do as they'd done: Minimize the potential spouse's exposure to our mother, lest he disappear into some dark abyss, like so many boyfriends before him. "Don't let Mom talk to him," my siblings warned me. "Especially without you there to monitor the conversation."

I followed their advice to the letter. I kept Eric away from Mom as much as I could. And it must have worked. Eric proposed to me just five months after we met. All was going as planned. Eric might have thought Mom was a little rough, but just a little. He was clueless, and I wanted to keep him that way until after we'd made things official.

But that was not to be. Just hours before our wedding, a freak cell phone accident messed up the plan, nearly costing me years of wedded bliss.

The morning of the wedding, my parents drove in from out of town and couldn't seem to locate the church, so my mom called Eric to ask for directions. He gave her the information, they chatted for a moment, and then my mom hung up the phone.

Or thought she did.

Eric was just about to hang up on his end when he heard my mom's voice. He put the phone back up to his ear and soon realized that she wasn't talking to him. But his curiosity got the best of him and he listened in.

"I told you to turn back there. You never listen to me, but you'd be so much better off if you would. After this many years of marriage, I would think you'd finally learn to do what I tell you to do."

Eric heard my father sigh and mumble something under his breath.

But Mom wasn't finished. "What did you say?"

"I said I just missed a turn. I don't think you need to make a federal case out of it."

"A federal case? A federal case? Are you kidding me with this stuff? You have not seen a federal case, mister. And if you would have just listened to me in the first place, none of this would have happened. You're not a very smart man, you know, and if you'd just do what I tell you…"

Eric gulped, then realized they might be able to hear him and quickly hung up. And, predictably, he called me.

"Hi, honey! Happy Wedding Day! I can't wait to see you!" I said in lieu of a simple hello.

"Um, babe," he said nervously, "how often do people tell you that you're just like your mom?"

Instant sinking feeling. "What happened? What did she say?"

He relayed the story to me and then said, "I have to be honest. I'm freaking out a little. You're sweet now, but after forty years of marriage, are you going to talk to me that way?"

"No, never," I said emphatically.

"But how do I know? Sometimes people change after the wedding."

Was this actually happening? I was sitting in the chair at the salon, and the stylist was pinning my veil into my up-do… the up-do I might no longer need.

Thanks to my mom, my biggest downfall.

"Eric, I'm sorry you had to hear that. My mom can be a little…"

"Demeaning? Condescending? Evil, even?"

I sighed. "I know it sounds crazy, but she really does mean well. Our wedding is so important to her, and she didn't want to be late."

"But the way she talked to your dad was terrible. I'm worried that you might turn into her some day." He swallowed hard. "And I couldn't take that."

I felt tears spring into my eyes. Was Eric considering calling things off? I wanted to ask the question, but I wasn't sure I wanted to hear the answer.

Eric interrupted my thoughts. "Oh, my gosh, I have another call—and it's your mom. What should I do?"

"Answer it, but act normal. She doesn't know you overheard her yelling at my dad."

Eric sighed and said he'd call me back. Then he answered Mom's call. "Hello? Martha? Did you find the church all right?"

"Yes, we did, but the flowers are all wrong. She ordered lilies; she told me that last week. I called the florist, and he said that he had a mix-up. We're on our way to the flower shop to pick up the right flowers." She seemed on the verge of tears as she added, "I just wanted everything to be perfect for her big day. She's my only daughter, and I love her so much."

"I know, Martha. We all love her. Thanks for fixing her flowers."

"Well, of course," she said. "It's what families do."

Mom's words echoed in Eric's head as he called me back. *It's what families do.* And families also overlook one another's faults, he realized.

I answered the phone, sure I hadn't breathed since Eric and I had hung up a few minutes before. "So everything's falling apart, isn't it?" I said, near tears.

"Nothing is falling apart," he answered calmly. "She's fixing the flowers as we speak."

I exhaled. "So you're not calling off the wedding?"

He chuckled. "No, of course not. Why would you think that?"

"Because my mom is horrible, and you're worried I'm going to turn into her some day."

"Your mom's not so bad."

"Not so bad? Are you kidding me?"

"Your mom was practically crying because your flowers were messed up. She's got a good heart, honey, and she really loves you."

"But the way she talked to my dad earlier, well, it's not exactly an isolated incident."

"Nobody's perfect, and she's part of my family now. So let's cut her some slack. After all, it's what families do."

I sighed. Eric was right. Mom had a heart of gold, despite having a tongue that sometimes went into slice-and-dice mode.

"So everything's okay?" I asked.

"Yeah, we're good. But, babe," Eric hesitated, "please, please, please don't ever turn into your mother."

"I promise."

"And one more thing: That woman is never, ever living with us."

I laughed and said, "You'll get no arguments here."

An hour later, Eric and I tied the knot surrounded by our families, friends, and dozens of simply perfect lilies, thanks to my less-than-perfect, but somehow still lovable mother.

~Marie Wells

Chapter
4

Family Matters

Happily Ever Laughter

Love is being stupid together.

~Paul Valery

30

The Butler Did It

If you never did you should. These things are fun and fun is good.
~Dr. Seuss

To beat the winter doldrums, my husband decided to throw an impromptu dinner party for his marketing group. "I know it's only two day's notice, but they'll come if they know you're making your famous lasagna," he said. "All they'll have to bring is a white elephant gift."

"I'll prepare enough lasagna, salad and garlic bread to feed an army," I chuckled as I recalled the group's previous parties at our home.

My husband's close-knit marketing group consisted of five men and five women. They'd never miss one of my husband's parties. Counting spouses and dates, the guest list would total twenty. And what a thoughtful bunch—they never arrived at the door empty-handed. They'd bring an appetizer or a dessert, a bottle of wine, and an outlandish white elephant gift, with everyone attempting to outdo each other's zany gift. It would definitely be another fun-filled evening, with shenanigans aplenty.

To amuse his employees, my husband donned butler attire for the party. And in butler mode with a white linen towel draped over his left forearm, he greeted the guests at the door. After everyone arrived, my husband poked his head into the kitchen, "Madam, it's 7:00 p.m. and all guests are accounted for."

"Dinner is ready," I said as I filled a big breadbasket. "Tell everyone to head for the buffet table. Hot garlic bread coming up!"

Toasts were made to good food, good conversation, and good marketing.

After dinner, we began the white elephant gift exchange. The elaborately wrapped gifts lined the family room floor. "Everyone take a number. Let the game begin!" my husband shouted.

The first gift chosen was a black oblong metal mailbox with caricatures of John, Paul, Ringo and George painted on each side. The second gift was a pair of red glitter-encrusted clown shoes. Since the object of the game is to choose, open, trade and steal, merriment, thievery and greed ensued. During the reclamation of the clown shoes, a bottle of red wine toppled from the buffet table and saturated the off-white carpet.

My husband, still in butler mode, shouted, "Madam, I'll take care of it!"

The party came to a halt. We watched as he poured white wine over the red wine spill. After each drenching, he blotted up the wine with the butler towel he'd been wearing over his arm. Suddenly, the red wine spot disappeared! My husband bowed to a round of applause.

The joviality continued until midnight, and the party was a huge success.

To our dismay, the spot from the red wine spill had returned the next morning. After breakfast, my husband called a professional carpet cleaning service. The experts assured us we'd never see the spot again.

However, two weeks later, the red spot reappeared. Again, the stain was removed, and we were promised it was gone forever.

But it was not to be. A month later, the phantom red spot was back, larger than the original spill.

After the owner of the carpet cleaning company refused to clean the carpet for a third time, we mulled our options. We made the decision to have the carpet and padding removed, and the hardwood floor underneath refinished.

"Since we have to look at that ghastly red spot for two more days, I have an idea," my husband said as he turned off the television after the 11:00 p.m. news.

He took two giant black permanent markers from the desk in the corner of the room and waved them in the air. His antics never ceased to amaze me. I howled as I watched him outline the ugly spot using one of the black markers. It was actually beginning to look like a body had once been sprawled on the carpet!

"You're crazy!" I exclaimed. "It's late. I'm going to bed." I blew him a kiss and headed upstairs to our bedroom.

That's the last thing I remember until the alarm awakened me at 6:00 the next morning. I got out of bed, put on my robe, skipped down the stairs and headed for the kitchen. I was dumbstruck with horror and disbelief when I glanced into the family room. It looked like an actual crime scene! Not only was there an outline of a body on the carpet, but there was yellow caution tape, two orange traffic cones, and one folding barricade sign, topped with two yellow flashing lights encircling the make-believe crime scene.

A wave of anguish and despair washed over me. Granted, my husband loved a good practical joke (so did I), but hadn't he gone too far this time with such outrageous behavior? Surely, a highway was missing its equipment. I had questions, but he was saved by the doorbell....

My husband had taken the day off from work for the occasion. He greeted the three workmen at the front door and led them into the family room.

"It's all yours, gentlemen," he said as he quickly removed the tape, cones, and barricade sign.

When the workers spotted the outlined section of carpet, one visibly shaken worker asked, "What happened here?"

My husband smiled, and then replied, "The butler did it."

"We have to go to our van to get our tools. Be right back," said the man in charge.

But no workmen returned. Several minutes later, we heard tires screeching as the van sped down our street. An hour later, the office manager called to advise us the workers had been called to another job.

"Please go to work tomorrow," I pleaded, "and return the cones and barricade sign."

My husband nodded and laughed uproariously. "You have to admit this was one of my best pranks."

Fortunately, the following morning, a new crew reported to work at our home. In five days, the refinished wood floor was shiny and beautiful, and looked brand new.

Yes, my husband thrives on chaos, hilarity and mischief, and I know striving for a predictable lifestyle is out of the question. So, I take deep breaths and enjoy the ride.

~Georgia A. Hubley

In Your Dreams

I have my own little world, but it's okay—they know me here.
~Author Unknown

My husband, Sam, is a big guy. At six feet, four-and-a-half inches tall, and two hundred and fifty pounds, when you meet him it's like shaking hands with a football player. In fact, in college, that's just what he was. But, like many men his size, Sam is also gentle. He gives great hugs, he's terrific to snuggle into on the couch, and when you are walking through a dark parking lot after a late-night movie, you don't have to worry about being jumped.

I love Sam's size, but it has come at one price: sleep. Along with the mere size of him in our bed, my gentle giant also happens to be an active sleeper. His sister assures me that he has always been this way, something she experienced often during their family trips as kids. While asleep, Sam regularly kicks out with his legs, flaps or flails his arms, talks to different people, and, from what I have been able to hear, he always tells the truth. We have a joke that if he cheats on me, he'll be the first one to tell me.

Thirteen years ago, in the beginning of our relationship, we shared a queen-sized bed. Almost every night I would wake up, alarmed and in pain after a kick to my calf or shin.

"Ow!" I would scream. "Sam! That really hurt!"

"Honey, someone was trying to attack you. I was protecting you. I am so sorry," he would say, and then roll over and go back to sleep.

"The only one attacking me is you!" I'd say, royally annoyed.

The third time his elbow came crashing down from over his head onto the top of my skull, I decided our queen-sized-bed days were over. Sleeping in a helmet was not in my future.

Now, seven years later, in our king-sized bed, I am safe from the kicking and the flailing—most of the time. It's only when he's on his side facing me, and my Bend-It-Like-Beckham takes a big kick at the goal during his imaginary U.S. Cup championship game, that I get nicked.

Along with the physical, his mouth is also active in sleep. Sam has a stressful job, and his subconscious takes over at night. I have heard him experiencing road rage, fending off the enemy during a war, and cursing like a teenage boy. In fact, I never know what I will hear.

One night, I woke up to roaring beside me. I looked over at Sam, growling like angry tiger. "Roooar! Roooaaar!"

"Sam," I said, "who on Earth are you roaring at?"

He flipped over and said, "Sorry, there was a polar bear at the window. I was trying to scare it away."

Of course there was a polar bear at the window.

One night, he was on his back, struggling to get out his words. He was angry, yet the anger was in how he said the words, not how loud they were.

"Get off... my property...." he said, brows wrinkled.

I wondered who was on our property.

"Get... off. Get off my property... with... those... cigarettes!" he yelled.

I smiled to myself. Who knew he was so anti smoking?

When Sam is fighting off an intruder or hurling curses at a nonexistent coworker, I like to save him from his dream. Why let him linger in misery? I'll wake him up. But sometimes I don't wake him up. I listen to the strange talk and try to go back to sleep. This is especially true when the dream appears to be a good one.

Not long ago, I woke up to a rhythmic movement from Sam's side of the bed. Sam was repeatedly thrusting his hips back and forth. Here we go again, I thought. Lucky him. He landed a good dream this time. As I waited, feeling the mattress move up and down, up and down, I started to wonder. Who is it? It's probably not me. And where is he? Probably somewhere good. Maybe the Caribbean. Despite the increase of speed and movement next to me, I waited. But after a while, I realized that the action was not dying down. Suddenly, he picked up the pace even more. His hips were racing, the bed was moving, and I was being bounced up and down.

"Sam!" I yelled. No nice wife this time. He rolled over onto his back.

I stared, waiting for him to explain himself. I knew enough not ask, "What were you dreaming about, honey?"

Then Sam burst into laughter.

"What!" I said. "WHAT is so funny?!"

"Honey," he said, "when you woke me up, I was just about to win the Kentucky Derby. I was making the last round to the finish line!"

Doesn't he know that a two-hundred-and-fifty-pound man can't be a jockey? Actually, in Sam's dreams, anything can happen.

~Gwen Daye

My Next Husband Will Be Normal

A man may be a fool and not know it,
but not if he is married.
~H. L. Mencken

"I'm taking a quick bike ride before breakfast," I called to my husband as he went out the door. "I should be back in twenty minutes." He turned to me, nodded, and headed toward the garage to tear apart a motorcycle.

For a moment, I hesitated, wondering if I should skip my morning ride. I had a migraine, and my fibromyalgia and arthritis were acting up, making it tough for me to even walk. But I was determined not to let my connective tissue disease get the better of me and alter my daily routine.

After pedaling only about a mile down a deserted dirt road near our house, I felt the strength draining from my body like air leaking from a balloon. I was weak, my ears began to ring, and things around me appeared to sprout black fuzz around the edges. Suddenly, my legs went limp like cooked linguini, and my body folded up like a cheap lawn chair. Then, everything went black.

I awoke in the ditch with the heavy bike across my chest. My head and ankle were throbbing. Bits of gravel were embedded in my skinned palms. When I tried to sit up, the world began to spin again, so I lay back down in the dirt.

Since I couldn't make it home on my own power, I had no choice but to wait for someone to happen along and help me. Knowing there was rarely any traffic on that road, I clung to the hope that my husband would come to my rescue.

"He'll be along any minute," I reassured myself. "He'll know something's wrong when I'm not back home at the usual time."

I assumed that when he realized I'd been gone too long, he would wonder if something happened and come looking for me. I was wrong.

I continued to lie there in a rain puddle with rocks and a discarded Pepsi can digging into my back. I felt like a marionette without strings. Each time I started to stand up, I felt faint, so I spent a good part of the morning lying there at the side of the road.

I pulled grass and a cigarette butt from my hair and spit the sandy grit from between my teeth while watching dead leaves, gum wrappers and other litter blow past me. When a McDonald's bag tumbled by, I wondered who had eaten their Big Mac here, in the middle of nowhere, and then recklessly thrown the trash out their car window.

After a while, the local bugs discovered me. Bees buzzed around my head, ants crawled up my shorts, and Japanese beetles tickled my thighs. Meanwhile, the sun grew hotter as it rose higher in the sky.

After a while, I felt my strength returning. By this time, I'd become painfully aware that my husband was not searching for me. Giving up hope of my knight coming to help, I muttered to myself, "If I want to get home before winter snows come, it's up to me to get myself there."

Using the bike for leverage, I pulled my woozy body up on quivering legs. I couldn't tell if it was the world spinning or just me wobbling. Half-standing and half-slumping over the handlebars for support, I trudged nearly a mile to get home. I mentally rehearsed what I would say to Sir Galahad when I got there.

Staggering into the front yard, I heard whistling in the garage. For a moment, I forgot the ringing in my head and the pain in my ankle. I dragged myself toward the whistling and said weakly, "I passed out in the road and waited for you to come looking for me."

My husband looked up from his project in surprise.

"Weren't you worried about what had happened to me when I didn't come right back from my ride?"

"I didn't notice that you were gone that long," he replied.

"I was gone most of the morning!" I hollered. He looked puzzled.

"I could have broken all my limbs or been flattened by a moving van!" I told him.

I was angry enough to spit hammers, but he just stood there silently. I wondered if, while I was gone, he'd been zapped by a lightning bolt and struck dumb. He wiped his hands on a greasy rag and shrugged.

"My inward parts could have been spilling out all over the road," I ranted. "I could have been devoured by wolves. My eyes could have been plucked out by vultures! All sorts of vermin could have been feasting on my flesh… but you didn't even notice I was gone!"

"Sorry," he whispered.

With a sigh, he turned back to his motorcycle. Then, as if he'd remembered something, he turned back. I waited expectantly for a delayed display of sympathy.

"Oh," he said, "let me know when lunch is ready."

I was too weak to choke him, but as I fell in a heap on the porch, I made a resolution: If I have a next husband, I will definitely try to find one who's normal.

~Marsha Jordan

Saturday Morning Crazy

The family—that dear octopus from whose tentacles we never quite escape,
nor, in our inmost hearts, ever quite wish to.
~Dodie Smith

The phone rang for the first time that Saturday morning when my brother called at ten o'clock. "I'm very upset," he began. I'd heard that before. I cradled the phone between my ear and my shoulder, reached for the dust rag, and started polishing furniture. I sensed this was going to be a long conversation. Certainly, I could console him and get some housework done at the same time. Twenty minutes later, my job was done. I had sparkling woodwork, and my brother was no longer "very upset."

In the meantime, a dull ache had started at my temples, so I sat down to finish my morning coffee, which was by this time, of course, cold. I placed the cup in the microwave and set the timer. Then the phone rang. Again. This time it was my father.

"Yeah," he started out, "I called the place, and they didn't get the thing for the thing."

Now, I'm usually pretty good at deciphering my father's cryptic speech. After all, I've had over forty years of experience. Yet, this remark was beyond even my level of comprehension. "What?" I asked.

"You know. The thing for the thing. The one we talked about the other day."

For a moment I felt like I was in a scene from the movie, *Goodfellas*, where several of the characters communicate in code just in case the Feds have placed a tap on their phones. "I can't understand you," I explained. "You'll have to give me a little more information."

"The thing that goes to the bank every month." He clucked his tongue. "You know. The thing."

The ache in my temples spread across the crown of my head. I closed my eyes in concentration. "The thing… the thing… for insurance." Suddenly, I got it. "Do you mean the automatic deduction for your health insurance premium?"

"Yes," my father huffed at my denseness, "finally."

"Did you call the insurance company to find out why?"

"No."

I'd better handle this, I decided. No customer representative, however well-trained, would ever understand an eighty-four-year-old man calling for information about "the thing for the thing." I ended our conversation and dialed his insurance carrier. A cheery recorded voice advised me that business hours were Monday through Friday, 8:00 a.m. to 8:00 p.m., so I disconnected and dialed Dad.

"What am I going to do now? What if I get sick over the weekend? Or have an accident?" he asked. "I won't have any insurance."

"Well, stay put and don't make any dangerous maneuvers," I responded in an attempt at humor.

Dad clucked his tongue again. "Everything is a big joke with you."

"Wait a second," I remarked. "What's today's date?"

"The third."

"And what day of the month does the deduction usually take place?"

"The sixth."

"There's your answer," I said.

"Oh… heh, heh. I just got the dates mixed up again."

Yep, you did, I thought, as I hung up the phone. I placed my cup in the microwave once more; maybe now I could finish my coffee. I sat down and took a few long sips of the warm liquid. Really, I thought, was I the only one in this family who could think clearly? Then the phone rang. Again. This time it was my cousin.

"Uh, hi, how you doin'?" he started shyly. "Umm, what are you doing for Christmas this year?"

"Same as always. Cooking for the family."

"Can I come to your house, too?"

"Of course," I answered.

"And could I bring a friend?"

"Sure."

"And could you make that rigatoni I like?"

"Yes, I'll make it."

I reached for my ever-expanding to-do list. Two more guests and one more entrée. Sure, no problem. No problem at all. I really wasn't counting on any additional work so close to the holiday, yet it came as no surprise; my cousin always did like my cooking best.

My stomach groaned, and my head throbbed. I checked the clock: 12:30. Breakfast had been a wipe-out. Maybe I'd have better luck with lunch. I spilled my stale coffee down the drain, grabbed a can of soup from the cabinet, popped the top, and poured its contents into a bowl. I set the microwave timer, and after its chirp, I sat and spooned the first comforting taste to my lips.

"What did you do with the sooooap?" my husband howled from the shower. "I need a new bar of sooooap!"

My spoon dropped with a clang, sending bits of vegetables and alphabets across the kitchen table. Oh, for goodness sake. I took a deep breath. I'm not going to react, I promised myself. I'm going to stay calm. I breathed again. Then, to use strictly clinical terms, I lost it.

"That's it!" I screamed as I pounded into the bathroom. I yanked open the cabinet door, grabbed a new bar of soap, and threw it into the bathtub. "I've had it with this family!" I cried. "I'm moving to a place where there is no family."

My husband peeked around the shower curtain. "Oh, yeah? And where would that be?"

"Over in no-family-land. Where I can eat and drink in peace, and the phone doesn't ring, and I don't have to cook at Christmas, and people like you can just find their own soap."

My head spun, and I could feel my blood pressure rising. I stumbled into the bedroom, turned on the radio, and lay down on the bed. After a few minutes, my husband tip-toed in and dressed quietly at the foot of the bed. Just as quietly, he left the room and returned holding my coat in his hand.

"C'mon," he said as he extended the coat toward me, "I'll take you out for lunch. Afterward, I'll drop you off at the airport. I'm pretty sure there's a flight to no-family-land leaving later tonight." He shot me a sly smile, "That is, if you really want to go."

No, I didn't really want to go. I didn't hate my family. I loved them. And I had to admit that their neediness was, in part, my own fault. In a way, be it rational or mad, I liked how they needed me. It made me feel useful, important. Whenever they asked for help or advice, I felt valued. And more importantly, when they gathered around my table, I felt loved, even if sometimes that love was overwhelming.

I shrugged into my coat and headed for the door. Then the phone rang. I grabbed my purse and stepped across the threshold. Whoever was calling would just have to wait until later to love me.

~Monica A. Andermann

A Brush With Disaster

It is foolish to tear one's hair in grief,
as though sorrow would be made less by baldness.
~Cicero

I n my scientist husband's perfect world of order, there would always be a place for everything, and everything would always be in its place. But, in our family of seven, that just didn't happen.

Neal had many pet peeves, but having to search for his brush each morning ranked among the highest. Sometimes, he'd find it in the boys' bathroom. Other times, it would be in the girls' toy box with Barbie hairs tangled in the bristles. On rare occasions, he might find it where it belonged in his bathroom drawer.

While looking through our local home improvement store, he hit upon an idea, a stroke of genius in his mind, to end this hide-and-seek routine with his brush. When he came home, I noticed the small bag he carried.

"What's that?"

"You'll see." His grin bothered me.

After a trip to the garage, he went straight to the bathroom. While I cooked supper, banging and drilling noises added to my misgivings. Finally, he called me to see his inspired solution.

He had chained his brush to the wall!

There, beside the sink, his brush sat on a pile of chain. He'd drilled a hole in the end of his brush and, to my chagrin, drilled a hole through my new wallpaper. It looked awful. But Neal's motto is "practical is better than pretty."

Every morning, the brush was right there beside the sink. His idea was working out just as he planned.

Or so he thought.

You see, spiking hair with gel was the "in" style for boys at that time, and every morning my youngest son, William, watched his brothers get ready for school. A few days after Neal attached his brush to the wall, I noticed William's hair. It looked strange. Kinda slick.

I asked, "Honey, what did you do to your hair?"

"Gelled it." His blue eyes danced. He was so proud of himself.

It didn't much look like gel. "Show me the gel."

He took my hand, passed the kids' bathroom, and went straight to mine. On the counter was an open jar of Vaseline and, lucky for him, a brush—chained to the wall. He explained to me that since he couldn't take the brush back to the boys' bathroom and use their gel, he used this other jar of "gel" that he found in our bathroom right next to the chained hairbrush.

I wanted to get that stuff out of my baby's hair. I tried shampooing it, but the petroleum jelly sucked in the shampoo like some kind of swamp monster, turning into a gelatinous mess.

Then I called my neighbor who owned a hair salon. I explained what William had done, and when he finally quit laughing, he suggested I try dishwashing soap, the kind that is supposed to cut through grease.

It did a fair job, but William still looked like a teen from the fifties. The kids came home, I made supper, and the whole thing was forgotten.

Until the next morning, that is.

While cooking breakfast, Neal yelled for me. I ran to the bathroom to find him, brush in hand, looking a lot like William did the day before. Giggles bubbled up in my throat and demanded to be let out, but I didn't dare.

"Look at me!" He stared in the mirror. "I can't go to work like this! What is this stuff in my brush?"

"Vaseline."

I couldn't hold the hilarity in any longer and erupted in laughter.

"I don't see anything funny about this."

By now, tears were rolling down my face. But I managed to get him the dish soap. It helped—a little.

There is a proverb that says, "There is a way that seems right to a man, but in the end it leads to death." Well, chaining his brush to the wall seemed right to Neal, and while it didn't lead to death, it certainly led to disaster!

~Linda Apple

Chicken Soup for the Soul

Battle of the Dishes

He who wants to change the world should already begin by cleaning the dishes.
~Paul Carvel

"Mom!" My daughter's cry echoed through the house.

"What now?" I asked as I entered the kitchen to find her rummaging in the drawers, ducking under an open cabinet door. Always drama with teenagers.

"He did it again. Daddy did it again," she cried.

I looked around the room. The countertops were free of clutter, and the appliances gleamed. A sure sign my husband had been in the room.

"Did what?" I asked. A second glance answered my question. The cupboard was bare. A lonely four plates, four cups, three bowls and four iced tea glasses filled the cavernous space.

"It's my fault. I'm sorry," Scott mumbled through a mouthful of Cheerios.

Hunched over the kitchen table, my son guarded his bowl of cereal. "I left my Coke glass and plate on the back porch, and Dad saw them."

"Mom!" Another cry erupted from my outraged teenager. "He's put our names on everything."

"Color coded," Scott said, as he drained the bowl of its remaining milk. He held it up. "Scott" was neatly printed on the side in dark blue marker.

"My name is in orange. I hate orange." Kathy plopped down at the table and buried her head in her arms. "Dad is so weird."

I picked up my iced tea glass to admire my name spelled out in bright rose. "You have to admit he has artistic talent."

When I married Harry, I was madly in love. Not once did I think to take notice of the fact that he grew up in a single-wide trailer. Living in a small space, Harry had "a place for everything and everything in its place" engraved on his soul.

"Does he love you?" my mother asked.

"Can he take care of you?" my father demanded.

"Does he treat his mother well? A man who treats his mother with love and kindness will treat his wife the same," my granny advised.

No one asked if he was a neat nut. I, on the other hand, was a pack rat.

"Less is better!" he said.

"It's my stuff!" I said.

The battle cries of war. A friendly battle with the kids on my side. Give me an empty tabletop, and I will find something to put on it. Harry, on the other hand, believes flat surfaces should remain bare. Knick-knacks should be banned.

Visitors to our house often departed with "my stuff." Admire the candlesticks, and Harry will say, "Here, take them."

Our attic was filled with boxes, items he deemed not necessary. It only made me go out and buy more stuff. The kids learned to hide their fast food toys.

"What if my friends come over?" I said. "It's a hundred degrees outside. I say, 'Would you like a glass of iced tea? Lemonade? Water?' No, wait, I can't offer them a drink. We have no glasses!"

"What if Patrick comes over?" my daughter cried.

The truth was out. Young love. My husband and I had a heart-to-heart talk. I understood that leaving dishes around the house and yard went against his grain. I knew that he had told the kids over and over and over again.

The crisis was solved. We now have a fifth glass in our kitchen cabinet. In front, in a place of honor, is a tea glass with VISITOR printed in large purple letters.

How to explain this to the relatives at Christmas will be our next problem!

~Jeri McBryde

36

Fit to Be Tied

*A lovely thing about Christmas is that
it's compulsory, like a thunderstorm,
and we all go through it together.*
~Garrison Keillor

Whoever said that second marriages are twice as hard as first marriages hit the nail on the head. When I met my second husband, I felt my dreams had been answered. We both agreed we wouldn't introduce our children to each other until we knew our relationship was serious. When we got married, I had no illusions that blending two families would be easy.

We were married in May. When Christmas rolled around, we wondered how we would fare with five kids between us, ranging in age from six to fifteen. Some days were pretty hairy, but we were managing.

Shortly after Thanksgiving, we made the decision to go on a search for the perfect Christmas tree. We hit a couple of tree lots, but nothing looked good. Finally, we found a lot where the trees were reasonable and well-shaped. We had four of the five children with us. They were full of Christmas spirit and starting to get on my husband's nerves. To me, they were just being kids.

We all jumped out of the car on this cold day, and the children immediately started wandering all over the lot. My husband, getting grumpier by the minute, ordered everyone back to the car.

It was evident his patience was wearing thin. I gathered the children, and we all sat in the car while he paid for the tree we had selected. We waited patiently while the man from the tree lot placed the tree on top of the car. The lot man gave my husband some rope to tie it on. Being a dutiful wife, I followed my husband's directions as he handed me an end of the rope and advised me to hand it back at the demanded time. This process was repeated several times.

By now, he was on the verge of going ballistic, so I dared not say a word as he completed securing the tree to the roof of the car. After checking it by tugging on the rope several times, he was sure it wouldn't blow off or move until we got it home, just a few short blocks away.

Then, he attempted to open the driver's side door. He pushed the button on the door handle and pulled on it. He had tied the door shut with the rope!

The children looked terrified. I, on the other hand, started to smile. The smile turned into an audible giggle, and the giggle sparked relief and amusement on the part of the children. My husband, realizing what he had done and feeling more than a little foolish, started to relax. But the calmness turned to embarrassment as the lot attendant stood watching while he untied the tree and re-secured it, tying it to the bumpers this time.

By the time we got home, we were all laughing so hard that tears ran down our cheeks. My husband, still not happy but not enraged, laughed along with us until we got home and took the tree off the car.

That happened more than twenty-five years ago, but we still retell the story every Christmas. And every Christmas my husband begs us not to retell it! But it is a fond memory of a particularly difficult time for all of us, which we recall with affection and love.

~Ann Williamson

37

Confessions of a Decorating Junkie

A good decorator not only plans and schemes,
but he also knows how the job is done.
~Albert Hadley,
The Story of America's Preeminent Interior Designer

It happens each spring. Walking home from the farmer's market, my tote filled with asparagus, strawberries, and lavender honey, I pass Irv and Patty's house. My neighbors have hauled an eight-foot-tall wooden Easter bunny onto their lawn. She's painted pink, wears a straw bonnet, and carries a basket of eggs in one paw. A picket fence laced with wooden flowers stands at her feet. I choke up at the sight of such decorating excellence. At times like these, I know I've found my spiritual home.

Go ahead, laugh if you want. I'm a decorating junkie. The neighbors may whisper about my husband and my continued childlessness, but no one suspects the holiday boxes I've hidden behind the tools in our shed.

What attracts me is the limitless nature of the sport. Anyone can collect a few things for Christmas or Chanukah—that's more or less expected. Halloween and Thanksgiving are also easy for the decorating novice. But it takes skill to decorate for April Fools' Day, Labor Day, and Columbus Day. Throw in Easter, St. Patrick's Day, and

Fourth of July, and you can see why I installed cabinets in the living room and added more shelves in the hall closet and garage.

I vow to stop, but then I see a trio of flag-waving metal ants in a catalog and lose control. My decorations accumulate in the attic and guest room, multiplying like tribbles on *Star Trek*. It's a good thing we don't have kids because I might toss their blocks and Tonka trucks to make room for fluffy yellow chicks and painted wooden eggs.

It doesn't end with traditional holidays. I've created decorations for Oktoberfest and Swiss Independence Day. This year, I've set my sights on summer solstice.

I'm telling you, it's an addiction. I console myself with the fact that decorations purchased on clearance after the holidays are way cheaper than crack and much easier to obtain than illegal prescription drugs. They're safer, too. But still, sometimes I'm ashamed when I buy red, white, and blue bunting and matching paper plates.

When Michael and I moved here, the neighbors warned us to expect 400 kids on Halloween. I don't know about you, but I need more than candy with that kind of attendance. First, I dusted off the headless horseman I made out of milk cartons in the sixth grade. (Horace is three feet tall, including the horse, carries a pumpkin head, and wears a white satin cape over his fitted black suit. Clearly, my illness started early.) I bought Michael a pumpkin carving kit and convinced him that real men do indeed use stencils. I pounded a sign in the front lawn that read "Scaredy cats welcome" and draped our bushes and porch with fake spider webs before I installed bats with glowing eyes.

Last year, I bought thirty yards of white tulle and made ghosts to hang from the trees. Michael, bored after transforming a pumpkin into Frankenstein's face, hooked up a fog machine and added a witch with a pointed green hat and purple velvet cape.

On November first, we moved on to Veteran's Day. I packed away the Halloween stuff and pulled out metal flags and tin soldiers reclaimed from Michael's childhood. A few weeks later, I stuffed them into cabinets and retrieved turkeys, gourds, and scarecrows from an overflowing footlocker. As I sorted through freeze-dried leaves and ears of corn, I thought ahead to Christmas. You need a solid decorating strategy for the mother of all holidays.

In our neighborhood, the sky's the limit. One neighbor constructs a twelve-foot-tall tumbleweed snowman. One has a working Santa train, and another a laser lightshow. It's probably dangerous for me to live here, knowing that no one, not even my husband, will rein in the decorating obsession, particularly in December.

Ten years ago, Michael discovered the Department 56 North Pole Village and purchased twelve porcelain buildings in one spree at the local Hallmark store. Since then, he's accumulated a staggering array of the toaster-sized buildings and their countless accessories. Eventually, he was forced to install a ceiling-mounted shelving system in the garage to house his collection. But the shelves can only hold so much, and now I'm embarrassed to open the door.

Last year, I spent two days setting up an intricate North Pole village on the kitchen buffet while my brother-in-law watched in amazement. Then I moved on to Elfland—an elfin spa complete with coffee shop, bakery, and wedding chapel—plus Santa's Visitor Center and ice skating rink.

Meanwhile, Michael hung the Christmas lights outside. Don't get me started on those. We've got white, colored, rope, net, and icicle lights. There are so many I'm sure you can see our home lit up from outer space.

As we decorated the tree, my brother-in-law said, "You two are a little obsessed with the holidays, aren't you?"

I was unwrapping a glass roadrunner that Michael and I had bought while on vacation in Arizona. I dropped the crumpled tissue paper and admired, as I did every year, the yellow sprinting feet. He had to repeat himself to get my attention.

I hung the ornament and stammered, "Another village, and we'll cross the line."

He looked at me incredulously. "Cynthia, it was out of control the minute you unpacked Santa's Woodworks and the lumberjack elves."

I knew he was right, so I didn't tell him I'd only completed the early December decorations. By Christmas, we'd have stockings, lighted garlands, and red lacquered pots brimming with poinsettias and cyclamen. Santas of every shape and size would be scattered throughout the house, along with an assortment of angels inherited from my grandmother. Upstairs, on the desk in the hallway, I'd assemble the North Pole ski resort using the latest of Michael's Department 56 collectibles.

I lay in bed that night and thought, "It's a sickness. It needs to stop."

I tried. I really tried.

Two weeks later, I bought a life-size felt snowman for the front porch and a pair of jeweled pewter trees to use as part of the dining room centerpiece. When I dragged the boxes through the door, Michael didn't ask why. He knows as well as I do that holidays were meant for kids. While we wait for our children to arrive, we decorate.

~Cynthia Patton

Reprinted by permission of Off the Mark
and Mark Parisi ©2006

38

It's Not Easy Being Green

Vegetarian—that's an old Indian word meaning "lousy hunter."
~Andy Rooney

I've always felt that it was our responsibility to care for our planet. So, like many like-minded souls, I adopted a new Earth-friendly lifestyle. But like Kermit the Frog, I soon learned that it's not easy being green.

My first mistake was trying to make a radical change overnight. Turning from a typical consumer into an eco-savvy citizen should be gradual. Instead, in my sudden fervor to keep the world from descending into the muck of human refuse, I wanted to be green all the way—and now. Of course, being married meant that my husband was going to have to go along with me. That was mistake number two.

My husband adjusted fine to tossing cans and bottles into the new recycling bin in the kitchen. We switched our light bulbs to CFL (compact fluorescent light) bulbs, a good trade that rendered cost savings as well as conserved energy. I went about the house flipping off lights and unplugging appliances that weren't in use. Our new cleansers lacked the same cleaning oomph of our usual toxic brands, but scrubbing harder was well worth avoiding a future generation of mutant flora and fauna.

So far, so good. I was learning new green lingo and we were

doing the Three R's: Reduce, reuse, recycle. But it wasn't enough. After all, the rate of global warming exceeded our snail's pace conversion to greenhood. So I pressed onward.

I tossed out cosmetics that were tested on animals, and for once felt relieved that my husband was too cheap to buy real leather. The kids and I even made our own solar cooker from cardboard and foil and a vermicompost bin, where red worms ate, or rather recycled, bits of celery ends and carrot tops while I envisioned a garden that would provide all our nutritional needs. And speaking of nutrition, one of the greenest things we could do, I decided, was to become vegans. Mistake number three.

For the uninitiated, there are different levels of vegetarianism. Lacto-ovo vegetarians eat eggs and fish but no red meat. The pescetarians abstain from all animal flesh except for seafood. Vegans refuse any animal flesh or commercial goods made from any animal byproducts such as milk or fats. And now, there are flexitarians who are vegetarians most of the time but who will eat meat on occasion. That would have been the wisest choice for newbie greenies like us, but I wanted to be a dedicated greenie so there was no other choice but veganism for us.

My family loves vegetables, so one wouldn't think veganism would be a problem except for one major obstacle: My husband was born and bred a Texan. He was weaned on beef. Something needed to have died a violent death for his meal or it wasn't dinner. I began with not-so-obvious vegan dishes like bean burritos, vegetable curry, and high-fiber vegetable stir-fry. It took a few days before he realized that he hadn't been eating any meat, but soon his biochemistry detected a total lack of decayed flesh in his intestinal system and it began to balk.

"I'm getting constipated," he announced. In our household, bowel movements constitute breaking news.

"You need to drink more water," I said, without mentioning the sudden enormous increase of fiber in his diet. He shrugged and drank a glass of water as I secretly added prunes to our grocery list.

"I feel like eating beef," he announced. In our household, in addition to bowel movements, food cravings constitute news as well as a family decree. So that night, I cooked up some delicious vegan chili, hoping he would not notice that the chunky texture in the spicy mixture was not beef, but a delightful medley of summer vegetables... actually just zucchini. Zucchini chili admittedly lacks the appeal of "Savory Vegetarian Chili" so I plunked down a bowl in front of my husband without an official introduction. He shoveled in the first mouthful and a curious look crossed his face. He peered into his bowl. Darn that Texan in him. He could taste beef—or the lack of it—no matter how well disguised it was.

"This is not chili."

"It is chili."

"Where's the beef?"

"Living peacefully somewhere on an open plain where it belongs."

"I knew it," he groaned. "You're going through one of your vegetarian phases again, aren't you?"

I'd attempted several times in the past to turn us all into vegetarians, but it never lasted more than a week. His taste buds were developed completely around the flavor of animal carcasses of every kind: cattle, pigs, deer, lamb, chickens, and ducks. Converting him was like feeding hay to a lion. Those who know their Bible stories believe this is possible because Noah allegedly did not feed meat to the animals on his ark for forty days and forty nights. But it doesn't actually state that in the Bible. Maybe a few pairs of animals didn't make it to dry land after all. In any case, my husband would have abandoned ship long before the rainbow appeared.

Before he could rage on about not wanting to give up meat, I quickly reminded him about global warming and how grain-fed cattle consume our dwindling resources of oxygen and release more methane gases.

"Do you know how much methane gas I'd release into the earth's atmosphere if I had to eat beans instead of beef?" he snapped. I tried to console him with some soy ice cream but apparently, he can taste the lack of animal byproducts as well because he spat it out and pouted for the rest of the night.

Now I'm all for preserving our planet, but what good would it do to save the earth for tomorrow's generation if today's died of starvation? The next day, we went out for burgers. I was very careful to place the paper bag into our recycling bin.

~Lori Phillips

39

Chicken Soup for the Soul

Joseph's Many Coats

Almost every man looks more so in a belted trench coat.
~Sydney J. Harris

I bought my teenage daughter a lovely designer coat to wear at my second wedding. As happens with fashion, the wool coat, with its billowing pleats, dropped sash, and velvet trim, was soon out of style. Several years later when my daughter—newly married herself, was spring-cleaning, the coat finally found its way into her discard pile. And as I'd offered to make the trip to the Salvation Army for her, she dropped her bags off at my house.

"Promise me you won't go through the bags," she implored, knowing that I was quite capable of salvaging half her castoffs for myself. I believe she envisioned, upon my demise, inheriting half the things she'd gotten rid of years earlier. I made an effort to stick to my promise, but a few days later when I put the bags in my car and was about to shut the trunk, I untied the bags and had a quick look. I couldn't believe my daughter was throwing out that gorgeous coat I'd bought her only two or three—well, maybe four years earlier. It was rumpled from being stuffed in the bag, and admittedly the lining was torn in several places, but it was surely worth keeping. I set it aside, and later, when my husband Joe and I returned from shopping, I hung it in the hall closet. I thought no more about it until nearly two years later.

Much happened during those years including Joe's being laid off. It was one of his job interviews that brought the coat back into our lives. Joe had been near retirement age when he was laid off, so job opportunities did not often come his way. An interview had been arranged for him by his friend Jim for a consulting position at the bank for which he was COO, and Joe was anxious to make a good impression, not only because he wanted the job but also for his friend's sake.

As it happened, Joe overslept that day. I had already left for work and assumed our several alarms would waken him. Alas, that didn't work. In a panic when he finally woke up, he threw on the clothes he'd asked me to select the night before, grabbed his electric shaver, shoved his arms into the new coat I'd given him for Christmas, and jumped into his car. To his credit, he did say afterward that he had thought the sleeves were a tad short. Shaving as he drove, Joe made it to the bank only a few minutes late. In through the revolving doors he flew and up to the reception desk where he breathlessly stated his purpose for being there. They directed him to the upper level. He hurried across the ground floor of the bank and up the marble steps, coat flowing gracefully behind him.

If the CEO noticed that Joe's attire was a little odd, he gave no indication as he ushered Joe into his office. Joe sat down, coat and all, and tried to gather his wits. About halfway through the interview Joe happened to glance down and noticed his coat had two large shiny black buttons in the front, which he didn't recall seeing before. But intent on making a good impression, he thought no more about it, and in fact, it wasn't until the interview was over and he was making his way down the stairs that it registered there was something really wrong with his coat as it dragged in an unfamiliar way on the steps behind him.

During dinner when we were discussing the job interview, the subject of the coat came up.

"By the way," Joe said, pushing his chair back and going to the hall closet. He returned, holding up the designer castoff. "Is this my new coat?"

"That?" I said in disbelief. "No. That's my daughter's old reject."

Joe looked nonplused. "I wore it to the interview," he said.

"You did?" I replied, starting to roar my head off. "Well you can kiss that job goodbye."

Joe was not amused. "What's it doing in the closet?" he asked indignantly.

"Didn't you notice the velvet collar?" I said, rubbing it in. "And the lovely belt across the fanny?"

Joe groaned. "Oh my God, I wonder if anyone noticed."

"Nah," I said reassuringly, once I could stop laughing long enough.

Eccentric though he may have seemed, Joe was hired and we both breathed a sigh of relief—until his first full day at the office, that is. It was late when Joe got home. Anxious to make up for any impressions he might have made earlier he'd stayed late updating old computer files. There was only one other man still in the building when he'd left. Feeling good about himself, Joe gave me a kiss and then ambled over to the closet to hang up his trench coat. When I didn't hear the customary squeak of the closet door closing, I looked up. Joe was standing there inspecting his London Fog, frantically turning it right side and back. He shoved his hand into one of the pockets and pulled out a set of keys.

"Oh my God!" he groaned. "This isn't my coat! These aren't my keys."

"Of course it's your coat," I said. "How could you walk off with someone else's coat?"

"But I have," he shouted, near hysteria. "What am I going to do?"

"Are you sure?" I asked, going over to form my own opinion.

"Of course I'm sure. This must belong to that other guy. And I've got his keys. He won't be able to get home."

"Well, call him up. You can take it right back."

"I don't even know who he is."

"Just call the bank then. Any number—until someone answers."

Joe began to get annoyed with my problem solving. "The switchboard is shut down—I couldn't get through if I wanted to."

"Then just go back. Maybe he's still there."

He sighed. "I won't be able to get in. And besides it'll take me forty-five minutes to get there. He's bound to have taken a taxi or something." Joe's mind was churning. "Oh God, he won't be able to get into his house."

So Joe called his friend Jim and explained the situation. Jim knew whose coat it had to be and called the fellow's home. All was well. He'd had a spare key. He'd worn Joe's coat home. His wife had let him in. No harm done. They could exchange coats in the morning.

"Whew," Joe sighed.

After we'd calmed down I said to Joe, "I hope you didn't have anything odd in your coat pockets."

"Like what? Of course not," Joe answered. "Besides the thing's so old and ratty, all the pockets are worn through."

I started to laugh again. "No wonder you took his coat."

That weekend we bought Joe a new London Fog and took the designer coat to the Salvation Army. And it wasn't just my daughter who never trusted me with her discards again.

~Juliet Bell

Toilet Paper for Valentine's Day

I don't understand why Cupid was chosen to represent Valentine's Day.
When I think about romance, the last thing on my mind is a short,
chubby toddler coming at me with a weapon.
~Author Unknown

I had recently moved from the cozy, tree-covered hills of western Pennsylvania to the rather stark flatlands of the Midwest. My heart told me it was the right thing to do, but my mind was rebelling against the statistical improbability of a relationship working out. A rather harsh winter brewed as I moved into my boyfriend's rented house, started a new job, and began to settle into a new life and surroundings.

Valentine's Day snuck up after only a couple of weeks. Since I worked at an office with all women, starting early in the morning, bouquets were delivered with their subsequent oohs and aahs. Finally, midday arrived, and I could sense the unspoken sympathy of my new coworkers who noticed the distinct absence of flowers on my desk. I tried not to notice their looks, and not being a huge fan of the holiday anyway, I quietly worked at my desk.

During my lunch break, my boyfriend and I ate together at our house. Although I tried to be nonchalant, he could tell that something was bothering me, so I finally spilled the reason for my rather unsubtle sullenness. He immediately expressed remorse for not giving gifts to me sooner, explaining that he had planned to celebrate after work when we had more time. Shamefaced, I said that I completely understood, but John had already scurried to get the stash of presents, asking me to close my eyes as he arranged them with care on the table. With his permission, I opened my eyes to see an odd assortment of unwrapped items, including… a large package of toilet paper!

Although I had taken some acting classes in my undergraduate days, nothing in my amateur training prepared me to mask the initial shock of receiving toilet paper for Valentine's Day. The other humble gifts on the table, such as a plain shower curtain, sat dwarfed by the tower of "ultra-soft." However, after I recovered a bit, I realized that here in front of me was the first person to actually listen and respond to my every little gripe. Having been accustomed to any minor (or major, for that matter) problems being ignored by a former husband, I assumed John hadn't even heard me comment that his bachelor pad was stocked with noticeably thin, rough bathroom tissue and that the faded, mildewed shower curtain could use a biohazard warning. In fact, I, myself, had forgotten that I verbalized any complaints. Yet, not only had John truly listened to me, he actually remembered and purposefully remedied each irritation.

We were married later that year, and we recently celebrated our eighth wedding anniversary where we now live in upstate New York. To this day, I have only received one bouquet of flowers from John, but I have never, ever had to remind him to take out the trash or mow the lawn. If I happen to mention any household problem or inconvenience, sure enough, it will be fixed within a week, if not the same day. If I warn him about our icy driveway in the winter, he'll want to buy ice cleats for me. If I remark on a doorknob not working properly, one will be bought and installed before I can blink. A casual comment about someday wanting a web camera to "visit" with my family resulted in him purchasing one the very next day.

In fact, to the chagrin of other women I know, I have the opposite problem of motivating my husband to do chores. Instead, I often find myself attempting to convince John to postpone his fixer-upper plans and to simply relax in front of the television. So, I will happily forego bouquets of flowers, being eternally grateful for a wonderful husband who actually listens and truly cares.

~Meghan Beeby

Define Normal

Divorce: The past tense of marriage.
~Author Unknown

The house is deathly quiet now, but I swear I can still hear my poor Jeep Grand Cherokee panting heavily out in the garage after toting seven-plus Reillys around town for the past seven-plus days. Ah, the out-of-town guests have left for home; they boarded a plane just this morning and I am finally free to sit down at my laptop in my skivvies with a tall Coke and a short line to the little girl's room.

For the past week I have been entertaining my out-of-town in-laws; I took them to and from the airport, hauled them around town, fed them my famous homemade fried potatoes and scrambled cheese eggs for breakfast, played board games and charades around the kitchen table with all of the kids for hours and employed every sleep-able piece of furniture I own. When the boys weren't at my ex-husbands house — taking full-advantage of the ultimate bachelor's pad — my cozy, little house was stuffed like a summer sausage.

My friends don't seem to understand this bizarre relationship I keep with my ex-husband's family, especially considering that I've been legally unbound from that particular contractual obligation for almost ten years now, the unspoken rule that states that I am to put up my in-laws whenever they're in town. I mean, it's not like I don't have the paperwork to prove it.

"It's just not normal," they observe.

Well, that may be true, but I like to think that I was granted joint custody of my quirky, well-meaning "out-laws"—as I like to call them—in the final decree of my divorce. My ex-husband doesn't seem to mind that I'm still close with them. In fact, I think he likes it; those are the ties that continue to bind us as a family, and I think it's been healthy for our boys to see that we can all still get along. And, besides that, whoever said that there was anything normal when it comes to family, anyway?

I happen to love my sister-in-law, a woman who was once married to my ex-husband's big brother. Over the years we've become sisters of sorts. I know it sounds kind of complicated, but she and her three children are very close to me and my two children. We all seem to get along great; it's as if, somehow, we belong together, in some crazy, not-entirely-dysfunctional way.

When I look at her two boys and her daughter—who are almost exactly the same ages as my boys—I see a strong family resemblance and I can't help but conclude that it is exactly as the old saying goes: Blood is, in fact, thicker than water.

All I know is that when I watch my kids hanging out with their cousins, laughing and enjoying one another in a way that only family can, I know that my decision to remain close with my out-laws is something I'm meant to do, if not supposed to do. The contented expressions on my boys' faces say it all, especially when we spend the day with friends and family—at the request of my ex-husband—consuming two lanes at the local bowling alley, scarfing down greasy food and making the Clampetts look more like the Kardashians.

The thing is my out-laws are good people—a little crazy sometimes—but then again, aren't we all?

And now that they've all packed up their bags and are headed for home, I realize more and more how desperately I miss seeing their faces. I realize how quickly time is getting away from us as our kids are growing up, graduating and grappling with their own futures.

Truth: Life is too short to be spent fighting with family—in-laws, out-laws and the like. This sweet time in our life should be spent wisely, say, playing board games around the kitchen table with a humongous dish of homemade chicken nuggets and French fries placed strategically within everyone's reach, while everyone is eating, laughing and clamoring all at once—pretending to be pseudo-normal, but really coming off as looking more like what a family is supposed to look like, and that is happy. At least happy is what my family looks like to me and that's what matters most.

~Natalie June Reilly

Chapter 5

Family Matters

Family Fun

There's no such thing as fun for the whole family.

~Jerry Seinfeld

42

Numb Skulls

It's a shallow life that doesn't give a person a few scars.
~Garrison Keillor

I come from a family full of adventure-seeking (aka injury-seeking) people, and I'm proud to announce that this is our key to achieving laughter-filled family gatherings. It may seem odd, but it's a fact that my family has grown stronger and stayed together simply due to the fact that we like to gather and share with one another our recent adventures—and, even more so, our resulting injuries.

Growing up in a Niezen household, one realizes quite quickly what is expected. From a young age, my siblings and I were thrown into the world of sports and were told to do our best. And if it didn't work out, at least make it a good crash. We found our family motto one day when my brother Derek walked in wearing a shirt that said, "It's only funny until someone gets hurt. Then it's hilarious." My family burst out laughing and realized someone had made a shirt about us.

I'm not sure what we find so funny about injuries, but if you ever want to see my father cry, just play an injury reel from a home video TV show (the skateboarder falling down stairs, the breaking diving board, the infamous dad-getting-sacked shot, etc.). These kinds of things are pure gold when it comes to laughter in my house. I'd like to say that it's not funny, and that I feel bad for the unfortunate person receiving my laughter, but I'd be lying—at least about the "not being funny" part. I blame it on my genes.

Perhaps Niezens enjoy the unfortunate injuries of others so much because they know better than anyone how injuries like that can occur and how it becomes a good story afterward as you proudly display your wounds, or "injury trophies." Ever since I can remember, going to family gatherings could be compared to watching *America's Funniest Home Videos* on repeat as family members vividly described their latest bruise, cut, stitches, sprain, cast, etc. If someone didn't show up with a sling, cast or significant injury, something wasn't right.

Niezens are known for having strong heads, which we just love to prove by continually crashing and then proceeding to use our heads to stop our falls. We believe scratched elbows and knees are for other families, the ones with weak skulls. We congratulate each other on head scars achieved by amazing acts of bravery, which just happened to end wrong. Good proof of this is my ever-growing collection of family members who have matching chin and face scars from various acts of "bravery" resulting in stitches. I'm proud to tell you that my very own sister, Melissa, is an owner of two chin scars: one from simply falling on her face at the lake and the other from falling off a countertop (why she was up there is anyone's guess). Did I mention the countertop incident happened the same day she got her previous stitches out? And that our babysitter panicked to the point that my oldest sister, familiar with head wounds, had to phone my mother to come home? Yes, these are the skills of my family. We push ourselves to find our limits and outdo one another.

When my brother fell off his bike in his early teenage years (doing some amazing, life-changing trick, I'm sure), he ended up with about a four-and-a-half-inch road burn up his jawbone and cheek. To prevent this injury from happening again, my parents did what every other parent would do. (This is where I would tell you that they made him wear a helmet all the time or taught him to put his hands out to block his falls, but see, ordinary helmets clearly cannot contain the Niezen skull.) They bought him a fancy new full-face, protect-the-entire-skull helmet because Niezens love falling on their heads, and you just can't stop us!

Again, I would like to say that I am immune to this love of skull-bashing, but again I would be lying. As a young, aspiring figure skater, I put so much focus on my graceful, artistic moves that I lacked the ability to simultaneously focus on where the skating rink boards were. I fell, slid, and smacked my head on the boards with a powerful thud… yes, right in front of my proud parents, witnesses to one of my first concussions. What's a loud thud if it doesn't come with a concussion? And, hey, since the first head-butting incident was so fun, why not do it again? And I did, two weeks later. Boastful stories for the next family reunion.

Sometimes, my parents liked to keep us on our toes or perhaps just help strengthen our skull invincibility, so they would challenge us. My oldest sister, Kristina, was unfortunately the target of one of my mother's challenges. My mother claims she "passed" the pool chlorine case to Kristina when she was swimming (about a four-pound gizmo), but my sister will tell you that the resulting two-inch welt on her forehead and corresponding concussion points to the worst "pass" in passing history. In the end, though, I believe Kristina truly benefited from this challenge. When my brother accidentally slammed a door on her a couple months later, the forehead welt came right back and we knew exactly what to do!

At the end of the day, the legacy of the Niezens' strong skulls is what keeps my family together. Whether we like it or not, we continue to hurt ourselves and find joy in describing to one another just how exactly we achieved our latest wound(s). I'm not sure why, and I'm not sure how long our strong skulls will be passed along, but I'm grateful and proud to have a Niezen skull.

~Sherylynn Niezen

"Don't just stand there, get the camcorder!"

43

The Sleepover War

A friend is a brother who was once a bother.
~Author Unknown

My sister Heidi and I couldn't have been much different growing up. She was smart, organized and somehow managed to still have fun despite these things. I was an utterly disorganized slob, and whenever I could I sought revenge against Heidi for being so damned good at everything. Boy, was she ever tough to annoy! She knew my game better than I did. I tried the typical ways a younger brother might annoy his older sister whom he secretly admires. I'd try, for instance, to follow her everywhere. To counter this, she put a lock on her door, and spent a good deal of time in her room. If she walked to the store, I tried to follow her, but she'd always simply run. She was very fast, and I could never keep up with her.

Heidi was disgusted by me, as she well should have been. I was, after all, her younger brother, and I maintained as squalid a standard of living as I could get away with. Anything that took away from my video game playing time was avoided as much as possible, including school, hygiene and chores. Of course, my parents would eventually force me to stop playing games when my eyes were shot through with crimson, and I looked like the very zombies I was trying to kill in my games. When I couldn't play games, my next favorite way to pass the time was to harass Heidi. And it just so happened that Heidi was having a massive sleepover party for her tenth birthday. Five friends were sleeping over, and from the way Heidi talked, she wanted to make a good impression on them. Five against one: I was going to need help.

I enlisted the help of my best friend Jason. Jay was well-versed in the art of guerrilla warfare. He was two years older than me, in Heidi's grade, in fact. He had a paper route, and he sometimes had to employ his substantial abilities to sabotage his non-paying newspaper customers. He came over early in the day, and we spent our time planning and fortifying the base of operations, which was my bedroom. We stockpiled canned food (while forgetting the can opener), built a fortress inside my room by arranging the dresser, desk, and bed into a wall, and prepared the equipment we'd use for our assault.

Around five o'clock, girls started showing up, and Jay went into action. While I sat angelically on the couch, Jay offered to take the girls' backpacks upstairs as soon as they arrived. I snuck upstairs, too, and Jay began rifling through the bags. I tied pull-string firecrackers to Heidi's dresser drawers and her hope chest. I also pulled her Barbies out of the closet and arranged them on the bed. With luck, they'd think she still played with them.

We retired to my room to play video games while waiting for the girls to leave the kitchen so we could enact the next phase of our plan. But my Nintendo's AC adapter was gone. I searched my whole room, but found nothing. Heidi. I went downstairs to ask my parents when I saw Heidi looking at me. She never looked at me. If anything, she stared directly above my head when talking to me, but she hardly ever made purposeful eye contact. I walked over to her. She leaned down to me and whispered:

"As long as you don't mess with me, I'll give you back your precious video game cord tomorrow morning. You pull anything, and you'll never find it."

Damn, she was good. But I was too proud to be treated this way. I'd find the video game cord and get my revenge at the same time. The girls filtered upstairs, and Jay passed them on the way down with my backpack. In the backpack was the girls' underwear. Once my parents were out of the kitchen, we ran all the underwear under the faucet, and then placed each pair in the freezer.

When we went back upstairs, Heidi's door was open. Her door was never open, so this meant trouble. She came out and said, "You're never going to get that cord back now. Did you go through my friends' bags?"

"No, I swear I didn't."

"You're such a liar," she said.

"Jay did," I said. "And they won't get their underwear back unless I get my cord."

"I'll tell Dad!" she said.

"I'll tell Dad you have my cord."

She pursed her lips, and I knew that dangerous sign. God gave Heidi that mannerism for the same reason he gave rattles to rattlesnakes. I ran into my room and turned to her, saying, "At eight o'clock, we'll do a switch at the top of the steps."

Just then, I heard a bang and a scream from Heidi's room. One of her "friends" was looking through her drawers apparently.

I showed up at the top of the steps at eight with a big smile. I had their underwear alright. Jay was armed, positioned in my door-way to provide covering fire. Heidi's door opened. Wrapped around her fist was my cord. Her eyes went wide.

"What the hell!" she yelled.

I heard my dad yell from downstairs: "Language, Heidi!"

At my feet was all the underwear except one Strawberry Shortcake pair. Heidi's. They were all frozen solid, stiff as cardboard. I saw her friends skulking behind her. They shrieked and giggled when they saw what had become of their underwear. Heidi pounced. She punched me hard on the arm and shoved me against the wall while her friends flooded around me and grabbed the underwear off the floor. Jay launched spoonfuls of sour cream at them, forcing them to retreat with their underwear. They'd got it all back, and Heidi still had my cord.

Luckily, I had a military genius on my side. "It's time to go nuclear," he told me. I nodded, but I had no idea what he meant.

He sent me downstairs for a brown paper bag. When I got back upstairs, he had my father's shaving cream. He sprayed the entire can of shaving cream into the bag so that it was completely full. He then laid the bag on its side and slid the opening of it beneath my sister's door. He looked at me, smiled, and then stomped with all his might on the bag with both feet. There was screaming, then incredulous laughter, and the door opened slowly. It looked as if someone had discharged a fire extinguisher in her room.

Jay and I didn't stop laughing, even when we were on our backs being punched and kicked, the victims of ten-year-old girl rage. The experience was the closest Jay and I had been to women yet. We decided maybe they weren't so bad after all.

Nowadays, Heidi and I are best friends, and her organization and intelligence served her well. Instead of investigating my pranks, she now investigates workman's compensation fraud. Woe to any lawbreakers who think they're going to outsmart that woman.

~Ron Kaiser, Jr.

**44**

Bonding over Bats and Bunfires

Camping: nature's way of promoting the motel industry.
~Dave Barry

We hadn't done it in years. I mean, with all these kids, who has the time—or the energy? My husband announced last week that it was high time we did it, and if we had to tie the kids to a tree, this weekend was IT.

Happily, I accepted this romantic invitation and spent two hundred dollars getting ready for it. Into the cart went the bare necessities: marshmallows, chocolate, fruit, tin foil and, oh yeah, mosquito repellent—lots of it! The more loaded my cart got, the more excited I became. I could already see the thousands of stars overhead, smell the clean mountain air, and feel the cool river. Ah, camping. It had been too long since we were one with nature.

I looked forward to finally being able to use those nifty fold-up chairs we had given my husband last Christmas, as well as the brand new tabletop tiki torches I bought on a whim. I couldn't wait!

Friday morning arrived, hot and sticky, and we all looked forward to higher elevations and cool mountain breezes. Landing the perfect spot next to the river, complete with a shallow swimming hole, we unpacked and were happy as wasps on a watermelon.

After settling myself in one of the technologically advanced fold-up chairs, soda in hand and feet lazily parked on the footrest, I began to let the beauty of nature relax me. I happened to breathe just ever so slightly in the incorrect direction, and BAM! The chair folded up with me in it. My soda landed neatly upside down, lid intact, but being all folded up, it was hard for me to pick it up (a major priority for me—I need my Diet Coke!). I only had one hand poking out of the chair, so all I could manage was to yell for help. Marty flopped around, laughing so hard that he couldn't help me get up (or so he claimed).

Eventually, I righted myself and the clearly dysfunctional chair, and saved my soda. What a woman! Feeling like a pioneer in the mountains of Utah, I now felt ready to deal with anything.

Suddenly, our tiki torches caught fire—not just the wick, but the whole bamboo part! We had to douse them several times because periodically they would catch on fire again. And again. The flames spread like, well, fire, straight down the sides of the torches until one of us, in panic-stricken hysteria, would trample, drown, or smack it out, only to have the whole thing begin again minutes later. The problem was that we needed those torches! Our camp swarmed with every type of flying insect, and the only thing that seemed to keep them at bay were those blasted torches. Heck, they scared me, too.

At last, it was close to bedtime, and somebody (they all claim it was me, but I don't remember it that way at all) had the bright idea to light sparklers—as if we didn't have enough fire in our camp. The children danced around, shooting sparklets leaping from their hands. It was wonderful, truly a Kodak moment, until I heard Marty say, "Uh, Sooz? Your butt is on fire."

Sure enough, my hiney had a little flame shooting out of it. I didn't even know! What does THAT say about the extra "padding" I have?! Immediately, I sat down, squashed it and was folded up in the chair again, all in one fell swoop. We figured my bum caught on fire because I was lighting sparklers for the kids, and the embers must have somehow found their way to my bootie. They burned a hole in that stupid chair, too. Good.

Leaving my husband to get the three-year-old to fall asleep in the tent (like that was going to happen), I sat outside with the other children, warming by the campfire and gazing upward at the summer night sky.

"BAT!" my fourteen-year-old son screamed suddenly in a perfect Shirley Temple voice.

"B-b-bat! Bat! Bat!" he screeched, pointing to the treetops overhead. Squinting into the night sky, I couldn't see a thing. Wait, there was something. Several somethings. Wings spread, tiny heads and pointy ears. Yup, bats.

"BAAAATTTS!" I screamed, running and tripping my way to the tent, dragging the eight-year-old behind me.

"Bats, bats, bats!" I screamed until I ripped the zipper open and threw both kids inside, stumbled in, and tightly zipped every last form of nylon protection between us and those fanged freaks.

It was a nerve-wracking night. Every noise seemed to be a bat-in-waiting. At long last, morning came, and we ended up having a wonderful day of hiking, waterfalls, eating dirt-covered food with our dirt-covered hands, and having fun. As nightfall approached, we packed up and headed for home. Another night in the woods was more than I was willing to risk.

In the end, we had a little bit of disaster, a lot of fun, and came home exhausted, but with a new appreciation for God's beautiful creations: showers, roofs, and sturdy chairs.

~Susan Farr-Fahncke

45

Scars and Legacies

Words—so innocent and powerless as they are, as standing in a dictionary, how potent for good and evil they become in the hands of one who knows how to combine them.
~Nathaniel Hawthorne

They try not to. But all parents scar their children in some fashion. Some children are luckier than others in the type or number of scars they bear. But even the lucky ones can be bitter for years.

My scar? A phobia that I am only now, after almost forty-five years, overcoming. And it's still hard to say in public, but here goes: I am *Scrabble*-phobic. Yes, that's right—I hyperventilate if anyone even says the word "Scrabble."

"B-A-G," I put on the board one evening long ago, proud that I had not only made a word, but used the high-scoring letter "B."

"Moira, that's a terrible move! You've left open a triple word space for anyone who can add an 'S' to 'bag,'" my father said.

I was crushed. I couldn't even see the remaining tiles because my eyes were swimming in tears.

My younger sister got it even worse. "Deirdre, you should never waste a triple letter space on a vowel." The poor thing barely knew what a vowel was! She burst into tears.

My parents played once a week with another couple who were also *Scrabble* fiends. They all knew the most obscure *Scrabble* words. They played with amazing strategy. And my parents played the same way when they played with us. Until one day we mutinied.

Holding my sister's hand, we stood just inside the doorway to the dining room where the *Scrabble* board sat, its smooth wooden tiles and bright red and blue double and triple spaces waiting. "Daddy, we don't want to play anymore."

He roared, "Why not?"

"*Scrabble's* too hard for us," I managed to squeak out. Deirdre just nodded.

He strode out of the room and down the hall. For such a small man, he could exude great power. And he never again asked us to play.

Recently a writer friend of mine sent me an invitation to play an online game. I clicked on the link. And there, seeming to pulsate in front of my eyes, was a *Scrabble* board. And there were the tiles, swaying in a taunting dance. And in the middle, a word. You can call it something else, but this was *Scrabble*. Spiders crawled down my spine. I clicked "exit."

But despite my *Scrabble* phobia, my dad had also instilled in me a great love of words and grammar. He loved to read his *Webster's International Dictionary* after dinner. He delighted in teaching me correct grammar and helping me grow my vocabulary. He is the reason I went to law school and am now a children's writer.

So I went back. I looked at my tiles. I saw a good word I could play on her word. I played it. It felt okay. Before I knew it, I had another invitation to play.

But this game was different. This player NEVER opened a triple word, NEVER played a low scoring letter on a triple letter space and rarely played fewer than three words at once. This player was from my father's *Scrabble* school.

Tentatively, I made a word. She immediately used it and made two more. I lost by a tremendous amount. But I kept playing. With her. With others.

I have five games going right now. And at the moment (although I know it won't last) I am beating her! And more importantly, I'm having fun. Because the legacy of loving words is stronger than my *Scrabble* scar, which, at this point, has faded almost to invisibility.

~Moira Rose Donohue

The Brisket Fairies

Call it a clan, call it a network, call it a tribe, call it a family.
Whatever you call it, whoever you are, you need one.
~Jane Howard

Well, of course everyone awaits the arrival of Santa Claus... but not too many can say they have been visited by the Brisket Fairies. Hanukah was imminent, a mere matzo ball away, and I decided to take on the holiday, whole hog (to use a non-kosher phrase). For years, I'd wangled my way out of the brisket preparation by hosting the party, making the latkes, side dishes and desserts; but now at forty-five years of age, I was about to face my coming-of-age brisket.

As a child, and for every holiday I could remember, my family ate this roasted fatty meat drenched in onions.

"Mmmm," they'd kvell and moan, wiping the oily gravy off their chins.

"Eeech," I'd say, pushing the meat to the far left of my plate, making sure it wouldn't make my crisp latke soggy.

"What? You'd think you were adopted," my parents would scoff. "Try it. It's delicious."

"See, that's what happens when you don't breastfeed," I'd retort, but it was too late. It was clear I was one brisket gene short.

Whether it skipped a generation or snuck through my husband's DNA I'll never know, but that gene clearly deposited itself in my daughter's young taste buds.

"Mmmm," she echoed the familiar kvell with her first bite. "Mommy," she said wiping her chin, "why don't you ever make this?"

Wow, I thought, there really is no escaping your cultural heritage; not only did she get the brisket gene, she got the Jewish guilt one, too. That was it—like it or not, I was going to have to learn to make brisket. So I headed straight for one of the many treasured things my mother willed me. Her cookbook.

As I thumbed through the sticky pages, breathing in memories of every oil- and chocolate-smudged recipe, it was obvious I wasn't going to find what I was looking for. Trying to decipher my mother's cryptic handwriting, cross-outs and arrows was something akin to solving the puzzle from *The Da Vinci Code*. So I called my cousin Susie in Dayton.

"Call my mother," she said upon hearing the trigger word "brisket." "She's the maven. I swear I think my parents are making ten briskets right now."

To know Aunt Lois and Uncle Gil is to know such pure unadulterated joy it's downright depressing. Married for fifty years and in their late seventies, they are excruciatingly ebullient, perennially perky, and nauseatingly nice.

"So I hear you're the goddess of grease," I say without a hello. "I mean the maven of meats. The best darn brisket maker in the whole family. Have I garnered your graces? Have I paid you due homage? What do you think? How about sharing your recipe?"

"Recipe?" Aunt Lois says, her voice sounding well-marinated in praise. "Recipe, schmecipe! We'll make you one and send it."

"You'll send me one? You'll make me a brisket and send it?" I repeat, certain that I heard this wrong.

"Of course," she says as if everybody does this. "We're mailing one to New York for Alex, one to San Francisco for Allison, one to Chicago for Ben and one to Boston for Michael. Oh, plus we're sending Allison a turkey."

"You're cooking and sending meat around the country? You're kidding, right? Is that legal? Is it safe?"

"Oh, honey, we've been doing it for years."

"Alrighty then, mail me a brisket. I'll have a party."

Each day I checked the mailbox. Nothing. As my party date

neared I made plans for the back-up salmon I might have to grill. Then, pulling into the driveway one day, my daughter yelled, "Mom, there's something big at the front door."

Sitting on my doorstep was an official U.S. mail basket, the type postal workers use to haul piles of letters. Contained inside was a package oozing a small odiferous puddle. It was either a brisket or a message from the mob, but one sniff and those onions gave it away. I rushed inside to open the package.

The brisket lay sliced and perfectly arranged in its oven-ready foil container. The meat was pretty frozen but the gravy was in definite thaw mode.

"Eeeww. I can't serve this, can I?" I poked at the meat imagining every festering foodborne cootie. I could already picture the newspaper headlines: "Hanukah Horror: Entire Party Hospitalized when Brisket Goes Bad."

"Uh, hi Aunt Lois. Umm the brisket arrived today. Well it looks great — really fabulous. Thank you sooo much. The only thing is, it's a little drippy, you know — defrosted."

"That's perfect!" she says and means it.

"Really? Don't you think it's a little scary?"

"Honey, we've never had a brisket go bad. Just refrigerate it and heat it up when you're ready. Enjoy!" she chirped and hung up.

Just to be sure, I called Susie again.

"What do you think? Is it safe?"

"I have no idea. My kids always get them drippy, but they eat them and they're okay. I think my parents are brisket fairies or something. I'm sure it'll be perfect. It always is."

That was four years ago. It was perfect and the only thing we suffered from was overeating.

Oh, I finally did face my coming-of-age brisket and as it turned out, it was pretty simple, especially because I could make it and freeze it long in advance, letting the flavors marry. But every year during our holiday preparations I enlist my daughter's help because you can bet I'll never be calling her to say, "the brisket is in the mail."

~Tsgoyna Tanzman

A Burning Issue

I once wanted to become an atheist but I gave up... they have no holidays.
~Henny Youngman

My family is Jewish. These days, many Jewish families have given in to the Christmas juggernaut by putting up Christmas trees. But when I was growing up, we weren't one of them. For a while we had a six-inch toy tree that my siblings and I attempted to decorate. But we were forced to hide it when my grandfather showed up, so it never really felt right. Besides, it could only hold about two Froot Loop garlands anyway.

Yes, we had Hanukah, but the truth is Hanukah is a very minor holiday in the Jewish religion. Just because it falls in December, it's gotten puffed up to compete with Christmas. But who are we kidding? It will never equal Christmas. How could it? Come December, the world goes Santa Claus crazy. We are deluged with images of the wonder and the glory and the letters to Santa and the many, many presents. Menorahs, potato pancakes and dreidels are fun, but they are no match for Christmas. Any attempt to make them so feels just creepy and sad. Like when we sang in the school choir and the choirmaster threw in "O Dreidel Dreidel Dreidel" as a blatant sop to the Jewish kids. It was so pathetic; we wished he had just skipped it altogether.

For the most part, playing second fiddle to Christmas didn't really bother my brother, two sisters and me when we were growing up. We knew who we were and we were proud of it. Pining for Christmas would be like a giraffe wanting the elephant's trunk. Sure it was cool, but really, what did it have to do with us? In fact, it was sort of nice to relax outside the holiday hysteria.

But we were just kids and it took us a while to get to this place. As little kids, for a while Christmas looked good. Really good. One year, when we were ten, eight, six and four, respectively, we did a full frontal push on our parents. "Just once? Puhhhleeeeeeeeez?"

Finally, they gave in—with one caveat. No tree. The little toy tree would have to do. "Sure, whatever," we said. We placed it in front of the fireplace where everyone could trip on it, and the dog could eat the Froot Loops.

Christmas Eve, we went to bed extra early at 8 p.m. Around 3 a.m., we snuck downstairs for a look, and oh! There they were! Piles of presents in four rows, one row for each kid. With ribbons and bows and fancy, unwrinkled paper that hadn't been saved from a previous gift! We just about collapsed. We went back to bed but rousted our parents around 6 a.m.

There was an explosion of energy as we ripped packages open and squealed with delight. But afterwards, a slight, slumping sadness set in. Was that it? All that build-up and it's over in five minutes? Trying to revive the momentum, we instructed our father, "You have to light the wrapping paper in the fireplace! That's part of it!"

Rolling his eyes, Dad threw the brightly colored paper in and lit it. But groggy at the early hour, he forgot to open the flue. A huge flame shot out and up, setting the mantelpiece on fire. We gawked for two seconds, then my mother grabbed my brother and me, my father grabbed my two sisters and we all ran out the front door into the frigid air. They dumped us, dressed only in our footie pajamas, into the snow, and ran back in to deal with the flames. We looked at each other in shock, all with one thought in our minds: Talk about your burning bushes! Clearly, God had spoken.

I can't remember if the firemen were called or if my parents managed to snuff it out themselves. But I do remember what came next. My father came stamping out into the snow to tell us it was okay to go back in. As we guiltily marched behind him, he turned to say, quite evenly, "See? This is what happens when Jews do Christmas!"

We never said another word about it.

~Beth Levine

Better Late than Never

A good holiday is one spent among people
whose notions of time are vaguer than yours.
~John B. Priestly

I wish that being late and disorganized were an Olympic sport because my family would be grinning from the front of every Wheaties box in the country. We are not timely, organized people. Well, let me retract that—we can be timely and organized, in our own way. For family parties, like Thanksgiving or Christmas, the general rule is to expect guests to show up roughly two hours after the agreed-upon time for the event. So, if dinner is set for four o' clock, you should expect family to start arriving around six. You cannot try to circumvent the rule by scheduling your event two hours later. You will just end up having people arrive four hours later than you originally wanted.

By some odd twist of fate, I married a German man, who is (true to the stereotype) fanatical about timeliness and organization. He gets edgy and tense whenever we have a plane or train to catch, even if we are leaving the house many hours in advance. He has embarrassed me many times by insisting that we arrive at a party exactly at the hour stated on the invitation. He gets this from his parents, who have an ability to be punctual that borders on the supernatural.

Obviously, coming from such an organized and timely family, my family's tardiness was shocking to my husband. Over time, he has learned to roll with our chaotic ways, though I can feel him trembling in frustration when we miss the first five minutes of a movie because we couldn't figure out who was supposed to be picking up whom.

Given my husband's sensitivities, I was relieved that he was away when, a few years ago, my family made a plan to go out to dinner. It was my sister's birthday, but because my mother, nephew, and I all have birthdays around the same time, we decided to celebrate them together. So, one Saturday evening, ten of us—my brother, his wife, their two children; my sister and her two children; and my mother, her companion and myself—set out to go to dinner. It started well. We met at my mother's apartment in a timely manner and decided that each family would travel in his or her own car, with me driving my mom and her friend.

The restaurant was about thirty minutes away from my mother's apartment. I had been following my brother's car on the highway for about fifteen minutes when I realized that he was going in the wrong direction. Just then, my sister Simone called me on my cell phone: "Where is Kenny going?" I told her that I thought he was going the wrong way. Simone responded, "Right, I thought so, too. I'll call Kenny."

A few minutes later, Kenny called me to say, "I made a mistake. I'm turning around." So, we all took the nearest exit and got back on the highway going in the other direction.

Forty minutes later, we arrived in the right neighborhood. I drove down the street slowly, scanning the storefronts for the restaurant, but I couldn't find it.

"I thought the restaurant was back there," said my mom, pointing behind me.

"I thought so, too," I replied, "but I don't see it."

I called my brother. "Where is the restaurant?" I asked.

"I don't know," said Kenny. "We have the correct address, but I don't see it. Veronica's going to call the restaurant."

We parked our cars as Veronica, my brother's wife, made the call. Soon, she called me back: "It doesn't exist anymore!" A collective groan rose from within my car, and I could hear my brother shouting in the background in his. My sister, brother and I got out of our cars to discuss where we should go next. Very soon, we were yelling at each other about whose fault it was that the restaurant was gone. Who was supposed to have made the reservations? How could we not know that the restaurant had gone out of business? My brother's five-year-old son began to cry. Finally, I cried, "Enough! It's Simone's birthday. Let's just calm down and choose another restaurant!"

We stormed back to our cars. I flung myself into my seat, glad that my husband wasn't there.

We decided via cell phone to go to a large family restaurant not too far away. By now, night had fallen. I drove staring grimly forward with my hands tight on the steering wheel. I wasn't sure where we were going, and it was growing difficult to follow Kenny's taillights since most taillights look the same in the dark—not to mention that Kenny was driving faster than usual because he was annoyed. To make matters worse, my mother, a nervous passenger in the best of circumstances, began to gasp with terror whenever I changed lanes, and slam on her "brakes" if she thought I got too close to another car. One gasp too many, and I'd had it.

"Mom," I shouted, "cut it out! You're making me nervous!"

My shouting enraged my mother's companion, Jacob. "Don't talk to your mother that way!" he roared. "Show some respect!"

"Oh, shut up!" I snarled.

Well, that did it. The remainder of the drive was rather unpleasant. Jacob ranted the entire time about my flagrant disrespect for my elders, while my mother defended me in an angry whisper. I drove in flinty silence, reflecting that the only bright spot in the evening was that my husband was not there.

When we arrived at the next restaurant, we were promptly told that the wait for a table of ten would be an hour and a half. Upon hearing this, both of my brother's young children began to sob loudly. Simone and Kenny began shouting at each other again. My sister-in-law, unable to bear the sound of her children weeping, shouted above all the noise in a maternal frenzy, "The children are hungry! We must get something to eat now!"

We decided to eat at a chain restaurant five minutes away at a local mall. We arrived at the restaurant exhausted, hungry, and many of us not speaking to the others. As soon as we were seated, my sister grabbed my hand and dragged me to the restaurant's bar, saying: "Come on. We need a drink."

One strawberry daiquiri later, my sister and I were in good form again, and we returned to the table. Appetizers had been served, the kids were placated with fries, and everyone was in high spirits. We ate heartily, laughing at our own ridiculousness. When dessert came, we sang the birthday song, harmonizing as usual, and the other patrons in the restaurant smiled and applauded.

As we prepared to leave, I looked around the table at the faces I loved so much and marveled at our ability to be genuinely happy to be together after so recently snapping at each other's throats. I knew we would always remember this night with amusement and affection. Suddenly, I wished that my husband had been there. I wanted him to see that timing isn't everything. Love is.

~Barbara Diggs

49

Brown Coffee and American Bread

The trouble with eating Italian food
is that five or six days later, you're hungry again.
~George Miller

As a child growing up in a suburb of New York City, I assumed there were only three ethnic groups in the world: Italians, Irishmen, and Jews. Likewise, I believed each person was a member of one of three religious affiliations: Catholic, Protestant, or Jewish. My family belonged to the first group, Italian Catholics. On my mother's side, my brother and I were second-generation Italians. Our maternal grandparents emigrated from the small town of Naro, on the island of Sicily, during the great European immigrant wave of the early twentieth century. Our father, on the other hand, was what some people referred to as "right off the boat." In 1948, at the age of twenty-three, he set sail from Sicily for a new life in America.

We were the quintessential demonstrative New York Italian family. Our lives revolved around food, family, food, weddings, funerals, and food—not necessarily in that order. With my mother's three brothers, their wives, and nine children among them, plus my father's five siblings and their assortment of fifteen offspring, there was hardly a weekend when our presence was not required for a christening, a first communion, or some other boring life event that other families celebrated on a much smaller scale. In addition, there was always Sunday dinner, a gastronomical feast that could bring a cardiologist to tears. To be absent from this weekly ritual was to risk disownment.

Sunday dinner was usually presided over by my Uncle Enzo, my father's eldest brother and the family patriarch. He was married to my Aunt Gina, a slow-witted and very buxom bleached blonde with a high-pitched laugh that sounded like Elmer Fudd after castration. I do not recall Uncle Enzo ever wearing anything but grey pants and a sleeveless undershirt. At every occasion and in all seasons, that outfit was his uniform. When he sat down to eat, he immediately tucked a napkin into the top of his undershirt; God forbid he should get it dirty.

In addition to his predictable attire were his even more disconcerting dinner habits. One of these involved holding a halved lemon in his palm, cut side down, and squeezing the juice through his nicotine-stained fingers. Another was his obsession with Parmesan cheese. He was never without a grater and a large block of Parmesan. Uncle Enzo assumed no one in their right mind would eat pasta without cheese. He was wrong. Moving around the table, grater in one hand, cheese in the other, he hovered them over my plate like weapons of mass destruction and released falling bombs of grated Parmesan that I neither requested nor wanted. That was it. My meal was ruined, and I let him know it—that is, until I caught my father's glaring eyes giving me the *malocchio*, the evil eye, that forced me to quiet down and eat my pasta, cheese and all.

We sat at the table and ate for hours, devouring course after course of tomato sauce laden dishes accompanied by several loaves of Italian bread. ("American bread" was that white stuff that was pre-sliced.) These were followed by pastries, such as cannoli and cream puffs, which always came in a white bakery box tied with string. At the end of the meal, someone would ask, "Who wants black coffee and who wants brown?" referring to the Americanized terms for espresso and Maxwell House, respectively.

We were constantly in each other's homes and faces. There was no such thing as a "private family matter." Everyone in the family knew everybody else's business and did not hesitate to give their unwanted opinions and advice. As if this weren't enough, we would get together every summer for a family reunion, something I viewed as completely illogical. I was more in favor of a family break, somewhere far from the word *mangia* (eat)!

By the time I was ten, thanks to my father's hard work and keen intellect, we became a demonstrative New York Italian family with money, a dangerous combination. All that money was shamelessly flaunted in front of friends and family members who "hadn't quite made it," as my mother would say in a hushed tone. In 1964, my parents had a new house built in an affluent Long Island neighborhood. It was an architectural monstrosity: a split foyer conspicuously displayed among well-maintained English Tudors and traditional colonials, as out of place as a tray of baked ziti at a wine and cheese party. The furniture was provincial and uninviting, complete with plastic slipcovers that stuck to our legs on hot summer days. Lamp bases were obtrusive sculptures of voluptuous Roman goddesses balancing cascades of grapes above their heads.

The front entrance was guarded by a ceramic jockey holding a lantern; his flickering light might as well have been blinking M-O-N-E-Y in Morse code. Out back was a large flagstone patio with plenty of room for gatherings of *la familia*, during which my father grilled the finest Italian sausage, and my mother served trays of homemade rice balls. Once, they even hired a musician who entertained guests by playing the Tarantella on his accordion until the neighbors called the police. We were a WASP's worst nightmare.

For all the time the family spent together, there was also a fair amount of feuding. On any given day, it was guaranteed that at least one family member was not speaking to another. This would have been tolerable if it involved only the two family members in question, but invariably their disagreement became a vortex that sucked in their spouses, parents, siblings, children, and the family dog. The causes of these feuds were usually trivial:

"My brother, Vinnie, borrowed ten dollars and never paid it back."

"Carmella brought a cheap gift to my daughter's wedding."

"The kids didn't kiss Aunt Nunziatta."

"Frankie didn't send flowers to my mother's funeral."

Like all arguments, there were always two sides: the Italian version and the very Italian version. Nearly every Sunday, Uncle Vinnie lost at least ten dollars during the family card games, so fu-get-about-it; all wedding gifts were cheap, and Carmella's was no exception; perhaps if Aunt Nunziatta took a bath and shaved her mustache before her visits, we would be more willing to greet her instead of hiding under the bed; and as for Frankie and his flowers, or lack thereof, he didn't know the difference between prize roses and chickweed, so it was no great loss.

I felt smothered and yearned to break free of all things Italian. My chance came in 1979 when I moved south to attend graduate school. As my car crossed over the George Washington Bridge into New Jersey, the Hudson River severed me from New York, and I breathed a heavy sigh of relief. I never looked back.

Or did I?

I must confess to a deep-seated sense of exhilaration when I meet someone who speaks with an unmistakable New Yawk accent, and whose expressive hand motions and voice inflections are a dead give-away to an Italian heritage. There is an instant bond, a shared experience we fully understand. When the conversation turns to Sunday dinner and family feuds, I recall the voices of my extensive family as they raised their wine glasses in a jovial "*Salute*" while simultaneously cursing their latest adversaries.

Most of the voices are silent now. It took many years of self-imposed distance and several funerals to begin to appreciate these people whose genes I share. I may never understand everything about them, but what I do know is that they loved life, they loved good food and, for all their feuding, they especially loved family.

~Laurel Vaccaro Hausman

50

The Clambake

Cooking is like love.
It should be entered into with abandon or not at all.
~Harriet van Horne

In 1969 I was a student at Syracuse University. That was the year of the campus riots when we were tear-gassed. It was a horrible burning sensation. My eyes flooded with hot tears and my throat felt like it was on fire. I couldn't catch my breath. This same terror of unleashed nasal passages and stinging tear ducts occurred when my husband, Bob, put together our Cape Cod clambake.

You see, Thanksgiving's at his sister's house. Christmas is at his folks'. Chanukah's at my brother's. So, some spiteful relative decided I need to host a family day too.

I assertively put my two cents in when asked to comply and here's what I said. "Sure!" So now Bob's family comes down from New Hampshire and my brother's family comes up from Washington, DC every Memorial Day for my very own seasonal to-do.

The day began well. Early in the morning, we drove down to the marina and collected seaweed. It was just about sunrise as we sat on the rocks and watched fishing boats, still with their lights on, depart from the harbor. When the lobster market opened, we bought steamers and mussels and seven lobsters weighing two pounds each.

After getting permission from the fire department to have a cooking fire, Bob dug a pit in the backyard. Then he lined the pit with rocks and started a fire on top of them. In a typical clambake, the seaweed goes on when the rocks get hot. Then the food gets placed and cooks under the cover of a tarp from the steam of the wet seaweed. Eventually Bob adds corn, still in the husk. Our feast was to be ready at two o'clock.

At six o'clock, we were well past the irritability stage.

The thing is—I love Bob's family, but the overriding theme of our gatherings is my Jewish-ness versus their pagan beliefs—oh excuse me, I meant to say Gentile-ness. Don't get me wrong. They love me too, but they worry about offending me, so they go overboard. At Christmas, instead of carols, they have a *Fiddler on the Roof* tape playing.

Truthfully, I'm uptight around them also, basically because they're in-laws—you know—part of the authority pack you spend your life kissing up to, all the while pretending you've outgrown this trait. But for this year's clambake, I decided to dip my tootsies in the maturity pool and I learned the following: there really does come a time in life when you stop caring about what other people think and you no longer need somebody else's approval.

And if I ever get there, I'll send you an invite.

Now, I don't keep kosher but Bob's mom needs to act as if I do. Hence, she doesn't put cheese on my hamburger, which is way up there on the drag meter. She knows it's not kosher to mix dairy products with meat products because, as I once told her, all Jewish people are lactose intolerant.

I had thought it would make his mom more comfortable if I made chopped liver for an appetizer. Bob was on the fence.

"I want the truth, Bob. You always loved my chopped liver."

"Well, it's kind of... liver-y."

"Your sense of taste is in the toilet."

"You asked for the truth!"

"You should know me by now. If I ask for the truth, it always means I don't want to hear it."

He tried to get away. A savvy, but unsuccessful move.

I grabbed his arm. "Did you know that I grew up without shellfish because it isn't kosher?" I frequently got on this childhood deprivation kick. "My mother said it's because lobsters eat sewage. And Christmas? Forget about presents."

"But Jewish people don't celebrate Christmas."

"That's right. We spend the holidays obsessing about mayonnaise. A dairy product or not? If I was kidnapped and my picture was on a milk carton, nobody in my neighborhood eating any meat would have seen it!" I couldn't stop. "Butterless bread with meat, Bob! All Jewish people know the Heimlich maneuver. Heimlich was probably a Jew who had to save his mother from choking on a dry wad of rye."

His mom, who always treats me like I'm Yentl, came to the clambake with potato knishes.

"I didn't think lobsters were kosher," she said.

"They're not. But it's okay to break the kosher laws if you eat outside, and besides, if God really wanted us to keep kosher, he wouldn't have put Swiss cheese on a sandwich with corned beef and named it after some Jewish guy called Reuben."

She gingerly stepped away from me with a polite but uncertain look on her face.

My brother examines everything he eats. You can imagine how this plays out when he's studying the innards of a steamed clam. Unfortunately, sausages were on the menu too.

I went to help Bob. Every time he picked up the tarp to see if the lobsters were done, they began to walk away.

"I don't think the fire's hot enough," I said. "Those lobsters have been doing the hokey pokey in there for about two hours." The look Bob gave me could only be described as akin to Linda Blair's facial expression when the nice priest came in to exorcise her.

And so, by seven o'clock, I put a huge pot up to boil on the stove. I gently patted Bob on the arm.

"It's time," I said. His shoulders slumped. "The lobsters have had a good life." With potholders, I retrieved the shellfish. "It will be quick... painless." He started to walk away. "You've got to think of them, honey. This isn't living. They wouldn't have wanted to have gone on this way."

And so, I steamed the lobsters and fried the sausage. I looked out the back window to see Bob standing by the smoldering fire. He carefully picked out a bunch of small black rocks about the size of ping-pong balls. I later found out that's what corn looks like when it's been on fire for eight hours.

And so, we had our clambake on the picnic table in the backyard.

We dipped the steamers and mussels in broth and drawn butter, as it's called. Not that anybody has any idea what that means. (Which reminds me—most fried clam shacks proudly put the following on their menu: "Our fish is fried in canola oil." What the heck is a canola?) We slathered the sausages with hot German mustard and ate them with our hands. The lobsters were perfection. Silky and luscious and dripping with butter too.

I saw Bob gazing over at the fire, now just pieces of charcoal. I knew he felt badly that he couldn't make a clambake. I got an idea.

On Cape Cod, the stars are so prevalent because there are no city lights to diminish them. Bob loves to go out on moonless nights and search for the Milky Way. After our feast, he went out back with everyone to sit on our glider swing. I got in the truck and went a block to a convenience store where I picked up graham crackers, Hershey's chocolate bars and marshmallows.

Later, I asked Bob to stoke the fire and add some wood. We roasted the marshmallows and put them in a graham cracker sandwich with a slice of chocolate wedged in. We sat on the ground, making up stories about noises we could hear in the woods. Everyone had at least three s'mores and a wonderful time.

~Saralee Perel

51

The Jokester

Family jokes, though rightly cursed by strangers,
are the bond that keeps most families alive.
~Stella Benson

"Make sure you hold your daddy's hand all the time on the trip," warned my brother's mother-in-law, Louise, to my ten-year-old niece, Jordan.

"I will!" shouted Jordan as she was about to get into the car where my brother, Jeff, had been "eavesdropping."

As they left in the car, my brother decided to play a "trick" on Jordan's "Mimi" (the name all of Louise's grandchildren lovingly called her)—with the help of my sweet, adorable niece.

Ten hours later, Jordan called Mimi and said with a face that would make the best poker player proud: "Mimi, I made it to Washington, D.C. It is so nice. But I don't know where Daddy is. I know you said to always hold his hand tight, but there was only room on the subway for one. So Daddy drove his car, and I took the subway. Daddy asked a very nice man who was already on the subway to help me find my stop. The nice man did, but Daddy's not here. What should I do?"

I could just imagine Louise fainting, dropping the phone as she fell to the cold, hard floor. Luckily, right then Jeff and Jordan screamed into the phone, "Gotcha!"

Yep, that's my brother—the "jokester." I'm sure many families have a family member who loves to play practical jokes on other family members. Often, it is quite humorous, but only in hindsight.

Jeff got his "jokester" trait many, many years ago. When Jeff was eight and I was six, we were driving with our father to Pennsylvania to visit our grandparents. My mother and sister had flown there because my parents agreed that the long car trip would be too difficult and stressful for my four-year-old sister. (The real question: "Stressful for whom?") So, Jeff, my dad and I headed out in my father's red Oldsmobile Cutlass station wagon on the long trip to Pennsylvania. My father thought the car trip would be a fun adventure for the three of us. However, he soon learned that an "adventure" did not necessarily come with "fun."

Jeff and I were sitting in the back seat, always fighting and bickering, even though our father tried to keep our minds busy by playing "road games" while we were driving. Finally, on a rural highway in Arkansas, my father screamed, "Enough! If you don't stop screaming, I'll drop ya'll off in the middle of the road!"

What do you think happened? Do you think we started acting politely? Of course not.

What do you think my father did? Do you think he kept his word concerning his "threat"?

Actually, he did. He slammed on his brakes on the barren highway in the middle of the cornfields in rural Arkansas and screamed, "Get out!"

I was very scared. I had never seen my father act so angrily. I was beginning to cry, but Jeff said nothing as he nudged me out of the car. My father then, seemingly still irate, puffed and "slammed on the gas" and drove away.

We were all alone. I began to sob, but not Jeff. He just said, "Mike, come on. Hurry up! Let's hide in the fields. You know Dad will be back in a second. He just wanted to prove a point."

Sure enough, thirty seconds later, I could see a red station wagon approaching from the fields where we were hiding. The car slowed down, then accelerated, and then slowed down again as if the driver was looking for valuable objects left on the side of the road. (Of course, those very valuable objects were us.)

The red station wagon screeched to a stop as my father jumped out screaming frantically, "Kids! Kids! Jeff, Mike, where are you?" My father quickly became hoarse from screaming, and his worried face was soaked with perspiration. As he quickly circled around, looking for us, he appeared to be in tears while thinking, "My precious sons! WHAT IN THE WORLD HAVE I DONE?" And then he crumpled to the ground.

Jeff nudged me again as he whispered, "Let's go!" He ran out from the fields to the road toward our father, who looked up and saw us. My father jumped up and started running toward us, screaming with happiness and hugging us.

Yes, my dad wanted to teach us a lesson, but exactly who was taught the lesson? And exactly what lesson was taught in the fields of Arkansas? To my father, the answer to those questions did not matter. His only concern was that he had his kids back safely in his arms.

So, Jeffrey was, and is, "the jokester" of the family. Now I wonder what tricks Jordan will play on Jeff in the years to come. I can hardly wait!

~Michael Jordan Segal, MSW

Tallyho!

It is the woman who chooses the man who will choose her.
~Author Unknown

My mother decided it was time — even though she'd said she could never love another, would never want another, would never need another man. Early on, she had heated a can of Campbell's and, forgetting, divided it between two bowls. When she realized her mistake, she poured them both in the sink and ran cold water until the last chunk of chicken and the remaining half noodle slithered down the drain. Her sobs drowned out the grind and growl of the garbage disposal.

She tried taking her meals at the Country Kitchen, but their home cookin' was as bland as an obituary that doesn't live up to the life it describes. Wendy's dollar menu worked, though: a salad or a bowl of chili at the drive-through. A meal-for-one. And, of course, a real value with extra packets of saltines and dressing. No need to change out of her sweats, comb her hair, or do her face. Or sit at a table, a woman alone.

Watching her fly solo after nearly five decades of living as a pair was painful. I couldn't fault her for drifting into The Pack.

She'd rolled her eyes at me each time the five gals appeared — en masse — at the Main Street McDonald's for morning coffee. And the free refills. And the complimentary weekend newspaper strewn across the booths. As tight-faced as they were tight-fisted, the widows hounded local events to see and be seen. To fill the hours.

Now, my mother was the latest inductee to their club, following them from retirement gala drop-ins to church revivals; from lectures at the community college to wedding receptions; from park concerts to grand openings of (take your pick) floral shops, branch banks, boutiques and gas stations, where they'd sniff out the refreshment table, hoping all four major food groups would be represented, thus eliminating the need for another bowl of bedtime bran flakes in front of the 10:00 news.

Then they all began frequenting funerals.

Mother was acquainted with the deceased—most of them. Or someone in The Pack probably was. Or, perhaps not. Nevertheless, in addition to the eats afterward, it was another opportunity to dress to the nines and accessorize. After all, "You never know who you'll meet."

"What do you mean?" I asked.

"Oh, you know. Divorced friends-of-friends. Widowers. Bachelor uncles."

At her age, single women far outnumbered available men. She repeated the stale line that all The Pack really needed was one good man to share between them. The only requirement? He must be willing to drive at night.

"The problem is," she lamented, "when you finally do track down a man-with-possibility and you're traveling as one with The Pack, complications arise before you can even get close enough to savor his after-shave."

While she was mining her oversized handbag for a crimson lipstick—Bold Seduction—among the packets of croutons, Italian lite dressing, and powdered saltines, three complimentary ink pens from the insurance agency and an emergency rain bonnet from the health fair tumbled to the floor. Her hangnail snagged on a crumpled Kleenex and dragged it, too, from the catacombs of her purse.... By then, the hungry predators had already surrounded the prey.

Badgering him with requests for household repairs.

Baiting him with invitations for outings.

Luring him with offers of home-cooked meals.

So she retreated. "After all," she reasoned, "no man is worth losing a girlfriend over."

"But..." I started to object.

She shook her finger in my face. "Girlfriends are vital; at our age, it takes all of us just to finish a sentence!"

Yet she admitted an overpowering urge to tuck her tail between her legs and hightail it out of The Pack. Away from the aimless social life. Away from the all-too-knowing eyes.

And, so, I watched her set out alone, on a hunt of her own, to bag her buck.

She planned her own ambush.

She posed before the "skinny mirror" on the back of her bedroom door. The mirror that gave her a boost of self-confidence while it subtracted ten pounds from her fat clothes.

She test-drove her smiles. Quick and flirtatious. Heavy-lidded and mysterious. Wide-eyed and innocent. Slow and seductive.

Leaning in, she finger-flattened the part in her hair to inspect her roots. "A touch-up, maybe?"

Huh, I thought. You can get as accurate a reflection in the sea of bobbing bald pates and wispy combovers that shine at every concert down at the Rialto.

She bared her teeth like a horse at auction. "Maybe one of those new whitening toothpastes?"

I pictured the church's monthly potluck with its side menu of dentures, partials, gold fillings, tobacco stains....

She stepped back for a full-length inventory and frowned. She'd made friends with elastic waistbands years ago.

"Do you think I ought to take Water Aerobics at the Senior Center?" She turned her backside toward the mirror, looked over her shoulder, and ran her hands over the full curve of her thighs.

I remembered the Center's standard fare of paunches, beer bellies, and suspenders.

She paused. She looked again, probing the mirror for flaws.

"Nah." She tossed her head. "I've got the bait. I just have to find my animal." She gazed once more at her reflection, crinkled her nose, and growled.

Let the hunt begin!

~Dee McFoster

Chapter
6

Family Matters

Relatively Strange

I wish I could relate to the people I'm related to.

~Jeff Foxworthy

53

Chicken Soup for the Soul

Lenny the Bunny

Animals are my friends… and I don't eat my friends.
~George Bernard Shaw

Okay, before everyone out there starts e-mailing me about the hazards of giving a three-year-old a pet for his birthday, let me say that you're right—it's wrong. I'll never do it again. I wish I had never done it in the first place—maybe not as much as Lenny, but I do regret it. Mea culpa.

My husband Prospero and I were still dating at the time of his nephew's third birthday. Never having shopped for gifts by himself, Prospero sought my advice on a memorable gift, as Leonardo was not just his nephew, but his godson—a very powerful bond in Italian families.

It was March, and stores were preparing for Easter.

"You know, the pet shop across from my mother's office has the cutest bunnies. I was over there looking at them today," I said to him with the enthusiasm of someone who has thought of the perfect gift.

My in-laws are from a rural part of Italy, and have kept rabbits and other animals on their property even though they live in a large city. I didn't think that giving a bunny to their little boy would be much of a burden to them, and it wasn't. In fact, Prospero's family was almost as thrilled with the gift as Leonardo.

"What are you going to name your bunny?" Prospero asked his nephew.

"Lenny!" announced the boy, proudly giving his new bunny the American version of his own first name.

And so spring became summer, and Lenny the Bunny had a lovely hutch of his own in the backyard. Whenever we visited, Leonardo would grab our hands and take us out to see Lenny. His love for that bunny was obvious to all. We would feed him carrots, lettuce, and other greens from my brother-in-law's abundant garden. Lenny was probably the best fed rabbit in the world.

Autumn brought a nip to the air, but we still went out back with Leonardo to visit Lenny. At least, we did until that fateful weekend. Leonardo dragged us over to Lenny's empty cage.

"Where's Lenny?" I asked.

My in-laws were of the philosophy that animals should be kept outdoors, so I highly doubted that they brought the rabbit into their warm home for winter.

Leonardo spread his arms in the air and looked totally baffled.

I turned to my future father-in-law. "Where's Lenny?"

"Heh, heh, heh," he replied.

The language barrier between us often made communication tricky so I turned to my husband's brother. "Where's Lenny?"

He just stood there smiling as if sharing a private joke with himself.

"Well, where is he?" I demanded.

As if placating a child, he replied in a sing-song voice, "He ran away."

With that, the two of them started chuckling.

I felt Prospero's hands on my shoulders firmly steering me away. "Come on, let's go," he said.

"But we just got here," I protested. "Where's the bunny?"

"Never mind," he said. "We're going."

As we walked across the lawn, his brother's voice rang out, "He was delicious!" Their laughter followed us. "But a little tough—he was old."

I looked up at Prospero. "No!" I gasped. But he kept leading me to the car.

Omigod, they ate Lenny the Bunny!

Seriously, this family raised and fed their child's pet for the sole purpose of providing a festive Sunday dinner!

The words of Euripides rang through my head: The gods visit the sins of the fathers upon the children. Thankfully, that wasn't true in this case. My husband is the family member who marches to the beat of his own drummer. He's the man who rescues a bird that flies into a window. His love and compassion know no bounds, and yet to this day he still gives me the same lecture.

"What did you expect?" he asks. "Did you think my family was going to let a rabbit run around their house?"

No, but…

"It's a cultural thing," he always continues. "They raise rabbits to eat. What did you think they did with all of those rabbits?"

But Lenny the Bunny wasn't a farm animal. We bought him in a pet store. He had a name! For what we paid for the bunny, we could have taken them out to dinner.

One thing is for certain—I will never buy a pet for another child. I learned that lesson the hard way. Well, it was harder on Lenny, but I'm still upset about it, and it's been thirty years.

Rest in peace, Lenny. Please forgive me for causing you pain. I promise you, we'll never eat rabbit in this household. Your relatives are safe with me.

~Lynn Maddalena Menna

54

Clear and Present Danger

Thanksgiving is so called because we are all so thankful
that it only comes once a year.
~P. J. O'Rourke

A holiday at my mother-in-law's house is never without drama. There was the Thanksgiving that her second, now ex-, husband was sharpening the carving knife and almost cut off my brother-in-law's ear. Then there was the year the Christmas tree was erected "the wrong way" very late on Christmas Eve. This almost resulted in a brawl between my husband and the same ex-husband. There was also the time when my mother-in-law invited people to stay at her country house—a three-bedroom home built in 1782—for Columbus Day weekend. Everyone said yes, and all fifteen of us showed up. One man ended up sleeping under the dining room table.

After thirteen years of marriage, I have learned how to say no. However, saying no on Thanksgiving and Christmas is not an option. The alternative is passive-aggressive retribution. I know, because I've already tried that.

Last Thanksgiving was especially memorable, probably because it was supposed to be "momentous." My mother-in-law had just finalized a bitter divorce in a legal battle that left her broke. Not long after the papers were signed, she met a man through an online dating service and decided to move in with him.

She wanted to host Thanksgiving at his—"their"—new

apartment in New York City, bringing together his family and hers so we could all meet. On her side were my husband and I who live in Connecticut with two children, ages six and four, and my sister-in-law, my husband's sister, and her husband, who live in New York State and have four boys, ages two, four, six, and eight. The beau has two grown children: a twenty-eight-year-old son, who is single, and thirty-year-old son, who had recently married a woman from the Ukraine. And because my mother-in-law is a "the-more-the-merrier" type of gal, she invited another couple and their autistic son.

None of our side had ever been to the apartment. My mother-in-law forewarned us that it was still a "bachelor pad" despite her moving in. Over the years, I have learned to arrive at least one hour after the invited time since a meal planned to start at 1:00 will be served no sooner than 3:30. I also know to feed my children before we arrive since none of us behave well with low blood sugar.

After an hour's drive to the city and a half-hour securing a parking space blocks from the apartment, we arrived with excited kids. We rang the doorbell, and the beau opened the door wearing a white undershirt with vibrant yellow sweat stains under each arm.

"Welcome!" he announced, red-faced and smelling of beer.

We walked into the two-bedroom apartment and made our rounds. Everyone, of course, had arrived before us.

My brother-in-law and sister-in-law stood together, she holding their youngest, while their three other boys were running through the apartment, sliding across the hardwood floor in their socks. We were introduced to the sullen single son, and the older son, who had a winning smile, and his Ukrainian wife. We shook hands with the other couple who were desperately trying to keep their son from banging on the keys of a nearby piano.

My kids pulled off their shoes and took off after their cousins, who were sliding into walls and doing somersaults on and off the couches. After a short tour of the cozy apartment, I decided to nip into the guest bathroom. From the doorway, I saw cracked tiles above a soap-scum-filled sink. A dirty hairbrush rested on the lip of the sink. I noticed that the toilet seat was up, and urine and hair were scattered around its rim. There was a bare roll of toilet paper and no replacement nearby.

The master bath would have to be better. And it was. There was toilet paper, and the seat and lid were down. As I gently lifted up the lid with two fingers, the lid and the seat slipped off the bowl and fell loudly onto the floor.

After grabbing a drink, I decided to chat with the winning son and his wife. She was lovely and smart, and he was handsome. After a bit, I decided to ask them how they met. It was quiet for a moment while they exchanged glances.

"Actually, she stalked me," he said with a smile.

I laughed. "That's funny!" I said. I had a few friends who had very bad stalker stories.

"No, really I did," she said, nodding like a bobblehead doll. "He used to play tennis near where I went to school, and I would go to watch him every day."

He nodded. She nodded. So I nodded.

"She really did," he added. "She followed me."

"And, finally, one day he spoke to me," she said and smiled up at him.

Two hours later, I was desperate to sit down and eat, mostly so the autistic boy would have to sit at the table and stop banging on the piano. I could feel a migraine coming on. I had noted the dining room earlier, a dark musty room with wall-to-wall bookshelves filled with books that hadn't been read — or dusted — in decades. The dining room also housed a three-foot-wide, flat-screen TV in one corner. The table for twelve was set for eighteen.

The apartment had heated up to about ninety-five degrees from the body heat and the cooking. Although I went into the kitchen occasionally to see if I could help get the festivities moving, it was only on my last attempt when I could. While lifting the bird out of the oven, I noticed that my mother-in-law was sweating so much that her foundation makeup had dripped off her face onto the turkey.

As she handed me side dishes to set out, I corralled everyone to the table. After the food was displayed, it was time to sit and enjoy.

My husband said a blessing before the carving. My mother-in-law has always liked "her man" to carve, so while the beau carved we got a full view of his T-shirt. I felt very thankful I was not sitting near him.

As we all watched the ritual carving and the doling out of food, it became abundantly clear that there was not enough turkey—and not enough of everything else either. Those guests with plates started filling them up with the accompaniments. Not surprisingly, when I got the last plate with one measly slice of turkey, the creamed onions and Brussels sprouts were the only side dishes left.

Now, I was mad. I can put up with a lot, but no heaps of stuffing swimming in hot gravy? No spoons upon spoons of sweet potatoes? I looked across the table at my oblivious and Brussels-sprout-loving husband. I knew this was almost normal for him. I caught his eye and gave him my evil eye. He smiled, cheek full of food (he was one of the first served), and lifted his Brussels-sprout-speared fork to toast me.

Fortunately, after my kids fled the table, I could feed off their plates. Mood slightly improved, I watched the beau finish off his second "forty," a forty-ounce bottle of cheap beer in a green bottle he proudly held up for all of us to see.

"Only $3.99 at the Korean market around the corner! Can you believe it?" he said.

Spit flew when he spoke, and when he laughed we got a view of half-chewed food as expansive as the Hudson River outside the window behind us.

After four hours, I had had enough. Although my kids' unspent energy was being tamped by the television, I was ready to hit the road. I stood up and called to my children.

"Time to go!" I announced.

Seated under a huge wooden wall shelf with glass panes that was filled with books, frames, and small figurines, they actually answered when I called. It seemed like they were ready to go, too.

Just as they reached my side, the wall shelf they had been sitting under pulled away from the wall. I gasped as gravity worked its magic. In a millisecond, the heavy shelf came crashing down on exactly the place where my children had been sitting mindlessly staring at the television.

The noise and chaos got everyone up and involved. I whispered in my husband's ear that the fun was definitely now over. Amid the "Oh my goodness!" and "Thank heavens they had gotten up!" and "I just can't believe it!" comments, I smiled and ushered my family out the door, waving thanks and blowing kisses all around.

Despite the long, cold, windy walk back to the car, the return drive on busy I-95, and the growls of hunger from my empty stomach, I felt truly thankful for the first time that day.

We had survived another holiday at my mother-in-law's house. It had been a close one.

~Gwen Daye

Huggy Bear Vs. The Iceberg

There's nothing like a mama-hug.
~Terri Guillemets

My favorite movie line is from *Dirty Dancing*. Johnny is trying to get Baby into shape for their big performance. Baby, falling for handsome Johnny and his moves, keeps trying to wrap her arms around him. Johnny finally shoves Baby away and says, while drawing an air bubble around each of them with his hands, "This is my dance space. This is your dance space."

I feel like that about the world. We would get along fine and move in greater harmony if others would stay in their own dance space... and out of mine.

Imagine then, if you will, the first time I went home to meet my boyfriend's parents. My boyfriend, well, was a guy. He shared pertinent details like: They keep the soda on the back porch, and be careful if you use the upstairs toilet because it clogs. Um, thanks. So I was flying blind when the door opened and I was enveloped by a continent of woman. By the time I realized what was happening, my nose was pressed between two enormous breasts.

Once this enthusiastic embrace was severed, I tried to duck away, but this woman had morphed into a multi-armed sea witch determined to keep touching me continually. An arm linked through mine, a hand on my shoulder, fingers on my back. I might have been more mentally prepared to handle these exchanges (and worn the body armor I keep on hand for just such an occasion) had my boyfriend warned me that his mother had earned herself the nickname "Huggy Bear."

I scanned the room for escape routes. Back out the front door? Could be a long weekend locked in the car. Into the kitchen? It's a pretty small space with lots of hot and sharp things. Dining room? Glass front china cabinet filled with breakables. Shaking my head in frustration, my bladder supplied the answer.

"May I use your bathroom?"

Huggy Bear walked me down the hall and into the bathroom. Yes, into the bathroom. Against the backdrop of the purple floral shower curtain, I was given a full tour. Of the bathroom. Right down to nose hair clippers, Nair, and extra feminine necessities.

This particular water closet had a pocket door that, when pulled, divided the sink and shower from the toilet. Unable to rid myself of hurricane Huggy Bear, I began to ease the divider closed. H.B.'s pair of prominent features hovered at the edge of the door as it slid across the entryway. My resolve and my bladder were set, however. I was closing the door, even if it meant giving her an extraneous mammogram.

I could hear her going on about shampoo and hot water, and thanked God for my brave bladder. By the time the flush, whoosh and fill of the tank had finished, the other half of the room was quiet and blissfully empty. I breathed a sigh of relief, locked the door that led to the hallway, and wondered how long I could wash my hands before a locksmith came to remove the door. My arms and back still crawled with radiating imprints where fingers and arms had pressed my flesh. A wave of goose bumps at the thought fluffed my arm hair and eased their impact. I was evaluating the wisdom of spending the weekend in the bathroom. After all, one only needed water to live, and I was sure at least one of the rainbow bottles of fruity body wash in the tub was edible.

Lest you think I was one of those children raised in a dog crate now shunning human contact, I will tell you that I appreciate a brief "nice to see you hug" from a friend or a firm, dry handshake. I'm

English, after all, and we—as I once heard it so aptly put—only show affection to horses and dogs.

I could hear voices in the kitchen, mingled with the sounds of pots and pans crashing together, and hoped that Huggy Bear now had five or six of her hands filled. Slinking from the bathroom, I came around the corner to the kitchen, straight into the waiting embrace of a second and third Huggy Bear offspring—my boyfriend's siblings, who had their mother's penchant for touching and her affinity for dessert. Sausage fingers squeezed my shoulders, patted my arms, and sent me into a minor panic attack as my boyfriend smirked at me. His hands were preparing supper, leaving his brother, sister and mother free to molest me.

The rest of the weekend became a bizarre version of *The Fugitive*. I chewed through satin handcuffs, changed my appearance, and crawled through sewers to steer clear of the many-armed woman. With true Tommy Lee Jones tenacity, she pawed through every car trunk, steamer trunk, swim trunk and tree trunk to keep me within an easy grab.

By the time we packed up and headed back to work on Sunday evening, I was exhausted. Physically and mentally, my space had been invaded, and I needed a week in my sensory deprivation chamber.

That boyfriend became my husband. Huggy Bear and her cubs became my in-laws, and my children have now taken up the mission of shattering my private dance bubble—their pure-blooded Swedish genes having taken over their affection centers. It was bad enough sharing my body with them for nine months. Now I've taken to storing the two adorable monsters in resealable containers so I can go to the bathroom or cook a meal without one or both of them grabbing or pinching parts of me.

They get along swimmingly with Huggy Bear. And while she lavishes them with embraces, I am released from the ritual. And Huggy Bear now seems content, if not happy, to wave to this Iceberg from across the room.

~Eden Arneau

Chicken Soup for the Soul

clomp, clomp, clomp

I like long walks, especially when they're taken by people who annoy me.
~Fred Allen

Okay, so I will be the only brave one in my family to admit this out loud: My brother has the worst taste in women in the world. He couldn't pick a mate to save his life. Wife number one was just evil, wife number two was nuts, and wife number three only lasted a few months, so it's hard to remember her at all. In between, there have been other women who have had their own peculiarities, too numerous to mention. Every time my brother calls my mom to tell her he thinks he has found "the one," she just about loses it. And my brother is no spring chicken—he is in his sixties. Shouldn't he know better?

But I think that this new one, wife number four, might be the prize winner. She is just, well, she is just the most obnoxious person on the planet. What was my brother thinking when he married her? She is very nice-looking, but she is very short. And to make up for this, she wears platform shoes with high heels. Huge platforms with huge heels. These shoes are impossible to walk in; they look like Frankenstein boots. She clomps around the house on these monster shoes. She makes so much noise and constantly trips over her own feet. And she lets out little yelps as she trips and falls down or bashes into the furniture. Clomp, clomp, clomp... yelp!

She has a teeny, tiny, squeaky, nails-on-the-chalkboard voice, and she talks constantly, even if there is no one around. When she speaks, she talks about herself in the third person and uses baby talk. "Gracie (her name) is getting a wittle bit hungry. Her wants some nummies. Gracie thinks she'll go into the kitchen and make herself some lunchie, punchie. Does Stevie (my brother) Weavie want some lunchie, punchie, too?" Oh, gag me. This woman is in her sixties, but I want to yell at her to grow up—and shut up!

She is terribly nearsighted, but won't wear her glasses. She goes to the market and shops by touch. She picks out what she thinks she needs. The only problem is that when she gets the stuff home and puts on her glasses, she is always surprised by what's in the bag. She finds that she has bought all of the wrong things. Duh, all cans feel the same; you need to read the labels. But she wouldn't be caught dead in the market wearing her glasses. Oh, no, not Gracie.

She is always breaking everything she touches. Dishes and glasses don't last long at her house. Since she can't see the tops of the kitchen counters, she constantly smashes things into the edges instead. She tries different recipes, but can't read the amounts of the ingredients, so almost everything tastes terrible. But will she wear glasses or contacts? Noooo.

We were all together this past summer to celebrate my parents' anniversary. Everyone traveled to my parents' house in Oklahoma. The fiasco lasted four days. By the end of the first day, we all wanted to lock Gracie Wacie in a closet—in someone else's house. We were so done with all of her quirks. She does try to help, but she is so clumsy that she is a danger to herself… and others. She decided that she would clear the dishes from the table, which was very nice. The only problem is that she took the plates before people were finished eating! "Where's my plate?" Oh, if I only had a nickel for every time I've heard someone ask that question. "Oh, you weren't finished eating? Gracie didn't know that. Sowwy."

Gracie is an early riser. Every morning, she would be the first one up and dressed. We all knew she was awake because she put on her monster shoes first thing and made so much noise getting ready that it woke the rest of us up. "Gracie thinks she'll wear this dress." Clomp, clomp, clomp. "Gracie needs to put on her make-up." Clomp,

clomp, clomp. "What did Gracie do with her wittle wed sweater?" Clomp, clomp, clomp. "Gracie wants coffee." Clomp, clomp, clomp. And down the stairs she goes. Clomp, clomp, clomp.

Since she is the first one in the kitchen, Gracie makes the coffee. And she makes the most horrible, disgusting, vile-tasting coffee in the whole world. It's either too strong or too weak. Can't she count? We have tried to sabotage her efforts, but she always finds a way to outsmart us. We hide the coffee; she finds it. We hide the filters; she doesn't use them. We turn off the water to the kitchen sink. She fills the coffee pot from the bathroom sink. Somehow, she always manages to prevail. She always spills coffee grounds all over the counters and the floor. Does she clean up? No, because she doesn't have her glasses on so she can't see what she's done. Coffee's ready, and Gracie pours herself a cup. She uses cream and sugar, but can she close the refrigerator door when she has put the cream away? Why should she when some poor soul will come along and do it for her?

What does Gracie do while she is having her coffee? She reads the newspaper. Or rather, she scatters it, page by page by page, all over the house. By the time anyone else tries to read it, it's just not possible. Page one is in the kitchen; page two might be in the living room; page three was probably ripped up and used for who knows what. The entire paper has been demolished so no one else can read it. Oh, and she rips pages out of magazines if she finds something she wants to save. Just try reading a magazine with pages missing. You know, it's kind of like reading a magazine in a doctor's office.

Gracie is a kleptomaniac. Is it on purpose? I don't think so, but she is just so oblivious that she doesn't think. We have lost many towels. Where do they go? What does she do with them? Who knows? We've asked her, but she pretends she doesn't know what we are talking about. We think she puts them in her suitcase, but when she gets home and can't remember where those extra towels came from, she throws them out. My mom has taken to putting old ratty towels or the towels we use to bathe the dog in her bathroom so that when she steals them, we won't care.

Four days are up, and it's finally time for Gracie Wacie to go.

Thank God! What will she leave for us to find this time? She always leaves something. (Maybe it's in trade for the towels she takes.) Her earrings, her make-up, her shoes, her underwear…

We always walk Stevie Weavie and Gracie Wacie to the car when they leave. And why is that? Well, it's not because we are nice or polite. Not a chance. We just want to be sure that they actually get in the car and leave. Bye bye.

~Madison Thomas

"NO, I'M NOT TALKING TO MYSELF!"

Reprinted by permission of
Dave Carpenter ©2007

Queen of Stealth Insults

Rudeness is the weak man's imitation of strength.
~Eric Hoffer

My mother-in-law is the queen of stealth insults. I am constantly amazed by how I unwittingly set myself up for her jabs. I am not a dumb person; by golly, I even graduated from college. Nonetheless, I never see those insults coming.

My mother-in-law's insults are not devastating, just irksome. They span the four to five range on the ten-scale. Not evil enough to condemn her, the jibes are just toxic enough to tax emotions. Never clearly straightforward, they are kind of right-flank-from-the-rear attacks. Often the insults are oblique enough to be misclassified as "general conversation." Fundamentally, they are subtle taunts exposing my soft side and encouraging me to show my worst side.

To avoid being predictable and therefore vulnerable, my mother-in-law has a large repertoire of insult modes. One mode is the No-Witness mode. During one particular visit, our men had gone outside and I was prepping to follow. She offered me a bit of advice, "Shouldn't you put a hat on? It's cold outside."

"Oh, my hair is thick enough for this weather," I responded sweetly. It was fifty degrees outdoors.

"Yes, I need a hair cut too," she said.

After twenty-two years, I have learned to view these unforeseen jibes as badges of honor and steps on a ladder. Each insult enables me to elevate my opinion of myself a bit higher. Not because I amuse myself by drawing fire, but rather because I feel a touch of pride in being able to raise myself above retaliation, however tempting that may be.

Hierarchy is crucial to my mother-in-law's supreme reign. She insists her status be recognized so Position-Coup is another of her modes. Granted, the woman's local community holds her in high esteem because of her benevolence and generosity. She inherently stakes claim to the superior position to which she feels entitled. When I married her son, I asked her by what name I should call her. She insisted on the significant name, "Mama." Strangely, even though I am supposed to call her Mama, when she leaves a message for me on my answering machine she always says, "Hello, Gretchen, this is your mother-in-law." I really do recognize her first name and even her voice. Her chosen words are subtle intimidations and elevations of position. If the Queen of England were to call me on the phone, I am sure she would say, "Hello, this is the Queen of England," rather than "Hey, this is Liz."

Sometimes Mama uses a combination of modes to put me in my place. The setup might include the Insignificance-Mode. Mama has never thanked me for any gift; au contraire, my feeble efforts of bestowing offerings are usually ignored. A lovely gift of premium scented bath soaps and lotions was once met with a grunt and a nod of the head. Initially I was ecstatic, as my gift was at least acknowledged. Thirty minutes later, when a group of her friends arrived, she showed me how I misinterpreted her gesture. She engaged the Protection-in-Numbers mode. I was duly admonished when Mama announced out of the blue to all her guests, "One gift I really can't use is scented soaps and lotions. I am allergic to them."

Was I supposed to be stupid enough to admit that I wasted a wad of money on a basket of useless smelly stuff? Or perhaps I was being taunted to say something unkind about Ms. Benevolence in front of her devotees. Maybe it was just her way of saying I was ignorant about her personage. Maybe the gift was too common. Who knows? Who cares?

Perhaps one of her most trifling modes is the You-Can't-Have-It mode. This is a seasonal mode occurring around birthdays and Christmas. Some years we have lived a great distance apart and in-person visits are very infrequent. At holiday time her phone call may start with a question, "What size are you wearing now?"

Being a person who is particular about what I wear and possessing fashion tastes very different from Mama's, I try to skirt the issue and explain that I am really hard to fit. Her persistence wears me down and I end up admitting MY TRUE SIZE, which of course is larger than it was twenty-two years ago.

After forcing my confession, her inevitable response is, "Well, I will probably get something else. What would you like?" This question runs in tandem with other conversations that have occurred throughout the years. When I compliment her on some material possession, she informs me that she may get me one for Christmas. Of course, I have never gotten anything I have ever said I liked or wanted.

Interspersed with her other surreptitious modes is her most frequently employed mode: You're-Dismissed. Feigning interest, she asks a question, "Do you have to give your kitty medication?"

Imagining that she might actually be interested in one of my passions, I repeatedly fall for her trap and begin to explain, "She's on a special diet. She has to have…"

I am promptly cut off and the subject is changed. I guess she is satisfied that she showed interest by asking the question. She really does not want to be bothered with my answer.

When I married, for some unknown reason I really did expect to have a good relationship with my mother-in-law. Maybe that is why I never see the insults coming. I keep expecting that she will like me and truly encourage me. I assure myself I am doing my part in maintaining peaceful family relations by redefining "standing up for myself," as "throwing return insults is unacceptable conduct." In other words, standing up for myself means learning to duck—or is that a bow to the queen?

~Gretchen Bauer

Queen of Stealth Insults : Relatively Strange   215

The Middle Child

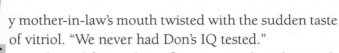

All negativity is an illusion created by the limited mind
to protect and defend itself.
~Ambika Wauters

My mother-in-law's mouth twisted with the sudden taste of vitriol. "We never had Don's IQ tested."

I leaned forward, my fingers strangling the couch cushion beneath me. "But you had your other kids tested—why not Don?"

"Didn't see the point." She eyed me critically while her mint green nails ticked against the glass she palmed. And as quickly as her venom set in, she rose from her seat across from me and shuffled into the kitchen for more iced tea, fungus-colored toenails leading the way.

A couple of months prior, my husband, Don, beamed when his parents phoned with the news they were paying us a visit. He had invited Mike and Karen several times, but in four years they had yet to come. This time they were attending a wedding in nearby Arizona and wanted to see their two sons who lived on the West Coast. Because Don's brother, Jim, was renting a room in another family's apartment, our house had been chosen as the meeting place.

Don's initial enthusiasm soon melted away as backhanded compliments filled any pauses between complaints. My in-laws had been in our house for a torturous twenty-four hours before Jim made an appearance. Cheers erupted as the golden boy strutted through the front door on his mission to demand everyone's attention. To my husband's parents, Jim shone as the epitome of all things witty and brilliant. Don, on the other hand, had been branded the "brainless" middle child.

While Jim passed gas in his mother's face en route to grab the remote control, Don tried to make conversation. Stories about Jim's life watching sports from his couch abounded betwixt burps and huge handfuls of chips. No one cared to hear about Don.

I escaped to the kitchen under the guise of dinner preparation, but mostly to ensure my tongue stayed safely in my mouth. To my dismay, Karen followed. No offer to help, of course; she was just looking for something worthy of complaint, namely my cooking.

"What's in the stuffing?" she asked while sliding her glasses back up the bridge of her shiny nose.

"Uh, sun-dried tomato, mozzarella, feta..."

"Oh, I've never liked *the* feta in anything really. But, I'm sure it won't be that bad."

She swallowed a gulp of her tea and refilled the glass for the tenth time. I returned my attention to the task at hand while she waddled back to the family room. I may have stuffed the chicken with more vigor than required.

Dinner consisted of open-mouth chewing peppered with laughter at anything Jim said. Don's attempts at conversing were rebuffed to the point where only I interacted with him. Meanwhile, Mike and Karen continued to dote on their older, jobless, unwashed son, Jim.

The rest of the weekend continued with more of the same, including jabs like, "Don't worry, we won't steal the silverware," when Don had to run to the store for more tea bags. Their youngest, and only daughter, called every couple of hours to check on them, effectively depriving Don of any leftover attention.

When the nightmare intrusion, I mean visit, ended, Don's mood remained sour. He asked a few days later, "Why are they so negative?"

"They're miserable and will always be. You don't need their approval."

His brow twitched as I took his hand and said, "I'm proud of you."

I often wonder how my in-laws can be so blind to the unequal treatment of their children. Perhaps they see it and just don't care. Whatever the case, I'm glad my husband was the middle child who had to work harder to be noticed. It's made him a wonderful man. And if they don't see it, I do.

~Avery Shepard

59

'Tis Better to Give than to Receive

Gratitude is the best attitude.
~Author Unknown

In late November, right after Thanksgiving, thoughts of dread and gloom used to start to invade the minds of my family. It's not that we didn't enjoy all of the holiday festivities. It's just that the holidays meant gift giving. And gift giving meant gift receiving. And receiving gifts from my Aunt Beadie was always interesting.

My Aunt Beadie was a really nice person and we did love her. She did tend to be a bit eccentric and always exaggerate the truth... just a tiny little bit. Like the time she told us she thwarted a bank robbery that was in progress and single-handedly detained the robber until the police arrived. Or the time she came screaming down the stairs at my house claiming that there was this huge hole in the floor of my son's closet and that both of my sons were going to fall through it down into the dining room below. Why hadn't any of us ever even seen this huge gaping hole in our floor? Why hadn't my kids fallen through it before? And then there was the time she swore she could hear the conversations going on in my neighbor's house through the heating ducts in OUR living room. She talked to her dog, too. And of course the dog answered her.

Aunt Beadie raised gift giving to a whole new level, or should I say lowered gift giving to a whole new level. The gifts she gave defied all common sense. Why would my two young sons, ages five and eight at the time, need valets? Now I'm not talking about the living breathing kind of valet who brings you breakfast in bed or irons your newspaper, but the piece of furniture kind of valet on which you hang your suit jacket and tie when you come home from work so they won't wrinkle. The kind that has a special safe place where you can put your cufflinks and tie tack so you won't lose them. What was Aunt Beadie thinking? But, I have to tell you, we did actually use those valets. They made a great tent frame. If you place them just so far apart and drape an old sheet over them, voilà—you have a tent.

The matching Hello Kitty nightshirts she gave to my husband and me one year were quite lovely. They were a kind of brown color with the perfect Hello Kitty logo right there on the front and they each came with matching coin purses. Fetching. She had bought both nightshirts in a large size… a child's size large. Not that we would have worn them anyway. And our boys would not have been caught dead wearing Hello Kitty nightshirts. We donated them, and the coin purses, and I'm sure two little girls were delighted to receive them.

One year we got a talking alarm clock. It didn't have a clock face but instead spoke the time in a very loud voice so you wouldn't have to put your glasses on to read it. That could possibly have been useful… if we spoke Russian.

We all got matching terry cloth shower wraps one year that were monogrammed with initials—not *our* initials but still quite lovely. The boys used them as Superman capes. Never mind about the very tasteful pink flamingo that she got for our yard one year. Now the Magic-8 Ball was actually quite useful. I used to ask it whether or not I should cook dinner. I loved it when the answer was, "My reply is no."

What do you say to a loving relative with the worst taste in the world? She would sit right there while we opened her gifts, with a big smile on her face. A mere thank you just didn't seem adequate. So we learned to ad-lib—meaning we learned to lie. "Oh Aunt Beadie, this is amazing. Thank you so much. I have never seen anything quite like this. Oh, the colors are dazzling. I just know this will come in so handy when… oh, I just love it!"

When Aunt Beadie reached her mid-eighties, she decided to stop shopping. No longer would she buy us useless gifts that we would never use. She started giving away useless gifts from her own home—all of the junk that she had been collecting for years and years. Old jars, some without lids, cracked dishes, ashtrays (for our non-smoking household), and much, much more. But the best of all was the jewelry.

None of her jewelry was real. Aunt Beadie knew that. And we knew that too, but she didn't know that we knew. She always claimed everything was real. The set of six huge spider pins was one of my favorite gifts. They were gold (gold-colored metal) with jade (cloudy green glass) centers. I hate spiders! The pins creeped me out—they went right in the trash but I wrapped them in newspaper first to be sure they wouldn't escape. The "ruby" earrings were so ugly and so heavy I was afraid they would pull my ear lobes off if I even tried to put them on. And where could I possibly wear them? Trash! Immediately! And how about the tiara? Please don't forget about the diamond (clear glass) and emerald (green glass) tiara. Now that was a keeper. I actually wore it… to a fiftieth birthday party when I went as the prom queen!

Sadly Aunt Beadie passed away a few years ago. Not to worry. Her daughter, my cousin, has taken up right where Aunt Beadie left off. Ethel is very busy "finding treasures" in Aunt Beadie's closets and drawers to wrap up and give to us as tokens of love. And although our sons are grown and have families of their own now, they still dread the "special gifts" they know that they, and their children, will receive. I, too, can hardly wait to see what is in store for us this year.

~Maddie Sohn

Bad Tidings to You

*I once bought my kids a set of batteries for Christmas
with a note on it saying, toys not included.*
~Bernard Manning

Many years ago, when I was engaged to Eleanor's son, Eleanor said something that I considered very odd. "Don't worry, honey," she said out of the blue. "I don't play games."

I had no idea what she was talking about. Parcheesi? Bridge?

"Head games," Eleanor clarified, seeing my confusion.

That didn't clear it up for me. I come from a family that could easily be called honest to a fault. Head games? I was perplexed and a little uneasy.

Turns out that Eleanor's family—and it is most definitely Eleanor's family—does indeed play head games. And what's more, the object of the game is to do whatever The Head dictates at all times or suffer the punishments. This great reigning toad of a woman can wield anything from a cold shoulder to a rude e-mail, but my favorite without a doubt is what I call "Punishment by Christmas Present."

It started after I had been married to Eleanor's son for a couple of years, when Eleanor's other son married Natalie. Eleanor didn't like the new bride, so everyone in the family dutifully shunned her. Everyone but me. I'd never met Natalie. How could I know if I liked her or not?

This did not sit well with Eleanor. On Christmas morning, she fixed me with her shrewish eyes as I opened my gift. It was... a cloth thing of some sort. I was twenty-seven years old and a size four, and it looked like a billowing tent made from yards and yards of gray fleece. It easily could have housed a family of three and some small pets. At the top was something that looked like a three-foot-tall, knitted chimney in candy cane stripes. That turned out to be a turtleneck. It rolled down and down until it looked just like a cross between a striped goiter warmer and a neck brace. Eleanor's gift was a muumuu that practically mooed.

Did her eyes twinkle, or did I only imagine it?

And then, the proverbial fly on the poop: "I thought it looked just like you!" she grinned. The horror!

As bad as my Punishment Gifts were, they were nothing compared to Natalie's. Every year, Eleanor sent each of her sons' families the ceramic pieces to a Christmas village. One year, Natalie's birthday gift was the five-dollar garbage cans that went with the set. Natalie cried.

Eleanor is not simply a bad gift-giver. She never buys bad gifts for herself or her daughter, but only for those who refuse to agree with her or stroke her ever-wounded ego. If Eleanor is pleased, the gifts are downright lavish. Whenever anyone does something that she considers a slight, they can count on getting the Punishment Gift at the next holiday. Or worse, their children will get bad gifts. If Eleanor is really angry, the gifts will be about three days late.

Ironically, Natalie and I became friends because of the way Eleanor divided her family. As a result, my gifts got worse… or better, depending on how one looks at it, since I've grown to enjoy the surprises.

One year, I couldn't figure out what the gift actually was. It was a small plastic square with a snow scene on it. Cap to something? Coaster? Tiny wall hanging of some sort? I had fun secretly polling friends. No one else knew, either. And I was somewhat proud of the way I got around the topic in my thank you note. Since I lived in a temperate climate at the time, I told Eleanor that her gift reminded me of the years I had spent in the cold.

Natalie took a different tack. "I will certainly think of you every time I see these!" she exclaimed of the garbage cans.

We figure Natalie will never get another gift from Eleanor again. She is not heartbroken.

~T. Powell Pryce

A Doll Dilemma

Christmas is not as much about opening our presents
as opening our hearts.
~Janice Maeditere

I t all began with a well-meaning gift from my mother-in-law, Mary, to my mother, Marilyn. Soon after spending Thanksgiving at my parents' house—during which she noted my mother's numerous collections—Mary instructed my husband, Mike, to give my mother a box that contained her childhood doll. Or, rather, what remained of the doll.

Peering in the box, my mother's jaw dropped as she studied the pitiful remains of the doll. Sawdust spilled from the torn and frayed kid leather body, twisted arms and legs were disconnected from the body, and a deep crack disfigured the smooth porcelain face that stared back from a hairless head.

It was nothing more than remnants of what had once been a beautiful Floradora doll created by the well-known doll designer, Armand Marseille.

Mary had decided she no longer needed it—small wonder—and thought my mother could add it to her modest doll collection—providing, that is, that she could fix it or locate someone with the skills to restore it.

Whether my mother saw its potential, or just the remains of a now rather unattractive doll, is difficult to tell. But soon after receiving the gift, the box and its contents disappeared into an upstairs closet, a potential black hole for any items that entered it. Childhood toys of mine had been stowed there years ago, never to be seen again.

Over the next six years, the doll was shuttled around the house in its cardboard box abode, from a closet to a bedroom and back to the closet again, all the while collecting dust and occasional cursory glances from curious passersby.

It was impossible to imagine how the doll had once looked. It was equally difficult to imagine the tragedy that had befallen the doll to leave it in this pathetic condition.

This past Christmas, when Mike and I were at my parents' house, we eyed a large box beneath the tree with our names on it. Cryptically, my mother repeatedly said, "The store only had one of these left, so if you don't want it, I'll keep it."

I was prepared to be the recipient of another appliance, like the coffeemaker she gave us five years ago that we had yet to open. Silently, I imagined the possibilities. A food processor? A bread machine? Expecting yet another gift that would see little or no use in our kitchen, we saved the large, cumbersome package for last.

Finally, Mike unwrapped the box and lifted out a long object wrapped in plastic. As he carefully peeled back the wrapping, I recognized it the instant the face was in view. Mike held the object aloft in amazement—his face expressionless—apparently wondering why my mother had seen fit to give us a doll.

A moment later, he, too, recognized Floradora.

She had undergone a truly amazing transformation, from the pitiful pile of remnants to the breathtaking, almost child-like doll now reflecting the soft glow of the sparkling Christmas tree lights. The porcelain face, with its real-hair eyebrows, glowed in the semi-darkness. Her piercing brown eyes were incredibly lifelike.

We passed her around the room for everyone to admire. We all stroked her long, soft curls and studied every last detail of her new outfit. Nearly an hour elapsed before the doll was finally laid gently back in its box.

My mother explained that a neighbor's mother, who once owned a doll hospital, agreed to take on this doll as a project, even though she was retired. Perhaps she saw it as a supreme challenge to attempt to restore this doll to even a semblance of its former beauty.

Later that day, we went to Mike's mother's house for yet another Christmas dinner. On the way, we decided to show her the doll and surprise her.

Before removing the doll from the box, Mike explained to Mary that Marilyn had given this to us as our main Christmas gift. Lifting the doll carefully from the box, he held her up in front of his mother. Suddenly, Mary clutched her hands to her chest, her face contorting as tears trickled down her cheeks.

"It isn't…," she stammered. "Is it? Is it? Is that my doll?"

She reached for the doll and carefully sat it on her lap. She continued crying as she caressed the doll's curls, stroked her dress, and studied her cherubic face.

The doll, in all its glory, closely resembling its original appearance, had been reunited with its former owner.

The roomful of people couldn't help but be touched by this unexpected reunion. Several were teary-eyed, while others simply looked on in amazement.

After admiring and exclaiming over the doll for another fifteen minutes or so, Mary held up the doll and instructed Mike, "Put her to bed. She's tired."

As he held the doll, he hesitated as we exchanged bewildered glances. I stared at him in stunned silence. A disturbing mixture of emotions swept over me.

Perhaps she had misunderstood that the doll had actually been our gift. As Mike placed the doll in a chair across from Mary's bed, I panicked as I imagined my mother's reaction to this unexpected turn of events. How was I going to explain this? My mind reeled as I contemplated the options.

Since I knew my mother was also understandably smitten by the doll, I had planned to leave it at my mother's house for her to enjoy, knowing one day it would return to us. After all, she had housed it for years until she arranged for its remarkable repair job. The doll would certainly be right at home there in my mother's extensive collection of old toys and antiques.

Suddenly, this situation resembled some twisted version of *The Gift of the Magi*. My mother's gift to us had been appropriated by a third party—albeit the doll's original owner—which prevented us from returning the doll to the person responsible for the doll's transformation, my own mother.

Such a bizarre ending to an otherwise memorable Christmas!

During the trip home, the future residence of the doll was discussed as we tried to determine our next move. It was decided to let the matter rest temporarily and hope that Mary would make the next move.

She didn't, however.

Nothing more was said about the matter until one day when Mike carefully broached the subject after sufficient time had elapsed.

Apparently, Mary had misunderstood who the recipient of the doll was. Once she found out, she said, "Well, that takes some of the glow off."

She insisted she never would have given the doll away to anyone, even in its poor condition. She maintained she had given it to my mother in the hopes she could fix it or find someone who could, which wasn't at all the way the other three parties in the transaction remembered it.

Things were becoming even more complicated, and we needed outside advice. Several people suggested doll-napping, while others simply said, "It's yours. Just ask for it." None of those options seemed viable.

Things, we knew, would eventually be settled… somehow, sometime. But there would certainly be someone who'd be less than thrilled with the outcome. But that, too, would be worked out sooner or later. Patience was required until the rightful owner of the doll was determined. Adults, after all, should be grappling with matters more weighty than the ownership of a doll.

But this particular doll evoked powerful emotions, particularly in its original owner, which made it much more than a mere plaything. To Mary, it symbolized poignant childhood memories and a means to recapture her youth.

To my mother, it was symbolic of an abiding respect for, and preservation of, beloved objects from the past, part of her overall appreciation of antiques.

Mike, in turn, was torn between joy in his mother's reunion with her doll while appreciating my mother's repair efforts and wanting her to have it. The newest owners were contemplating drafting a custody agreement between the two mothers.

The urgency of the situation dwindled with time. But, one day, the true magnitude of the situation became apparent. It's often said that things happen for a reason, even though the reason may not be obvious at the time.

Almost three months to the day of the doll incident, Mary was declared legally blind.

All of a sudden, everyone, especially me, had a new perspective on what had so recently been a particularly thorny issue. It was sobering how a mere three months could so dramatically alter one's opinions on an emotional issue.

At first, I was struck by the miraculous nature of my mother's decision to choose this particular Christmas to get the doll repaired after it had been lost in oblivion for so many years. In so doing, she had allowed Mary one last chance to see her childhood doll as she once was. Certainly, plenty of fond childhood memories had been revisited as Mary awoke each morning to the sight of the doll sitting in a chair by her bed.

Perhaps my mother expressed it best when she said, "Thank the Lord she got to see her doll one last time."

After all that had transpired these past few months, none of us will ever "see" Floradora in quite the same way ever again.

Not long ago, Mary suggested that Mike take Floradora to our house since she could no longer see her. He shrugged off her suggestion, knowing the time was not quite right for the doll to finally come to live with her adoptive family.

After all, Floradora was home.

~Debbie Dufresne

Dressed to Impress

What a strange power there is in clothing.
~Isaac Bashevis Singer

My future mother-in-law. She was a tough nut, all right. My mother could only repeat, "Thank goodness, there's only one of her," whenever my fiancé Phil's mother, Helga, was mentioned. As a result of her "commanding" personality, Helga's niece called her aunt "The General" when she was safely out of earshot. And when my godmother met Helga at Phil's and my engagement party, she leaned toward me, kissed me on the cheek, and whispered into my ear, "Good luck with that one."

In the years leading up to Phil's and my engagement, his mother made her assessment of my appearance perfectly clear: my nails were too long and too brightly polished; my heels were too high; my jeans were too tight. Once, despite having no training as a beautician, she even offered to cut my hair, commenting, "Why don't you let me fix that style up for you?"

So when I learned that Phil's father, my future father-in-law, was to be honored at a party hosted by his genealogy club, I had my share of concerns. As outgoing president, he, my future mother-in-law, and the balance of their family, including me, would be seated at the head table on a raised dais for all to see. This was to be my first introduction to my father-in-law's friends and associates. Certainly, I wanted to look my best. More than that, however, I wanted to avoid any further criticism at the hands of Helga. So I embarked on a citywide search for the perfect outfit.

For weeks, I made my way through malls, badgered boutique owners, and ransacked racks of evening wear in search of the appropriate garment. Finally, my insecurities brought me home with not one, but two possibilities. The night of the party, as I readied for the big event, I held up the two outfits for Phil to inspect: one, a fashionable silk suit with a black skirt complemented by a simple white jacket; the other, a form-fitting little black number accented by a floral scarf.

"Which one?" I asked. Phil chose the suit.

I must admit that Phil's choice surprised me. Of the two, the suit was more no-nonsense, while the little black dress with its bright scarf was more frivolous, sexy even. I would have thought Phil would have preferred for me to wear that one. However, I accepted his advice willingly. Certainly, he was a better barometer of his mother's likes and dislikes than I was. Still, as I stood before the mirror adjusting my jacket, my lungs tightened and my stomach rumbled.

"Well," I thought, "if Helga has anything to say about the way I look tonight, I'll just tell her that her son chose my outfit."

Bolstered by my false confidence, I walked tall out of the house and into Phil's car. Yet as we drove toward the venue, my anxiety only worsened. I twisted my hands and made the annoying throat-clearing sound I always made when I was nervous. Recognizing my tension, Phil quickly put me at ease with a good-natured impersonation of his mother's heavily accented speech. "I vill cut your hair und you vill like it," he said, reminding me of one of his mother's more over-the-top comments.

By the time we reached the parking lot, Phil and I had both succumbed to a bad case of the giggles. As we approached the building, though, I quickly sobered. After a deep, cleansing breath, I entered through the ballroom's elegant glass double doors. Then, from way across the room, my mother-in-law and I spotted each other. Even at several paces, I could see her jaw drop. When she regained her composure, I watched as she turned to her husband, pointed toward me, and howled out, "She's wearing the same dress as me!"

With shaking knees, I approached her. "We're wearing the same dress," she repeated. I stood there, speechless, the air sucked from my lungs by the sight of my fashion-twin. Then she lifted her hand above her head and brought it down on my shoulder.

"That's all right," she said. "At least people will see we have good taste in common."

Silently, I prayed that good taste was the only thing people would think we had in common. Yet, as my fiancé sat at the dais flanked by two women wearing identical outfits that night, I realized that my mother-in-law and I had something else in common: we both loved her son very much. And that one fact, and that fact alone, has kept my mother-in-law and me at peaceful odds for well over twenty years.

~Annie

Chapter
7

Family Matters

Kids Will Be Kids

A characteristic of the normal child is he doesn't act that way very often.

~Author Unknown

Music to Soothe the Savage Beast

Music hath the charm to soothe a savage beast, but I'd try a revolver first.
~Josh Billings

My legs hang over the arm of the couch. Inches away from my head, my eight-year-old daughter plinks away at her electronic keyboard. "Yo, monkey," I say to her without turning. "What's the name of that song?"

"I Dropped My Dolly in the Dirt."

I smile and continue reading my magazine. I also smile at my own pleasure. It was not always possible for me to enjoy young children playing instruments. In fact, once upon a time I detested it.

Many moons ago when I was sixteen, my mother wheedled a white baby grand piano out of my half-brother's grandparents. Mom was great at wheedling. Dear ol' Mom had plans for her herd. Great plans. Mom placed my six-year-old brother on a pedestal so lofty that he often fell back to Earth with such a clamor that all felt the reverberations.

Much to my horror and that of my five-year-old sister, Mom had decided our brother Mark was a musical genius. Thus, logically, the only possible next step for our beloved sibling was to follow in the footsteps of Mozart. This translated into a small fiery-red-haired brat practicing at ungodly hours on a piano. That the showpiece white baby grand sat in the living room — and that my bedroom was on the other side of a wall by said instrument—further infuriated me. Each morning, my cherubic brother plinked on his scales at the predawn hour of 6:00 a.m.

I'd shove my pillow around my head and curse, but the noise continued. Teenage fury rose in me.

Eventually, I'd give up, get up and mumble the same thing I always did as soon as I saw Mom.

"WHY does he have to play SO EARLY?"

And dear Mom had her pat melodious reply: "Markie is a morning person."

I wanted to kill or at least gag him. Or, better yet, destroy that piano.

My stepfather went along with all the musical shenanigans. After all, it was his parents who had been bamboozled into buying the piano. He never said too much, but he was constantly on edge. To be fair, Mom kept us all pretty much on the edge. She'd fly off the hat at real or imagined offenses. She had called the cops on neighbors so many times that I hung my head low whenever I walked the neighborhood. Once, she had smashed a neighbor's front door window because their dogs had come in our yard and eaten my sister's rabbits.

As I saw the world from my sixteen-year-old eyes, I got grief, Markie got a piano, and my sister got animals. In fact, she had a hamster called Hammie.

Now, Mr. Hammie was a normal hamster, orange-ish, fluffy, way overweight, and didn't have much of a personality if I recall correctly. He was kind of skittish. Oh, yeah, he didn't like being held. But if you think about it, who would like to be manhandled by five- or six-year-olds? And, to be honest, we were all kind of skittish.

Anyway, one fine day Markie was not at his piano. My sister was letting Hammie explore the wondrous white instrument. First, he was on the keys on the left side, sitting comfortably on a nice solid C note. He was taking short hamster steps, testing whether or not the keys would support his weight. Hammie got a feel for it and hauled hamster butt. He zoomed to the far right end of the keyboard. And with each step, he plunked a note. This caught the pointy ears of our brother, the king of the white baby grand.

"Hey, who's messing with my piano?" my brother yelled from somewhere in the house.

I smelled a disaster, and that is good for a non-involved, eternally pissed off sixteen-year-old. Bodies from all over the house converged on the sacred piano zone—a stepdad body, a six-year-old Mozart impersonator body and, worst of all, THE MOTHER BODY!

My sister, reading the writing on the wall, knew she would pay for trespassing on the sacred and holy piano. She attempted to scoop up Hammie. Ah, but Hammie had a different vision of the world. The lid of the piano was open. How else to impress the neighbors and occasional visitors? Hammie jumped into the guts of the piano. He worked his way under the many miles of strung wire. My sister was horrorstruck. But her timing was just a little off. His Royal Highness Markie had arrived on the scene, just in time to see Hammie's furry hamster hindquarters leap into the heart of his piano.

"MOM! HAMMIE'S IN THE PIANO!" he screamed.

Our house was never far from hysteria, and like a tornado picking up speed, the winds of chaos were now swirling. I continued peeking from the safety of the kitchen, wanting to see, but at least be near an exit. I had two exit options—the front door or the sliding glass door.

Hammie did his best to burrow deeper into the core of the piano. But as he ran across the inner strings, the keys would pluck, and the sucker played a song of flight. I loved it. My sister paled. My brother was mortified. Mom, well, Mom freaked… but that was pretty predictable.

"Oh, my God, my GOD, the hamster is in the piano. Roger! Roger!"

Stepdad was named Roger at birth. The only time we ever heard his name was when Mom wanted him to solve some crisis. Like a hamster in a piano. We heard his name pretty regularly.

"Roger, Roger. Oh, my God, what can we do?"

My brother added his calm voice to the din. "I HATE YOUR HAMSTER! GET IT OUT OF MY PIANO. NOW!!!"

Hammie kept up the music and took a quick turn to the left, playing a descending scale — actually better than what I normally had to listen to.

"Roger, do something. Do something!" demanded Mom.

Now, Roger was a quiet guy. He worked for the state, loved solitude, and had married my mother when his hormones got the better of him. All this pressure was building for him to do something. My sister sniffled and then broke into a howl. Markie was jumping up and down at the edge of the piano.

"There he is!" Markie said, pointing. "There he is. Get some cheese and get him out."

"He hates cheese," my sister sobbed.

Hammie kept up a good tune. Mom's arms were in the air, flailing.

"Roger, Roger! Get the hamster out. What if he poops in there?"

"No!" screamed my brother. "He better not poop in my piano!"

He turned to my sister. "Stupid! You aren't supposed to touch my piano!"

Recriminations usually were part and parcel of our domestic storms.

The chaos factor had kicked in. How do you make it stop? What could one person do to end such a situation?

Roger figured it out. He watched Mr. Hammie's handiwork on the keys. They'd depress as a result of the fast-footed critter's movements. Roger anticipated two keys ahead of Mr. Hammie, raised his hand, made a fist and WHAM! Eeek!

My sister hit the floor legs spread wide. Her arms were the same, kind of like a kid making an angel in the snow. She started screaming. Next, my brother went nuts.

"THERE'S GUTS EVERYWHERE!!" he screamed and tried to attack my sister.

Roger pulled him off. Mom was quiet, but her eyes were big. She looked at me in the kitchen. "Why did YOU let her do this?"

I said nothing, just backed out the sliding glass door into a crisp Connecticut November day and ran.

It's taken me a few years to enjoy hearing my daughter play the keyboard. But then again, we don't have a hamster.

~Paul H. Karrer

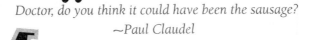

A Love Affair With Sausage

Doctor, do you think it could have been the sausage?
~Paul Claudel

My brother Gary had a love affair with sausage. From his first tiny nibble as a baby with three front teeth until he started school in the first grade, Gary's love of sausage was intense and passionate.

Most children have a favorite teddy bear or blankie they drag around throughout the day and without which they cannot sleep at night. Gary's passion was sausage. He wanted to eat it. He wanted to carry it around during his waking hours, and he wanted to sleep with it at night.

Night after night, the routine never varied. The only way to get him to bed was to let him cuddle up with a two-pound roll of raw, uncooked sausage, which was stuffed into a thin gauzy casing and wrapped in white butcher paper.

My mama tried without success to substitute stuffed animals, toys, blankets, or quilts, but to no avail. Gary stood in his baby bed, one hand on the rail, crocodile tears rolling down his cheeks, his other hand reaching and grabbing toward the doorway, gesturing and crying, "'ont sausage."

My mama finally conceded and placed the roll of uncooked sausage in his little arms. A wide smile appeared on his wet face, and he lay down without being told. Sausage to neck, he fell asleep immediately and never made another sound throughout the night.

What can it hurt, my mama thought, if he snuggles with the sausage for a little while? She and Daddy tried to remember to pull the sausage from his grip before they went to bed. Many times, however, when Daddy opened the refrigerator the next morning to get the sausage, it was not there. He would have to tiptoe into Gary's room where he found, more often than not, that Gary had laid on the sausage during the night, flattened it out, and wet on it repeatedly. Often, the butcher paper had come completely off, and raw sausage had been squashed out of the thin gauzy bag.

There were no disposable diapers in the 1940s. There were only cloth diapers and rubber sheets to puddle the pee.

Surely it can't hurt us, my mama reasoned. Cooking kills germs. So my parents cooked the sausage that Gary snuggled up to, slept with, and wet on.

For years, we teased my brother about sleeping with and wetting on the sausage. He always got the last word, though.

"I slept with it and wet on it," he admitted, "but the rest of you ate it!"

~Judy Lee Green

Lemon Tree

The world only goes round by misunderstanding.
~Charles Baudelaire

It was a bright and sunny spring afternoon. As I washed dishes, I looked out my kitchen window and saw Pat, my roommate, admiring her miniature lemon tree. It had been three years since she planted that tree, and each year she would baby it, hoping it would grow lemons. The tree had reached approximately four feet. There were three leaves growing on a single branch. Pat looked so happy and content. This year, it seemed it would finally grow those long-awaited lemons.

"Grandma, do you have any work for me? I need fifteen dollars."

I asked, "What do you need fifteen dollars for, Anthony?"

My twelve-year-old grandson wanted to make some extra money to go to the local amusement park. I was a little hesitant to pay him for doing work that I felt he should have done for free. After all, I was his grandmother.

After thinking for a while, I decided it would be nice for him to mow the backyard. I also wanted him to mow around the stone walkway close to the hedges and trim around Pat's lemon tree.

"Okay, Anthony, I want you to mow the backyard. I want you to mow everything, especially the stone walkway and as close to the hedges as possible."

Anthony was a little more excited than I thought he would be.

He said, "You want me to mow everything?"

I told him yes, mow everything. I had to go to the store for an hour or so, but I would pay him when I got back. In exchange, he had to promise that he would take his time and do a good job.

He said, "Okay. So, you want me to mow everything?"

Again, I said yes, "Everything."

Pat was also on her way out. She said she would be back in a few hours.

As I drove up toward the driveway on my return from the store, I noticed three little leaves on a lone branch sticking out of the trash can. I quickly parked my car and ran to the backyard.

"Oh, my goodness!" I was almost in a state of panic. I couldn't believe what I was seeing. The tree was gone. The whole tree was gone!

I could imagine how Pat would yell. "You always have to be specific with children because they can only do what they comprehend," she'd say. This was one of those moments; I should have been specific with Anthony. I should have told him to mow everything except the lemon tree.

"Anthony! Anthony!" I yelled, but no answer. What the heck had this kid done?

I ran back to the trashcan and looked inside, hoping to replant the tree, but it was cut up into six little pieces. I shoved all the pieces back into the trash can. I had to do something, but what? I decided I would buy another tree and plant it before Pat returned.

Rushing around town, I went to three home improvement stores, but no luck. I could not find a tree that remotely resembled Pat's lemon tree. Oh, no! It was getting late, and Pat would be so angry if she got home and saw her tree missing. I had to do something, and I had to do it quickly.

"A nursery… I could go to a nursery."

As I hurried toward the neighborhood nursery, I said a little prayer. "Please let there be a lemon tree." My prayers were answered. There was a tree that kind of resembled Pat's lemon tree. I asked the owner to cut a few of the branches and pluck the leaves. Not perfect, but it looked a lot like Pat's tree.

As soon as I got home, I rushed to the backyard to plant the lemon tree. I had to replant it once because I planted it with the leaves on the right side and remembered they had been on the left side. Just as I finished replanting the tree, Pat came home. I heard her calling my name. I yelled back and told her I was in the backyard. As soon as she came outside, I could see her eyes focused on the tree.

"I can't believe it!" she yelled. I couldn't believe it, either. She had noticed the tree. I should have been honest with her. I should have told her the truth. I should never have wasted my time and money. That's what I deserved for trying to cover for my grandson.

"I can't believe it!" Pat kept yelling. She looked at me and said, "I told you that you have to be specific when telling kids what to do." She was shaking her hand, pointing to the tree. "You have to keep an eye on kids. You have to monitor them because they do what they want to do." I could see the expression on her face, and she was reaching a state of anger.

"Where is Anthony?" she asked. "Don't you pay him a dime!" She walked away toward the house. "Anthony! Anthony!" she yelled.

How could she have known? I thought I had trimmed the tree to look exactly as the old one. I was physically exhausted from running around town looking for that tree. I was also becoming emotionally drained. No matter how hard I had tried to replace that tree, Pat had noticed. Now, I had to hear her complaining for hours, maybe even days.

As soon as I entered the house, Pat looked at me and said, "I can't believe Anthony didn't listen to me." She was angry. "Where is he?"

Just as she started to walk toward the living room, Anthony walked in the door. Pat said, "Anthony! Why didn't you do as I told you?" Anthony looked confused. "Didn't I tell you to cut down that tree?" I almost fainted; I couldn't believe what I had just heard.

Anthony said, "I did cut it down."

"Well, if you cut it down, then what the heck is that in the backyard?!"

~Irene Estrada

The Crying Machine

If your parents didn't have any children,
there's a good chance that you won't have any.
~Clarence Day

When my nephew, Anthony, was fourteen, he decided never to have children. He had seen the enemy, and he didn't want to go back and study parenting anymore. Why? He enrolled in Family Studies.

In Family Studies, teenagers learn about interpersonal relationships, fighting fair, negotiating the emotional whitewater rapids of home life, and caring for children by carrying around an egg or a five-pound bag of sugar. This supposedly teaches them the responsibility of having a baby. With computer technology, the days of carrying around eggs and bags of sugar are past; lifelike dolls have taken their place.

Girls usually choose the dolls. Boys choose simpler tasks, like cooking or writing a paper, or caring for a hamster or a plant. Anthony is an unusual boy. He plays sports, but he's not a fanatic. Given the choice, he would rather read a book, play computer games, or just watch television. Anthony chose the doll.

Unlike babies, the doll Anthony chose has an internal clock and mechanisms that provide hours and hours of scenarios you might encounter with a real baby. They even weigh about the same as a one-to three-month-old infant. Anthony's baby was named Scott, and he was fully equipped with a baby carrier, diaper bag, bottles, diapers and a change of clothes.

My sister forgot Anthony was bringing the baby home that weekend; when he did, she was surprised and fascinated. The baby was lifelike and heavy, about the size of a newborn. Anthony had a key attached to his wrist to stop the baby's crying, and the baby cried very loudly and often.

All through supper and washing the dishes, the baby was silent. After dinner, the family went to the tack shop in town; they needed supplies for their horses. Just as they turned into the shopping mall, the baby started crying. Tracy stayed with Anthony to help him stop the baby's cries. After ten minutes, she gave up. She told Anthony he was on his own. Anthony pleaded, but his mother ignored him.

"The baby is your responsibility," she told him. She disappeared inside the tack shop, and Cody, who usually sticks close to his brother, followed her.

"It's too loud," he said.

When they returned to the car, the baby was silent.

When they drove to Walmart, Tracy gave Anthony a choice: either stay in the car with the baby or bring him into the store. Randy felt sorry for his son and didn't think the baby would cry again. "Just leave it in the car."

Tracy didn't agree. "You're teaching him bad habits. That baby is his responsibility." Anthony left the baby in the car.

In the two years that Anthony's family lived in that town, they never saw any of the boys' classmates in the stores, but they didn't count on Murphy's Law.

"Hey, Anthony!" a girl called just as they walked into the store. "Where's your baby?"

He told her he left it in the car. She hurried away as though afraid of being contaminated or because she couldn't wait to tell her mother or their teacher. But Anthony didn't care. He shrugged his shoulders and went to look at the video section, almost as though he were relieved.

Just after they got home, Tracy called her mother, and the baby started crying again.

"What is that?" Mom asked. Tracy explained. "Can't you turn that thing down?"

"Can you turn a real baby down?" Tracy asked.

"Well, I can't stand to listen to that," Mom said and hung up. Anthony turned the key. The baby cried.

Tracy had worked overtime Saturday, so she went to bed early. She had just fallen asleep when she heard a baby crying. Slightly dazed and still half-asleep, Tracy got out of bed to take care of her child. Suddenly, she realized she was getting up to take care of a doll.

Tracy found Anthony in the family room. He turned the key. The baby cried. "Anthony, I have to work tomorrow. I need to get some sleep."

"Mom, I want to go to bed, but it won't stop crying."

He cranked the key over and over. The baby cried and cried.

"It has to stop sometime," Tracy said as she went back to bed.

Anthony cranked the key. The baby cried. When Tracy got back into bed, the baby's crying sounded muffled.

Tracy got up again. Anthony was still on the couch. Although she could hear the baby crying, Tracy didn't see it.

"Where's the baby?"

Tracy followed her son into the laundry room, and he pointed under the table. Muffled cries came from under a pile of clothes.

"Get that baby out of there and take care of him."

Anthony dug it out and cranked the key. The baby cried. Tracy went back to bed. And the baby cried.

A few minutes later, Anthony climbed the stairs to his bedroom. He didn't have the baby.

"Where is that baby, Anthony?" she asked.

"I put it in the car."

"Get that baby and put it to bed."

"But, Mom, I locked the door."

"Go get that baby."

Everyone was asleep when Tracy left for work the next morning. She called home a couple of times to check on the kids—and the baby. It hadn't cried all day. As soon as Tracy got home, the baby started crying. Anthony cranked the key. The baby cried. Off and on the rest of the night, Anthony cranked, and the baby cried.

When Tracy went to bed that night, she watched Anthony climb the stairs to his room. He didn't have the baby. She called him back downstairs.

"Where's the baby?"

"I put it in the car. It wouldn't stop crying."

"Go get that baby, Anthony."

Anthony took the baby to his room, but it didn't cry all that night. It didn't cry all the next day. No one was sure whether they should be relieved or worried. They jumped at every sound, sure the baby was about to cry. The baby didn't cry.

Anthony took the baby back to school Monday morning. The baby's internal computer recorded the amount of time it had cried and how long Anthony took to respond. The computer reported the baby had been neglected eleven times. It would have been more, but the batteries died.

Cody told Tracy he didn't want a brother or sister. "They're just too noisy."

"You don't have to worry. I have all the babies I want," Tracy assured Cody.

Anthony tried parenthood. He didn't like it. "I'm never having kids, Mom. They're too much trouble."

Parenting isn't for the faint-hearted; neither is caring for a computerized crying machine that tattles. Family Studies are like the scared-straight program for juvenile delinquents or, as in this case, cried straight.

~J.M. Cornwell

Waffles

A waffle is like a pancake with a syrup trap.
~Mitch Hedberg

"Mom? Ummmm, Mom?"

I roll over. In which direction? Away from my interrogating child.

He persists, "Really, Mom, you are going to want to hear this."

Fairly certain that I am NOT going to want to hear what Max has to say (he and I have very different communication styles at 7:00 a.m.), I pull the covers over my head and attempt to hide.

"Max, unless there is a hippo tap dancing in our bathtub, I want fifteen more minutes of sleep."

"Well, okay but…"

"No buts, Max. It's early! It's Saturday! I haven't had any coffee yet! You should be sleeping in, too!" Nothing like pointing the Mom finger to get your day up and moving.

Max yells down the hallway to his brother. "She's not getting up, Alex! Maybe there's more spray stuff in the basement."

Under my warm, cozy fortress of covers, I open one eye. Spray stuff?

Now, let me rewind. I vaguely remember being tapped on the shoulder at an ungodly hour by someone asking for breakfast. However, I am a gal who has some pretty trippy adventures in dreamland, so when the beautiful vase of flowers I was arranging started to talk to me, I was not alarmed. When that vase of flowers started speaking in a voice that eerily resembled the one my seven-year-old uses, I didn't even bat one dreaming eyelash. It wasn't until the icy cold hand of reality reached very rudely into my dream and yanked me quite forcefully into the present that I started to worry. Spray stuff? My attempt to enjoy a luxury most moms surrender upon childbirth was thwarted by spray stuff. I make a mental note to write a scathing letter to whoever made children such happy little morning people, and I ask Max with the kind of hesitation reserved for walking through a landmine, "Did you say 'spray stuff,' Max?"

"Uh-huh."

Reluctantly, painfully, I pull the covers down from my head. I look to my right, and there is Max, wearing nothing but Spiderman undies and a smile.

"Hi, Mom." He's holding a near-empty bottle of Windex. I conclude, with much brilliance, this is the spray stuff of which he speaks. Not really wanting the answer to what I am about to ask, I realize it's my parental duty to suck it up and do it anyway.

"Why are you holding a Windex bottle, Max?"

Max is a bright child. He knows in most cases how to properly handle a situation. He doesn't always choose that option, but he clearly knows right from wrong. I can see the wheels spinning in his head, mulling over what to say. He makes his choice, and does what any respectable five-year old would do. He totally throws his brother under the bus.

"You gotta talk to Alex about that, Mom. This was HIS idea." And with that, I am forced to get dressed and start my day.

I go downstairs, knowing I'm in for something, but not sure what. As I descend the stairs to my life, I notice that it's strangely quiet except for the "shhht-shhht-shhht" sound of a spray bottle. I close my eyes and ask for patience. Deliver it immediately, please.

Alex is bent over, backside to me, spraying something on the couch. I close my eyes and change my original request. This time, I ask for patience, guidance, and the willpower not to flip my lid.

I have to give the kid credit: whatever he is trying to do, he is doing it with a crazy, focused passion. He didn't even hear me come down the stairs. "Shhht-shhht-shhht" is all there is.

"Alex, can you tell me what you are doing?" I believe I will require a medal for my calmness this morning.

He turns around, bottle of 409 in his left hand, wad of paper towels in his right. He, too, wears nothing but his skivvies. I notice that my living room smells like an IHOP.

"Well, I made breakfast for me and Max. I made waffles, but the plates were too small, and we kinda got syrup on the couch."

Okay, no big deal, I think. This is okay. I can handle this. A few drops of syrup are no big deal. Right?

Then I look at the floor. I think I might cry.

Two tiny plates and an EMPTY bottle of syrup reside there. Our kitten Roxie is perched in the middle, paws covered in syrup. Sensing that I am not at all happy, she looks up at me, and then takes her syrup-covered paws and bolts through the living room, the kitchen, up the stairs—you get the idea.

Shock is starting to set in. I look at the couch and realize it's not just a drop of syrup that was spilled. It's more like an entire maple tree exploded in our living room. And now, it's not just syrup covering the couch; it's syrup AND Windex AND Formula 409. Since the living room is overwhelming me, I decide to go to the kitchen to clear my head.

Roxie has come to a rest in the middle of the kitchen floor. At least she isn't tracking syrup through the house anymore. But what I realize on further inspection is that she didn't really come to a willful rest where she now sits—she is most likely STUCK there. I try to cross the kitchen, but my feet are sticking to the floor as if I am walking across flypaper made for humans.

I try to recite the serenity prayer in my head, but I can't remember the words. Roxie intently tilts her pretty little head in the direction of the trash can, and I look to see why. There, in front of the can, is a nice-sized puddle of the goo that is covering my house… and it's moving. I can see why she was so interested. Moving syrup? I need to contact the people who handle all those "Virgin Mary in the

French toast" sightings. Moving closer to the "miracle moving puddle of syrup," I come to the understanding that it's not really the syrup that's moving, but rather a bevy of ants now invading my house to take a swim in the sugary mess on the floor.

I turn and look behind me. There in the doorway to the kitchen are my two boys — dressed in underwear, covered in syrup, and holding household cleaners. If I had been mad, it dissolved in that moment. They were trying to handle the situation on their own. They were trying to be independent and make their own breakfast. They were ultimately trying their hand at spreading out their wings a bit. And, after all, isn't that what being a parent is about? Giving our children roots so that they can grow wings? Granted, I need to tweak their culinary skills a bit, but, really, if you look closely, this was a pretty clear picture of them moving forward in being responsible for their actions.

I hug them both, grab some paper towels and my own bottle of cleaner, and together we tackle the mess. But while wiping up ants and sticky kitten paws, I realize there was a lesson for Mom in this morning's events, too. When a vase of flowers asks you for breakfast, you'd best get up and make it.

~Jody A. James

"DON'T WORRY. I'M USING CARPET SHAMPOO."

Reprinted by permission of
Martha Campbell ©1998

The Forgetful Fairy

*The tooth fairy teaches children
that they can sell body parts for money.*
~David Richerby

I should have been saving more money this past summer, not just for vacation and camp, but for those visits from the Tooth Fairy... or "Toof Fairy," as one of my twins, Emily, affectionately calls her. The past few months, my three kids have been spitting out baby teeth left and right. When my oldest, Aaron, lost his first tooth, it was such a momentous event. As soon as he drifted off to sleep, I tiptoed into his bedroom, carefully leaving under his pillow: two dollars for the first tooth lost, a new toothbrush, a small tube of toothpaste, and a wonderfully crafted letter from the Tooth Fairy. The next morning, he was thrilled at what the Tooth Fairy had left for him. Ha, I thought. This is fun! I'll be so good at this. Well, that is until the next tooth fell out...

A week later, Aaron was having a pillow fight with his Uncle Jimmy. His second tooth was dangling out of his mouth, ready to fall out. Uncle Jimmy swung the pillow at Aaron. Wham! Out came tooth number two. That night, Aaron put the tooth under his pillow and fell asleep. And then... Mom forgot! I woke up around 3:00 a.m. in a complete panic. Darn Tooth Fairy! I stumbled to the kitchen and grabbed my purse, but all I could find was a twenty-dollar bill. Are you kidding me? I love my son to death, but he was not about to get twenty dollars for a tooth. So I scraped together whatever change I could find in the house and literally dumped the coins under his pillow. Aaron was thrilled the next morning to receive a huge pile of coins. Whew, that was close!

Two weeks later, Emily lost her first tooth, and I was back on track: two dollars for the first tooth lost, a toothbrush, toothpaste, a note. Good to go. A week later, Emily lost her second tooth. Mom forgot. This time, it was midnight, and I awoke again in a panic. I rushed to the kitchen and rummaged through my purse to find no cash at all. This time, I went through the closet downstairs. It contained some Christmas gifts the kids hadn't used yet, and I found a Little Mermaid game. Thankfully, Emily didn't remember that gift. The next morning, she was thrilled, yet confused about the whole board game idea. Emily had a broken leg at the time, so I said, "Well, the Tooth Fairy knew you'd be laid up and wanted you to have something to pass the time." Mom, you liar you. But it worked!

Another couple of weeks passed, and Aaron's top tooth was very loose. He was having a sleepover with two of his friends, and they decided they would pull out the tooth and stay up to see the Tooth Fairy. Their tooth-pulling event began around 9:00 p.m. I had to intervene at one point because they came up with the idea of putting Aaron's head in the doorway, and then trying to shut the door on his tooth. Then, apparently, we ran out of dental floss and they began looking for rope. On top of that, my hand mirror was mysteriously broken. I was told later that Aaron's friend was trying to spank the tooth out of him with my mirror! These kids were definitely creative.

I went to bed around 11:30 and could hear the kids still whispering and working on the loose tooth. Finally, one of his friends pulled the tooth out for him. I could hear the whispering excitement. "Aaron's tooth fell out! Now let's set up base and wait up for the Tooth Fairy!" They all went to bed, waiting. I fell asleep. Around 4:00 a.m., I woke up, frantic. I had forgotten AGAIN! I grabbed a dollar from my purse and snuck into Aaron's room. Luckily, everyone was fast asleep. I slithered over each sleeping child and slipped the money under Aaron's pillow. The next morning, one of Aaron's friends claimed he saw the Tooth Fairy. I said, "Oh, really? What did she look like?" He simply said, "I don't remember." Ha!

A month went by. Emily lost a second tooth, and now her top tooth was very loose. One day, she yanked it out and came to me crying. "Mommy, I don't want the Tooth Fairy to take my tooth. I want to keep it!"

I said, "Don't worry, Emily. The Tooth Fairy is a wonderful, kind, caring fairy, not to mention smart, beautiful, funny (okay, maybe rambling a bit there), and she would not take your tooth from you unless you wanted her to."

Together, we crafted a letter to the Tooth Fairy to come and view the tooth, not take it with her, but still leave Emily her surprise. Of course, Emily made sure it was fully explained in the letter. All went well. The next night, however, Emily wanted the Tooth Fairy to visit again and take the tooth. I told her, "Well, Emily, she can come and take the tooth, but she can't leave you anything this time around."

Emily looked at me bluntly and said, "Never mind. I'll keep it."

Oh, my gosh! She was planning to double-dip the Tooth Fairy! I couldn't believe it!

Last but not least, Sara finally lost her first tooth last week. It was such a treat. She was my last one to lose her first tooth. She had waited so patiently, watching Emily and Aaron getting all the Tooth Fairy surprises. When she woke up the next morning and saw what the Tooth Fairy had left, she was beaming so proudly. It was the sweetest thing to see. She felt like she was part of the club. Good memory, Tooth Fairy!

Today, in addition to scouring the "Help Wanted" ads for a second job to pay for all the lost teeth, I am also playing Memory games with my kids so I can improve my recollection skills. This is one of the many journeys with my kids I want to remember!

~Michele Christian

69

Tripping Out

In the long run the pessimist may be proved right,
but the optimist has a better time on the trip.
~Daniel L. Reardon

O n a hot August morning, after waking me up way too early, my dad handed me a red T-shirt with orange lettering on it. "McCheesey?" I grumbled.

"McChesney." It was his mother's maiden name.

"Looks like McCheesey. These are McDonald's colors. It looks like we're selling cheeseburgers."

Mom chuckled. Dad scowled. That pretty much set the tone for the rest of the trip.

The reason for the shirts (we each had one) was to identify which branch of the family tree we fell off at a reunion. In rural Wisconsin. I wasn't even trying to pretend that I wasn't miserable.

From the moment we arrived, parking our car between a compost heap and a tree stump, my worst fears were confirmed: I was at a picnic. I don't "do" nature. I appreciate bike rides and walks, but only on pavement. Put dirt in the picture or, God forbid, bumblebees, and I'm out. I've camped twice in my entire life—once in the pouring rain (bye-bye sneakers) and once at a Christian camp, where I didn't last three days. Dragging me to a family reunion in the woods was just plain cruel.

"Why didn't they host the reunion up there?" I whined.

"Up there" was a modern lodge on the top of a hill. It had bay windows, through which I could clearly see banquet tables, indoor plumbing, and a snack machine.

"Because this was cheaper," my dad replied curtly.

"This" was a creaky cabin with picnic tables crawling with daddy long-legs.

To be fair, I wouldn't have been much happier in the lodge. Thermostats or not, I don't like family reunions. I think they're dumb. I know everybody complains about them. I know nobody looks forward to old people jabbering on about insurance or new moms insisting that their big, barfing baby is adorable. But my distaste for family reunions runs deeper than simple annoyance. I am opposed to them on principle.

It's the same way I feel about networking. Anybody I actually care about is someone I met naturally and is a friend of mine on Facebook. These people in the woods were folks I never e-mailed and barely knew the names of. Spending an entire day with them just seemed silly.

"Put on your shirt," my dad said. He'd finished unloading the car and apparently had time to nag me again.

"It's goofy."

"We all look goofy. Put it on."

I mumbled something and wandered into the cabin without my McCheesey shirt.

Inside, I came face to face with my next gripe of the trip: the menu. Countless Tupperware containers filled with unidentifiable casseroles and the occasional Jell-O mold littered the dining area. But for all the food, none of it looked edible. Not to me. I was a picky eater. Growing up, my parents and I had an arrangement: any time the adults ate weird food (i.e., something other than a hamburger), I got McDonald's on the way home. That day, we were too far from civilization to observe the pact. There would be no French fries.

"Have a Sloppy Joe," my dad suggested.

"I don't like Sloppy Joes."

"It's meat and ketchup. It's basically a hamburger."

"That is NOT a hamburger."

"Then have a SALAD."

He knew I hated salad. Out of spite, I put a small dollop of Sloppy Joe on my plate, the kind that said, "See, I TRIED it." Then when he turned his back, I filled the rest of my plate with potato chips.

Throughout lunch, I was passed around to a variety of family members who I had either met once, met several times, or never heard of at all, and they all asked me if I remembered them. An uncle talked vaguely about the time he spent in Egypt working for the government. An aunt asked about college. A cousin filled us in all too thoroughly on his recent stomach stapling procedure. And that's when I decided it was time to use the bathroom.

I really did have to use the bathroom, but I also really needed an excuse to escape. My plan was to pee, then hide. I could read behind a tree until it was time to leave. I could listen to my MP3 player. If anybody asked, I could tell them I'd been in the bathroom the whole time. I could blame it on the Sloppy Joes. No one would doubt me.

Little did I know the bathrooms would not be my salvation so much as the last straw. The bathrooms, if you can even call them that, were squat, square boxes of concrete that looked like above-ground bomb shelters. They were comparable to rest stop bathrooms, the kind you find along interstates, but these were cleaned far less frequently and didn't have running water. They were damp, dark, cobwebbed cubes with toilets. And, for some reason, there were no doors or sinks.

That sealed it. I stomped back to the cabin, sunburned and full-bladdered, and begged my dad to drive me to the nearest city. I needed a toilet. I needed McDonald's. I was getting mosquito bites and totally creeped out being this close to a green lake. We'd made our cameo. We'd eaten some food. Couldn't we leave?

But instead of caving under the weight of his little girl's misery, my dad exploded.

"I ask you to do ONE THING for my family. Can't you deal with it for ONE DAY?"

I recoiled.

"I don't want to be here either, but I never ask you to do ANYTHING. I was hoping you could put up with it for ME."

I was speechless. I'd never been yelled at like that before, certainly not for my behavior. I was a good kid. I did my homework. I said thank you for everything and never hit my cousins. I was freakin' charming.

The rest of the trip, even our stop in the Wisconsin Dells the day after, was soured by the argument. Sure, the backwoods of Wisconsin are not the most ideal vacation destination, but the whole outing was a bust—all because I refused to let it be anything better than that. I made the day lame by refusing to swim in the lake. I made it boring by not even tasting the potato salad. I made it regrettable by remaining bitter.

Somebody on the family trip always makes things difficult. That trip, I realized the pain in the butt was me.

~Jess Knox

The Magic of Mercurochrome

Laughter is the best medicine.

~Proverb

There were no boo-boo bunnies or character Band-Aids when I was a little girl, but there was the magic of Mercurochrome. Iodine burned. Mercurochrome did not. Mercurochrome was like a little pharmacy in a bottle. An antiseptic as well as a psychological healer, Mercurochrome was good for cuts, scratches, scrapes, bumps, bruises, abrasions, gashes, or more serious wounds. It did not have to be injected—no pain. There were no doses or pills to swallow—no bad taste. It was not a messy ointment. Application was easy. Paint it on. Blow on it. It dried instantly. Anything that my mama put Mercurochrome on immediately became better, and the bright red color was a badge of courage.

"I didn't even cry," I would boast for several days until the red finally wore off.

My brothers, my sister and I tested and proved the restorative powers of Mercurochrome many years ago. Gary, Donna, Ronnie, Dana, and I were small. We ranged in age from nine down to three. It was summer and hot. The windows were up, and the doors were open.

Mama was not feeling well and had become extremely tired. She

The Magic of Mercurochrome : Kids Will Be Kids   261

latched the screen doors and told us that she was going to lie down on her bed. We were to play together quietly, no fussing, no arguing, no pestering, no annoying. She was not going to sleep, but was just going to close her eyes and rest.

Only a few minutes had passed when Ronnie, four years old, noticed a scratch on his knee that needed immediate attention. We tiptoed into Mama's room and asked her if we could put Mercurochrome on Ronnie's scratch. Flat on her back with one arm flung over her head, Mama had fallen into a deep sleep. We reasoned that since she did not say no, her answer was yes.

We scooted a stool into the bathroom, climbed up and retrieved the Mercurochrome from the medicine cabinet. We painted Ronnie's knee, and he immediately began to feel better.

We were being so good and so very quiet. Since the Mercurochrome was already down and open, each of us started noticing scratches that needed doctoring with our magic cure-all. Soon, we five kids all had Mercurochrome in several different places.

Quietly, we tiptoed into Mama's room to show her that we had taken care of our scratches without bothering her. We knew that she would be so proud of us. She was in an exhausted sleep. We whispered that since Mama didn't feel well, perhaps Mercurochrome would make her feel better. We had to look very carefully to find a scratch, but after the first one, the rest were easy to locate.

Twenty minutes later, we were back in the living room playing Cooties on the floor. We had painted every scratch, every freckle, every mole, every discoloration of our Mama's skin that we could see. She had Mercurochrome on her toes, feet, legs, hands, arms, neck and face. At Donna's urging, we had even tried to paint her fingernails and toenails.

When Mama shrieked in horror, we knew that she was awake. Proud of ourselves, we ran to her room and asked, "Are you feeling better?" We expected her to tell us what good kids we had been while she rested.

With all the yelling, it didn't seem at first that she was feeling much better. But her disbelief and shock soon turned to humor as she stared at her polka-dotted image in the mirror of the bedroom vanity.

We laughed a lot the next few days as the Mercurochrome slowly wore away. If anyone had asked us kids, we would have insisted that the Mercurochrome had made Mama feel better. Hadn't she laid down feeling bad and woke up laughing—after a while, anyway? And hadn't everyone who saw her laughed and laughed at our red polka-dotted mama? Yes, we were sure. Mama had been cured by the magic of Mercurochrome.

~Judy Lee Green

71

A Voice Above the Vacuum

The best gift you can give is a hug:
one size fits all and no one ever minds if you return it.
~Author Unknown

It was our first Thanksgiving in the new house, and I wanted everything to be perfect. Perfect food. Perfect house. Perfect conversation. By the time I hit the forty-eight-hour countdown, my vision of a table with pressed linens, fresh flowers, and a smorgasbord of homemade desserts had already dissolved. I was just hopeful that I'd find a clean tablecloth and eight matching dessert forks.

Our family "plan" for everyone to chip in with the necessary prep work had been torpedoed by my husband's new job in retail. To make matters worse, a critical project for me that week had claimed two days of planned vacation. John Lennon was right: Life is what happens while you are making other plans.

By Wednesday night, while my husband was selling camping gear as Christmas gifts, my children and I were at home and into full-blown vacuum-mania. I was thankful that a kid's allowance didn't constitute a salary as I put my six- and eight-year-old to work, violating all child labor laws. For my part, I was swooshing around in the toilet bowl, headed for a meltdown. I started ticking off all the ways my holiday was falling short as if it were a long list of personal injustices.

It was already too late. In my perfect Thanksgiving, there wasn't going to be any orange zest in my cranberry salad because it hadn't made the grocery list. There would be no perfect family photos to record the day because I had forgotten to buy batteries. The hand towel that matched the new bathroom paint had not been laundered. And then I saw it and exploded; it was the last straw. Someone had brought home the wrong toilet paper. Two-ply or not two-ply: that should never be the question.

I don't remember what my son asked me as he was trying his best to finish the vacuuming, but I do remember twisting into that mean-and-tight mom-face before barking out an angry answer. This combination of sound and fury is a universal signal to kids everywhere that their real mom has just been abducted by aliens, and it's best to duck and cover until she gets back. But he didn't.

Instead of darting out of view, my second-grader turned off the vacuum and walked the whole way around the stairwell to face me. He never said a word. He just wrapped his arms around me for a hug that makes me feel ashamed of myself to this very day. My son—my shrink—took a risk to teach me that sometimes we need a hug most when we are least huggable.

It was the perfect Thanksgiving. The people I loved gathered around my table where a pumpkin covered up last year's stubborn gravy stain. We dined on just one choice of pie, and my dad used a mismatched dinner fork without complaint. My daughter drew a picture of us on a paper plate where no one had their eyes closed.

I learned a lot from an eight-year-old that holiday, and I've tried hard to remember it. As the holidays approach now, I try to celebrate all of our blessings, especially those that come disguised as inconvenience. And if you find a grump circling your Thanksgiving table complaining about her job, his gallstones or her dress size, sidle up and give them all a hug. It just might be what they need most.

~Mitchell Kyd

72

The Joy of Birthmas

There is still no cure for the common birthday.
~John Glenn

Is it a curse or a blessing to have your birthday close to the holidays? I think it's a little bit of both. It's a blessing because we spend half the time celebrating the birth of Christ and the other half celebrating the birth of Becca (that's me). It's a curse because I spend half the time agreeing with my mother that it is better to give than to receive, and the other half wishing that I could have a normal birthday, like the kids born in April.

I didn't always feel that way about my birth date. It all started one November, about ten years ago, after my mother read an article about a little girl in Florida who gave all the birthday presents she received each year to the homeless. Mom decided that her little girl should do the same. However, my mother, being the innovator that she is, wasn't content to just copy someone's idea; she was going to expand and improve upon that idea.

"Honey, I've been thinking. You already get so many presents for Christmas... you really don't need that many more for your birthday. It's only two weeks later. Wouldn't it be nice for you to do something for your birthday for people who don't have as much as you do? You already get so much, and you have parents who love and care about you, so it's time for you to start thinking of other people who are less fortunate. How does that sound to you?"

What could I say? To an eight-year-old, her argument was

infallible. I agreed, and her brilliant plan was set into motion. The next few years, my birthday invitations were accompanied by phrases like "Come prepared to bake brownies for the homeless" and "Bring some fleece material to make hats and scarves for the homeless." The year I turned eleven, my mother's inventiveness reached all new heights when she presented me with an invitation that read: "No GIFTS NECESSARY!" (No gifts?!) "Instead, please bring a package of any type of men's underwear to donate to the homeless shelter." (Men's underwear?!)

Everything came to a grinding halt. No presents? I had gamely gone along with the brownie baking, the scarf knitting, and the hat crocheting because, although they weren't typical birthday activities, they were still fun, but the idea of having a birthday party with no presents was just a little too much for me. Mom relented slightly by altering her sentence to simply say: "Please bring a package of any type of men's underwear to donate to the homeless." But, still, men's underwear? She explained that while shelters have a steady stream of donations, for some reason men's underwear was one of the least frequently provided by donors. We would be doing a great service by providing them with some underwear. Fine.

The very next day, she took me to JCPenney to pick out a package of men's underwear for my donation. She left me standing alone in the aisle as she browsed through the packages, checking for things like price, cotton percentage, elasticity, durability — you know, the boring stuff. I tried to participate. Really, I did. But I was easily distracted by more interesting things, like counting the tiles on the floor.

When I ran out of floor tiles to count, I tried again to marshal my interest. I firmly directed my eyes toward the underwear packages, and surprisingly enough, my attention was caught. I gave a quick glance around to see where my mother was, and then inched closer. Who knew that there were pictures of men modeling the underwear on the underwear packages? If someone had told me that, I probably wouldn't have argued about coming! I never saw the packaging on the underwear that my dad wore. Come to think of it, I had never actually seen a guy in underwear before. These pictures were so...

interesting. They were all so… so… handsome. And muscular. And… my gaze dropped to the only clothed part of the models. Whoa.

"Becca? Where are you?" called my mother as she came around the corner, stopping as she saw my wide-eyed, open-mouthed expression. Following my focus, she sighed with a grin.

"Oh, dear," she murmured as she steered me out the door.

The next day, I had a chance to see the birthday invitations printed out by our trusty computer right before we sent them to my friends.

"Please bring a package of any type of men's SOCKS to donate to the homeless."

~Rebecca Davis

Reprinted by permission of Off the Mark
and Mark Parisi ©2002

An Angel at Our Table

The reason angels can fly is because they take themselves lightly.
~G.K. Chesterton

Aunt Felicia was a sour woman. The only person for whom she showed affection was my little brother, Mikey. It unnerved him. "What's wrong with me? She likes me! What's wrong with me?!"

I suspect it went against my aunt's principles to demonstrate her true feelings for her own little brother. As a boy, my dad had been a prankster. As a man, he had donned the cap of the court jester. Yet each Passover it was my father who led the Seder service, even though it was held in his brother-in-law's house.

Raised to become a rabbi, Dad had turned to socialist rebellion. He could recite the Haggadah backwards, forwards, with full expression, and at any speed he chose. One year, Aunt Felicia informed my male cousins that they could be excused from the table to watch the hockey play-offs if the service ended before the game did. Hockey play-off games go on forever—but the Seder service goes on longer. Auntie's mistake was to make this promise within earshot of my father.

At first, the shift in rhythm was imperceptible. Dad began chanting more quickly than usual, and the uncles dutifully picked up the pace. Incrementally, his chanting grew faster and louder and faster still, until he was hurtling through the Haggadah at the tongue-twisting pace of a Danny Kaye patter song. Daddy kept his head down, his face straight, and his eyes fixed firmly on the Hebrew text before him. The uncles were forced to follow as best they could. Aunt Felicia fumed in helpless fury. The boys beamed. Before the evening ended, they got to see the last part of the hockey play-off game.

It is the role of the youngest child to open the door for Elijah — prophet, angel, and protector of children — so he can enter the household and drink from the goblet of wine that has been prepared for him. By rights that task should've been performed by my little brother, but when the moment came each year for the participants to dip their pinkies into their wineglasses ten times to symbolize the ten plagues that had befallen Egypt (this comes before the entrance of the angel), my little brother would cuddle up to our mother and merrily dip his pinky into her wineglass along with her. Whereas my mother would then wipe the residue onto a napkin like the rest of the grown-ups, Mickey would remove the wine from his finger by licking it off.

Ten drops of Manischewitz would knock out Mickey, and he'd spend the rest of a very long evening curled up on my mother's lap, his pudgy palms clasped as if in prayer and pressed against a cheek, his yarmulke askew on his flaxen crew-cut and a beatific smile on his cherubic face. Thus, the role of gatekeeper fell to me.

"You mean to tell me that he comes to our house and to everybody else's house all at the same time?" I would query when instructed to stand watch.

"Well, he's an angel. He can do that. Except in Israel. In Israel, he gets there seven hours later because of the time change."

As my aunts and uncles and older cousins remained at the long dining room table continuing the recitation, I was told when to open the door, when Elijah had finished his drink, and then when to close the front door to my aunt's duplex because Elijah had just made his exit.

"But I can't see the angel!" I complained.

"Look harder," urged my father.

I squinted my eyes. "I still can't see the angel!"

Daddy smiled his warm, gentle smile. "*Shepsaleh*, you have to look with different eyes."

My big cousins snickered. The entire tribe insisted they could see Elijah clearly. It occurred to me that if I joined my relatives at the table, I'd be able to see the angel too.

"Why can't I just come back to the table and watch the angel drink the wine? Why can't he let himself out?"

"It's not polite to let a guest leave alone. With an angel, you have to be a lady."

I had no answer. Yet.

By the time I was eight, I was fed up with this game.

"I don't care if I'm a lady or not! After I open the door, I'm coming back to the table! I want to see him drink!" I was adamant.

Daddy quickly improvised. "Okay, you can come to the table, and you will see the angel drink." (Mikey still couldn't hold his liquor.)

When cued, I opened the door for Elijah, as I did every year. I marched back to my aunt's dining room table. Maybe I walked behind Elijah, maybe alongside him. If I bumped into the angel, I didn't notice.

I stood among the adults in front of my aunt's table, which held a large, ornate silver drinking vessel filled to the brim with a deep burgundy-coloured wine. The moment of truth had arrived.

"Okay," my father instructed, "watch. The angel's going to drink."

I held my breath. My father slipped his knee under the table and shook it. The silver vessel shimmered under the twinkling crystals of the chandelier. Within the confines of the oval-shaped cup, the dark liquid trembled. I lowered my head and peered.

"It didn't go down!" I scowled. "When you drink, there's supposed to be less in the glass! It didn't go down!"

My father's frustration was beginning to match my own. He pursed his lips and pointed to the goblet.

"Watch again. The angel's going to drink again!"

This time, my father kneed the bottom of the table with such force that the wine spilled over the rim and onto the tablecloth—my aunt's snow-white tablecloth with the lace trim that she displayed only on special occasions. Auntie stared in horror at the deep burgundy-hued stain.

I gazed at the goblet in wonder and awe.

"Oh!" I gleefully clapped my hands, convinced at long last. "What a sloppy angel!"

Daddy was satisfied. Auntie sat stewing over the ruin of her finest linen. She glowered at her youngest brother. Daddy met her smouldering glare and reminded her softly, sweetly, and in accented English, "You can't get mad from an angel."

The last Seder my father led was held in his own home. Our last Seder was our last supper. A week later, Daddy was felled by a massive coronary. My mother found him. He was wearing a smile. He had been getting ready to attend a hockey play-off game.

~S. Nadja Zajdman

Chapter 8

Family Matters

On the Road

Sometimes the road less traveled is less traveled for a reason.

~Jerry Seinfeld

One Crappy Road Trip

I don't like boys. They're kind of annoying.
~Michelle Wie

Anyone who's raised a boy or grown up with brothers can relate to the car trip I recently endured. Once in his life, every boy discovers a word, which from the first time he hears it completely enchants him. For my five brothers, it was the word "booger." For my son, Hewson, it's "turd."

In the late 1960s, there was nothing funnier to my brothers than taking any sentence (song title, slogan, whatever I just said) and slipping "booger" in place of another word. I can still hear them crooning, "I'm looking over a four-pound booger," and then collapsing in laughter in the back seat where I was trapped with them for our annual endurance trip from Kansas City to New Orleans and back.

The more they used their word, the harder they laughed. The harder they laughed, the madder I got. I caught a glimpse of my parents once in the rearview mirror as they pretended to scold my brothers while snickering to each other. I felt completely betrayed.

Now I'm the mom of four kids, including one red-blooded eight-year-old boy and one far-too-serious eleven-year-old sister. As much as I've tried to reason with her and explain, "If you don't let him get to you, he'll get bored and stop saying it," she doesn't listen any more than I did.

Last Thursday, the three of us piled into the car and set out in search of a new minivan. It wasn't Kansas City to New Orleans, but for my daughter, Molly, it might as well have been, as Hewson set about using his newfound word with a gusto that would've made his uncles proud. He began with highway signs: "Turds May Ice in Cold Weather," "Turd Limit 70," "Caution: Falling Turds," and my own personal favorite, "Highway Workers, Give Them a Turd."

Molly's pleas of "MAAA-MAAA, make him stop!" started a tug of war inside me. On one hand, I remember too well the booger days of the 1960s. On the other, when I looked from my new vantage point in the rearview mirror and saw the impish look on Hewson's freckled face as he sang out, "Unlawful to Turd and Authorized Turds Only," I felt a laugh boiling up inside me. I thought about my brothers singing, "She's Got a Booger to Ride," took a deep breath and told Hewson, "All right, buddy, enough turd talk for a while. Find something else to do."

He did for a few miles, but then we hit a populated area and the billboards began. A national motel chain offered "Free Continental Turds." An airline invited customers to "Come Turd with Us." I disguised a chuckle as a cough.

Molly turned red in the face. "Mom, I'm going to clobber him if he doesn't shut up!"

We passed a truck warning, "Caution Wide Turds."

Another truck offered "Quality Refrigerated Turds." A good one!

"Mom, aren't you going to say anything?"

I swallowed repeatedly, made myself think of something sad, and tried changing the subject. "Whatcha reading there, Sis?"

She cut her brother a look and held up the book in her lap. "It's for school. A collection of poems by Edgar Allan Poe."

"Oh," Hewson retorted, "Turdy Allan Poe. I've heard of him." And then he broke into a rousing rendition of "Hail to the Turd." (Better than "Turd to the Chief," I thought. But I didn't say it.)

We passed through a "No Turd Zone" and a car with an "I Brake for Turds" bumper sticker. That's when Molly walloped Hewson. He didn't miss a beat, "Caution… Steep Turds Ahead." She punched him again. I tried to referee from the front seat.

"Molly, if you'll stop pounding your brother, I'm sure he'll stop talking turd for a while. Right, buddy?" Nobody heard me.

"Yield to Oncoming Turds." POUND!

"Center Lane for Turds Only." POUND!

"This Turd Stops at All Railroad Crossings." DOUBLE POUND!

I threatened to "Pull this car over and you'll both be sorry." I was talking to myself. That's when I saw it, clearly written on the passenger side mirror: "Turds in Mirror Are Closer Than They Appear." No, I couldn't. I owed it to Molly, to sisters everywhere, to take her side on this. I willed myself to remember how badly I'd wanted to open the back door of our old Impala and kick my brothers out onto the highway.

The fray in the back seat continued as we turned off the interstate and into a residential neighborhood, "Slow, Turds at Play."

"I'm gonna kill him, Mom. I MEAN it!"

"Quiet! Turd Zone."

"All right, I warned him."

"Fines Higher in Turd Area."

"Mom, you're just gonna let him say it?"

No more signs, but Hewson was on a roll.

"A turd in the hand is worth two in the bush."

"Yeah," I thought, "the early bird gets the turd."

I tried my hardest to conjure up a picture of my brothers after we got home from New Orleans and they recruited a few neighborhood boys in singing, "The booger, my friend, is blowing in the wind."

"Got turds?" Hewson asked.

"The squeaky turd gets the grease," I thought.

That was last week. Molly hasn't killed her brother yet, and we still haven't found a new minivan. We're setting out to shop some more today. Things aren't looking too good, though. I can hear Hewson in his room getting ready by singing, "Who let the turds out? Who? Who?"

~Mimi Greenwood Knight

Stoplight Fire Drill

Right now, my daughter's just rolling her eyes at everything I do;
I'm just an embarrassment.
~Elizabeth Perkins

There is a point in a teenager's life when parents become annoying and embarrassing by dancing at parties at home or just by being parents. When my mother got on the stoplight fire drill kick—jumping out of the car at stoplights, running around the car and jumping back inside—all I wanted to do was crawl under the seats. I was a dignified teenager and far too mature for silly games. Mom should have been more dignified and mature, but she wasn't, and that little bit of fun came back to bite her in the backside.

The Saturday before Memorial Day in 1970 when I was fifteen, we piled into the car to drive up to Alger, Ohio to the cemetery where my Uncle Jack, who had served in the Navy, was buried. My younger siblings, Carol, Jimmy and Tracy, cousins, Lonnie, Dave and Earl, and I were spread over all three seats of the station wagon. I was in the back seat with my brother and youngest sister, Carol in the front with Mom and the cousins in the third seat facing traffic.

We stopped for the light at the corner of Sullivant and Burgess on our way out of town and Mom called, "Stoplight fire drill." Everyone jumped out of the car, raced around and dove back in just when the light turned green, everyone except me. People in the cars around us laughed and pointed and I wanted to die, slumping lower and lower in the seat, a hand propped up in the window to hide my face.

"Mom, why can't you be normal? Why can't you act like other mothers?"

"You need to loosen up and have fun." Mom kept driving and everyone teased me about being a drag.

"Yeah, it's fun," Jimmy said. "Everyone laughs and points. They like it."

"They're laughing *at* us. Probably think we're insane." He didn't know any better. He was only ten.

Mom called two more fire drills at small towns we passed through, one when we stopped for gas and another at a stoplight across from the fire station. I stayed in the car until we stopped at a rest stop for my brother to go to the bathroom.

"Why didn't you go before we left?"

"Didn't have to," he said.

When Jimmy returned, Mom yelled, "Fire drill. Three times around the car."

Lonnie tried to coax me out. "I'm not getting out."

"Oh, yes you are, miss. There's no one here," my mother said.

Another car pulled into the slot next to ours. "What about them?"

"We'll never see them again."

My cousins tugged and urged and finally dragged me out and hauled me around the car three times. I grabbed for the door every time I passed it, but Mom helped them pull me around. When the boys dove into the back, they let me go and I walked the rest of the way to the open door and got in. My face was red, not from exertion, but from shame.

The people in the car next to ours goggled open-mouthed as though watching the antics of lunatics. The woman rolled up her window and locked the door, probably afraid we'd try to drag her out of the car to join us. Mom took her time getting into the car and catching her breath. She started the car, backed out and cheerily waved, then drove off.

When we got to the cemetery, I helped unload the flowers. Every other year Mom's parents came with us, but Grandma had to work and Grandpa seldom went anywhere without her. For the first time I could remember, we decorated the graves without them.

A few other people meandered along the rows of headstones in the old cemetery where Mom claimed the teenagers used to go parking. "It was fun," she insisted. I shuddered. The idea of kissing a boy in a cemetery felt creepy.

"How about another fire drill?" My brother turned hopeful eyes on my mother.

"Not here. It's disrespectful."

So, I thought, there were limits.

A car drove past us and parked a few feet farther up the road. It looked familiar. "Mom, didn't you say we'd never see those people again?" I pointed at the car and the man and woman walking toward us.

Mom shaded her eyes from the sun and watched them approach. "Oh, Lordy," she said.

Not only did we see them again, but she knew them, had grown up and gone to school with them. It was Mom's turn to be embarrassed. I smiled and leaned up against the car with my arms crossed.

Mom called me over and introduced me to her old neighbors. The other people didn't mention our fire drill at the rest stop. Neither did Mom. She acted as if nothing out of the ordinary had happened. They reminisced about Uncle Jack and caught up on family gossip. They asked about my grandparents and Mom asked about their parents.

"Here they come now." Their parents had been in the back seat of the car with two young children.

Mom's cheeks flushed bright red. I did not doubt the story would get back to my grandparents and to everyone in town. Grandpa had been the mayor and the sheriff. Her cheeks might stay red for a while.

On the way home, there were no more fire drills, and there were no more ever again. Mom had finally outgrown them.

~J.M. Cornwell

The Ideal Parking Spot

The misfortunes of mankind are of varied plumage.
~Aeschylus

My husband, Frank, loves cars. It is just that simple… and that difficult. He talks about cars, he reads car magazines, he belongs to car clubs and he tenderly washes and waxes his cars… by hand using only special soaps and cloths. And he has rules: no eating in the car, no drinking in the car (well water is okay but only on long trips), don't take the car through a car wash, and try your very best not to park in parking lots. This last rule is a little bit flexible because sometimes the only available parking is in a lot. But, if you must park in a lot, park as far away from other cars as possible so that no one opens his car door and dings the side of our car.

It was a nice summer day. We had a date to meet some friends for lunch. Frank got the car ready—tires, windows, mirrors and all—and then we drove off. We checked the streets in the neighborhood surrounding the restaurant for parking, but with nothing available, and following his rules, we pulled into a parking lot and parked as far away from everyone and everything as possible. No cars were on either side of us and no cars were in front or in back of us. We were safe. That also meant that we were three long blocks away from the restaurant, but we walked fast and got there on time.

We had a nice relaxing lunch with our friends, said goodbye and started walking back to our car. Way off in the distance we could see it… his beautiful car. It was still by itself with no one nearby. What luck. Frank was so pleased; his precious car had enjoyed another dingless outing. Never mind that his precious wife was now limping in her dressy shoes because of the long distance between the restaurant and the car.

But, wait. Something was not right. Our car was a medium silver blue color. The car we were heading towards seemed to be a different color — kind of a creamy color. And wait. What was wrong with the windows? They seemed kind of opaque rather than the sparkling clear windows Frank had washed carefully before we left. Frank started to walk a little faster and then started to run towards his car. I did my best to keep up but soon I was half a block behind. I couldn't see his face when he reached the car but I sure could hear him yelling. #&%$#!*%&*@*! or something to that effect.

I arrived at the car, huffing and puffing. And what did I see? Was it our car? Oh yes, it was our car and it was parked right where we left it — inconveniently far away. But… oh my… it was covered in pigeon poop! COVERED!! Can you picture it? Thick, gloppy, runny pigeon poop. What Frank hadn't realized when he found his ideal spot was that he had parked beneath a whole host of electrical wires. And you know that birds love to congregate on wires. I think that while we were in the restaurant, a whole flock of pigeons, probably seventeen generations of them, had a family reunion on the wires above our car and then they let go with everything that they had. Do you think that was why we had this perfect dingless portion of the parking lot to ourselves?

It was a sight to behold. Frank couldn't speak and was beyond being rational at that point. He was sputtering, spewing, yelling and was practically in tears. And I, his loving, devoted, understanding, caring wife was… in hysterics. This was the funniest thing I had ever seen.

Now I had been married to Frank long enough to know that the one thing you don't do when he is upset is laugh. It's best to just be quiet and let him process what is happening. I tried but… I couldn't help myself. I was screaming with laughter. You know, the kind that comes from your toes and explodes. I was doubled over with laughter and gasping for breath.

We still had to get home. How? The front window was totally covered; there was no way to see so Frank could drive. Another question: how were we even going to get into the car? The doors were covered too. Frank checked and found that one of the back doors was not as bad as the others and so, using a tissue I found in my purse, he opened that door very carefully. We both got in and then we had to climb over the seat to get into the front. I was trying to control myself and was doing a pretty good job.

Then Frank turned on the windshield wipers and pigeon poop flew everywhere! It's a good thing that no one was parked near us. Frank turned on the engine and slowly backed up, since he couldn't see out the rear window either. Then we slowly made our way forward, out of the parking lot, onto the street and headed for home. Frank had to sit at a funny angle the whole way home in order to see out the front window through a tiny poop-free opening.

The ride home was slow, long and not very pleasant. Frank was mumbling to himself and I just kept my head bowed and stared at my knees. But every once in a while I would look up, try to look out the window, see all of that poop and just burst out laughing. Frank would mumble louder and say in his angry voice, "Barbara, it's not funny." Of course that made it even funnier and I'd laugh louder.

We did make it home. Frank immediately washed the car. The car survived the attack of the pigeon poop and so did our marriage. Every once in a while I'll tell the story about the pigeon poop. It still makes me laugh. (I'm laughing right now.) Frank, on the other hand, still doesn't find it amusing at all and still mumbles, "Barbara, it's not funny."

~Barbara LoMonaco

77

Lost in Conversation

Never go on trips with anyone you do not love.
~Ernest Hemingway

while back, our family was on a trip to visit my parents, who had retired and moved to Idaho. My wife and I were having one of those great conversations that parents sometimes have when the kids are asleep in the car. We were laughing as we recalled fun memories, while trying not to wake up the two sleeping angels in the back of the minivan. We were talking about current events, and looking ahead to our goals and hopes for the future. Somewhere in the midst of our conversation, I realized the freeway sign overhead read "Salt Lake City." (Note: In case you have never driven from California to western Idaho, you should know that there is no reason to see a large overhead sign that reads "Salt Lake City" on the way. If you do see a large overhead sign that reads "Salt Lake City," it means you are nearly in Utah, which isn't a bad thing, unless you are attempting to visit your parents in Idaho.)

Suddenly, I felt like the hunting guide in Washington State whose hunting party became hopelessly lost while he was leading them. The group was very unhappy and let him feel their distress. "You told us you were the best guide in Washington!" they yelled. "I am," he said, "but I think we're in Montana now."

Thankfully, we came prepared with maps—a map of the western U.S., a map of each state, and one of those maps the Auto Club puts together that is a flip chart of your whole journey. (Or at least

286   On the Road: *Lost in Conversation*

your *planned* journey. They didn't put Utah in my flip chart for this trip.) Those maps allowed us to reduce our extra time on the road to seven or eight hours.

But before getting back on the road in the right direction, I had to make "the" phone call. Maybe you know the one I am talking about. It's the one you make to tell your parents you've driven hundreds of miles out of the way en route to their house.

"Hello, Dad," I said. "We're going to be a little late." I was hoping I could just say we were a little behind schedule. There was no need to get into the details.

Then he asked, "Where are you?" I don't think I had finished answering before he wanted to know, "How did you get there?" while trying not to laugh too hard.

I found out what it's like to be in your thirties but feel like a teenager who is calling home because he ran out of gas in the middle of nowhere with not a cent in his pocket, standing at a payphone to make a collect call home to ask Dad to bring him some gas. Not that this actually ever happened, of course.

There were a couple of good lessons learned on that trip. First, great conversations with your wife are to be prized, as is a really comfortable seat in your car. Second, I am thankful for road maps. In fact, without them I might be driving through Canada at this very moment, still searching for Idaho, instead of sharing this story with you.

You might be happy to know we finally did make it to my parents' house. Along the way, we discovered that the town of Elko, Nevada, is the Home of Cowboy Poetry. It says so right on the sign coming into town.

~Cecil Swetland

78

Dinner To Go

No chaos, no creation. Evidence: the kitchen at mealtime.
~Mason Cooley

Buckle up, because you're in for a wild ride... kind of like our turkey on Thanksgiving Eve seven years ago. These are the actual events of that day. It's the kind of experience that will only happen once in a lifetime, and no matter how many Thanksgivings we have from here on out, this will always be my family's favorite Thanksgiving memory.

Thanksgiving Eve morning, I arrived at my mom's house at about 8:30. Mom and I plunged right in and started to make the Thanksgiving feast for our family. Being of Italian descent, we not only make the traditional dishes, but we add an Italian flair. This included dishes like stuffed artichokes, fried cardones, and stuffing from scratch. So Mom and I were busy multitasking, stuffing this and frying that. I also made my famous banana split cake. Thanksgiving would not be the same without these dishes.

Since it was a very cold day, we used the garage as a second refrigerator, and put everything we finished cooking on the trunk of my parents' car. My mom got the twenty-three-pound turkey out of the fridge. We gave him a saltwater bath and placed him safely in his roasting pan. He was all set for his date with the 350-degree oven the next morning at 6:00. I brought him out to the garage and put him on the trunk of the car, next to the artichokes, cardones and banana split cake.

My dad came in and said he had to go to the store. We didn't really hear him. Although we love him dearly, we often block him out.

Hours went by, and Mom and I finished the homemade stuffing. I went to the garage to put the stuffing on the trunk of the car, but there was no car. My mind began to race. Where's the car? Where's the food? I glanced at the end of the driveway and screamed. My banana split cake was laying there — upside-down. Artichokes and cardones were in the road.

My mom came outside, saw the carnage, and began to bite on her index finger the way old Italian women do. I went to the end of the driveway in shock. My Aunt Kay, who lives next door, came outside and helped me gather the artichokes and cardones that had escaped their tinfoil homes. She tried to comfort me by pointing out that a few artichokes didn't look so bad. "Just brush off the stones. No one will know."

As I crouched there picking up all the food, it hit me: There was no turkey. I looked down the road… no sign of the turkey or the roasting pan. My mom was in a panic. Where would we get a twenty-three-pound turkey that was ready to cook the day before Thanksgiving?

I decided to search for the turkey. I drove about three miles down the road, but there was no sign of the turkey. I turned back and reassured my mom that Dad surely noticed the turkey and put it inside the car.

My mom, Aunt Kay and I sat at the kitchen table in shock. No normal person could possibly pass by all that food piled on the car and not see it. However, we were talking about my dad. Although he is the best dad in the world, he does live in a fog.

I called my four sisters and told them our turkey was missing. We became hysterical, imagining the people driving behind the "fog man," beeping their little hearts out to get my dad's attention, only to go unheard since Dad is oblivious when he's driving.

About an hour later, my dad pulled in the driveway. He walked into the kitchen holding the turkey still inside the roasting pan. Dad informed us that this poor turkey had made it on the trunk of the car all the way from Churchville to Gates (approximately nine miles). My father finally noticed it when it flew off the trunk as he was turning onto Manitou Road from Buffalo Road. He slammed on the brakes and blocked the whole intersection. He got out of his car to rescue the turkey, which, according to him, only bounced once. He picked up the turkey from the road, put it in the roasting pan, and ran back to the car. On his way home, he found the lid to the roasting pan a few miles from our house.

Once again, Mom and I were plucking stones from our Thanksgiving dinner. We gave the turkey another saltwater bath, placed him back into the slightly dented roasting pan, and put him on a shelf in the garage. My sisters showed up with bags of artichokes and cardones, and we began the task of preparing them… again.

I don't remember a Thanksgiving before or since our "road kill turkey dinner." The laughter around our dinner table that day was truly beautiful. And I am thankful for my father, who put aside his pride and chased after our turkey rolling down the road.

P.S. In my father's defense, he wants it known that he lives in a fog because he raised five daughters.

~Lori Giraulo-Secor

Big Yellow

A child is a curly dimpled lunatic.
~Ralph Waldo Emerson

The discussions began during the heat of the Arizona summer, months before our only child was scheduled to leave the nest for the first time and head off to kindergarten. The controversial topic? The big yellow school bus.

Cody and I thought school buses were pretty cool. My wife, however, felt that school buses were The Great Satan. I argued that the familiar vehicles were an important part of the school experience, and were critical to our son's social development. She countered that they're hot, dangerous, driven by ex-cons, and are always being buried underground by terrorists.

I countered that they're bigger and safer than cars, the school board doesn't specifically seek to hire dangerous criminals, and reminded her that the terrorist thing only happened once a long time ago.

After weeks of the verbal equivalent of a Texas Death Cage match, Cody and I won the day.

At 11:45 a.m. on the fateful first morning, we all gathered at the designated pickup spot a block away, snapping photos while waiting for the historic arrival of the big yellow bus. Among the children buzzing around was Nikki, a tiny neighborhood girl also starting kindergarten. I told Nikki that she and Cody were now bus buddies, and to make sure they came home together. Nikki agreed and made a pinky promise.

We continued to mill about and wait. And wait. A half hour passed and no bus. It was closing in on 110 degrees outside in our Phoenix suburb. Cody and Nikki were wilting like daisies. The only thing hotter was Cody's mother.

The bus finally arrived. It was being driven by—SANTA CLAUS! No kidding, the driver was the same guy who played Santa Claus in all the area festivals because he has the real hair, girth and beard. Cody and Nikki were thrilled. I shot my wife a classic, smug, know-it-all-grin.

That afternoon, Cody's still-anxious mother and I took our place on the corner waiting for the equally historic first trip home. The bus arrived only fifteen minutes late. The kids piled out. No Cody. I hopped on the bus. No Cody. No Santa. Different driver. A scruffy-looking guy.

Cody's mother was starting to go into cardiac arrest. I cautioned her to stay cool. I spotted Nikki still sitting passively on the bus, clueless as to where she was supposed to get off.

"Nikki, where's Cody?"

"I dunno."

"What do you mean, you don't know? I told you that you were bus buddies! We made a pinky promise! Did he make it to school?"

"I dunno."

"Did you see him in class?"

"I dunno."

My wife was now frantic. "But I told Nikki to watch him," I lamely pointed out.

"Nikki's got the brain of a gnat!!" she screamed as she ran home for the phone.

I remained on the bus, convinced I could solve the mystery of our missing son. I heard over the radio that the dispatcher was looking for a lost girl name Katie. Katie? Cody? Cody? Katie? Maybe a switch? "Is there anybody here named Katie?" I asked a sea of children. There was no answer. The driver radioed back that he didn't have Katie. I heard the dispatcher give a description of Katie. Blond hair, freckles, white dress with red roses. I spotted the exact munchkin sitting two feet in front of me.

"Are you Katie?" I asked.

Silence.

"Is your name Katie?"

The little girl finally nodded.

"Get up here, you little knucklehead!" I said, a bit too forcefully due to my exasperation. The petite child walked forward and stood wide-eyed at my side. Meanwhile, the driver continued to radio that we didn't have Katie.

By that point, my wife had determined that Cody was still at school in the office. In the confusion of all our previous discussions, he thought his mom was going to pick him up. In a flash, she was in her SUV and on her way.

Meanwhile, I grabbed the radio from the driver and announced to Katie's hyperventilating mother that Katie was indeed here and was fine and dandy.

Katie giggled at the commotion. The two of us exited the bus. I got into my car and drove Katie back to the school. I was a big time hero with Katie's relieved mother. Unfortunately, my own wife didn't remotely share that view. That evening more fights ensued. I argue that it was "just a tiny little snafu." She called me an "insensitive oaf," which further deflated my hero status. "Try it one more day," I pleaded. "What can go wrong?"

The next morning, all went well—until the phone rang. Cody never arrived at school!

More panic set in. My wife was now making yesterday's hysteria seem like a trial run. "He's got to be somewhere," I assured. "I mean, aliens couldn't have abducted him from the bus." After a few more scorching glares, off she went in the car again.

I began pacing the house, feeling like the world's worst dad. The phone rang again. Bingo! Cody was now at school. Seems he was so mellow about the whole ordeal that he promptly fell asleep on the ride over. Nikki strolled off without bothering to wake him. Santa drove to a holding terminal five miles from the school. As he was about to depart the oven-baked vehicle, he heard a whimper. Searching the seats, he came across Cody snoozing away. He cranked up the banana-colored machine and drove Cody back to school.

A half hour later, my wife returned. She was, suffice it to say, ballistic. She was ready to kill Nikki. She was ready to kill me. She lowered Nikki's brain capacity to that of a one-celled animal. She lowered mine even more.

The following afternoon, the bus was nearly forty-five minutes late. Apparently, Santa's long hair and beard got in his eyes and he couldn't clearly see the dashboard gauges. The bus—a vehicle that only had to travel two miles!—ran out of gas halfway home. The kids had to sit in the 110-degree heat and wait for a second bus to pick them up and finish the journey.

Eleven years have since passed. My son, a high school junior, is nearly six feet tall and holds a black belt in Tae Kwan Do and martial arts weapons.

His mother still drives him to and from school every day.

~Dary Matera

80

Uncle Bernie

If it's not fun, you're not doing it right.
~Bob Basso

Our Uncle Bernie was a true Mr. Malaprop, and he was invariably funny and outrageous, and at the same time always lovable and kind. He was not a real uncle, but a very distant cousin of my maternal grandmother. However, I did not know that until I was an adult. He was always with the family at every holiday, wedding, funeral... come to think of it, he was there every weekend, too!

He was great fun and loved being with the children, but he never got all of our names straight. To make it easier for him, Uncle Bernie gave all of us nicknames. In this way, he could remember who we were and who we belonged to.

"Okay, you are Penny, daughter of Jenny, and you are Skinny, daughter of Minnie," and on and on until all of the children had a new name and a permanent label. Those nicknames stayed with us throughout our childhood and, in some cases, until today.

He loved watching the evening news, especially during the days of Huntley and Brinkley. Uncle Bernie would go on and on about the intelligence and dignity of those two commentators. Unfortunately, he never got their names quite right. To this day, we laugh at his admiration of that famous team, "David and Brinkley!"

Uncle Bernie was always very generous. However, he was never quite sure about the actual date of anyone's birthday. So, to cover himself, he kept wrapped presents in the trunk of his car. When he arrived at Grandma's house for Sunday dinner, he was ready in case it was someone's birthday.

As the birthday cake was ablaze with candles, Uncle Bernie would rush out to his car to retrieve a gift. The problem was, he never identified the present, so he was never sure what was in the box, or whether it was for a male or female.

This led to many laughs for the adults and much confusion for the children. On my tenth birthday, I received a brightly colored tie from Uncle Bernie. My cousin, who had a birthday close to mine, received a pair of lovely earrings—not especially appropriate for a twelve-year-old boy. Needless to say, we swapped gifts that day.

Uncle Bernie prided himself on his driving ability. He was the self-appointed family driving instructor. As I look back, our parents were foolhardy to give this responsibility to Uncle Bernie. However, it was probably easier for them. Besides, what could possibly happen?

It was the 1950s, and schools were just introducing driver's education classes. In New Jersey, you had to be sixteen to get a permit and seventeen to get a license. Since we were from a large, extended family, there were five cousins eligible to get permits that year. Uncle Bernie decided he would be our driving instructor.

What qualified him for this position? Nothing, except for the fact he had never had an accident, or so he said.

So one Saturday, he put all of us in his 1956 Chevrolet Sedan, and off we went to a nearby open field. When we arrived at the field, Cousin #1 got into the driver's seat with Uncle Bernie riding shotgun. The rest of us were in the back seat patiently awaiting our turn at the wheel.

The car had a stick shift on the steering wheel. None of us had any experience with Uncle Bernie's car. He quickly explained the steps to us: turn on the ignition; step on the clutch; put the gear shift into first; slowly step on the gas and release the clutch; and go. Boy did he go! Cousin #1 went so fast, he hit a tree. Fortunately, no one was hurt, but we were scared.

Uncle Bernie was very calm and told us not to worry. He would take care of everything. He told us to get out of the car and walk home, and we would all meet at Grandma's house where we were expected for dinner.

As we gathered for dinner, Uncle Bernie said he would like to say grace. With our heads bowed, he said, "Let us all give thanks for family, friends, and trees. If that tree was not planted just where it was, I would have hit the cow wandering in the field."

Giggles were buried in our hands, and the incident was never discussed again. We all took driver's education in school.

Uncle Bernie is long gone, but never forgotten. He is remembered fondly, and his stories are repeated time and time again at family gatherings.

~Helen Xenakis

"What makes it even more exciting is that I forget what's in half of them."

81

DriVing LessonS

Giving your son a skill is better than giving him one thousand pieces of gold.
~Chinese Proverb

The severe winter storms we remember from our childhood always seem to be noted for wild tales of ten-feet-deep snowdrifts and families trapped in their homes for a week at a time. Just how often that occurred in southern New England is purely speculative, but during the 1950s my family sometimes waited a day or two before the snowplow showed up.

We lived in the last house on a mile-long dead-end road that crisscrossed the town line. Every time there was a major snowstorm, the adjacent towns squabbled over whose turn it was to plow. As a youngster, I didn't care if we ever got plowed out, but my father wasn't so accommodating. He'd get angry and phone in a complaint even before it stopped snowing. That tactic sometimes worked, but at a price. The snowplow drivers usually did a lousy job, leaving the travel lane too narrow for oncoming vehicles to pass each other. This new problem only further annoyed my father.

To ease his frustrations, Dad took it upon himself to widen the travel lane by flattening the snow banks with his pickup truck. Driving at thirty miles per hour on the wrong side of the road, he'd skillfully gouge a tire path through the windrow until the truck lost momentum or a hapless motorist coming the other way ran into a ditch. The few times he got stuck were rationalized as a small price to pay for making the road passable.

One afternoon, Dad drove into a snow bank with a little more aggression than usual and flipped the truck onto its side. Dad wasn't hurt and the vehicle suffered only minor damage, but it cost him twenty dollars to borrow a neighbor's tractor to right the truck.

My father refused to believe that he was at fault for the accident. After all, he had been knocking down snow banks for years and considered himself somewhat of an expert. Determined to find the cause, he reconstructed the mishap by driving through the same snow bank again. Everything seemed normal for the first fifty feet (whatever "normal" is for people who drive through snow banks). Then the front wheel hit a solid object, sending the truck airborne and then, once again, flipping it onto its side.

Unhurt, Dad climbed out of the wreck and began digging in the snow to find what the truck had hit. It was the stump of an oak tree that he himself had cut down a few months earlier because he thought it was growing too close to the road.

Word spread fast about Dad's driving escapades, and everyone joked that flipping a truck over twice in one day in the same spot had to be some kind of a record.

When it was time for me to learn how to drive, my father didn't want me wasting money on a formal driver's training course. Instead, he taught me. Naturally, I mastered most of his vast driving skills, especially how to knock down snow banks.

Several years later, while transporting a pickup load of firewood, I was confidently plowing through snow banks as if I were in command of an Army tank. I was doing fine until the front wheel hooked on a buried chunk of ice and spun the steering wheel out of my hands. The truck slid sideways and flipped over, scattering firewood into the middle of the road. I was a little shook up, but not hurt.

After composing myself, I began to clear the wood off the road before I caused a real accident. Two friendly men stopped to offer assistance, which I gratefully accepted. They continued to move the wood while I went to the nearest house to call for a wrecker to right my truck. I left the scene for no more than ten minutes. When I returned, the two men were gone—and so was all my firewood.

I quit knocking down snow banks after that.

~Arthur Wiknik, Jr.

Man and Car: A Love Story

When a man opens a car door for his wife, it's either a new car or a new wife.
~Prince Philip

The year the PT Cruiser came out, my husband, David, fell in love. Not with another woman, but with the automobile he'd been looking forward to his whole life. Or so he claimed.

The waiting list for the car was long. For the next seven months, life at our house centered around the Coming of the PT Cruiser. Someone gave David a toy model of the vehicle he talked about all the time. That year, our manger scene consisted of Baby Jesus, Mary, Joseph… and a PT Cruiser.

David was at a business meeting in Baltimore when the PT Cruiser was finally delivered to the dealership. It was late when he called me from the airport. I could hear the fatigue in his voice.

"The airline's overbooked my flight, and I'm ready to drop. Should I just get the travel voucher they're offering and stay here at the airport hotel tonight?"

"Sure," I said. "Oh, and by the way, your car's here."

All signs of exhaustion miraculously disappeared as David answered, "I'll be home as soon as I can."

Early the next day, David and I went to the Chrysler dealership. The salesperson handed David a slip of paper.

"Here's the invoice you signed. Remember, it says that you'll pay the sticker price—no matter what it is—when the PT Cruiser is delivered."

"YOU WHAT???" My shriek bounced from one glass wall of the showroom to the other. "There has to be a mistake. My husband graduated from Cal Tech. He would never do anything that stupid."

David grew suspiciously quiet.

"Look at the signature," the salesperson smirked.

When I saw the unmistakable evidence that my frugal, practical husband had, in fact, put his John Hancock on the document, I could only wonder if the world was coming to an end.

"They wouldn't order my car unless I signed it," David offered weakly.

"If you'll just step outside, I'll bring the Cruiser around," the salesman told us, victory shining in his eyes.

After a few minutes, he pulled up in a cranberry-colored, 1930s gangster-looking car and left it near where we were standing. I looked at David. He didn't notice me… or anything else. He was too busy admiring his new purchase.

David held open the door so I could climb into the passenger seat.

"This is so great," he sighed. "Have you ever seen a more beautiful car?"

"Well, there's the 1957 Chevy, the…"

"Be serious. Have you ever seen a car like this one?"

"No," I could honestly reply. "This car looks as though people should be hanging out the window shooting Tommy guns."

He grunted. I settled back in the seat.

"Hey, where's my armrest? David, there's only one armrest in this car."

"That's not a problem. I'll share mine. This was *Motor Trend's* Car of the Year, you know."

"It was *Motor Trend's* Car of the Year and it only has one armrest? Obviously, they didn't test the passenger side."

I started inspecting other parts of the interior.

"David, there's no drawer under my seat, just a big, gaping hole."

"The salesman promised he'd throw in a drawer for free."

"So, in other words, you paid higher than top dollar for an automobile with no armrest for the passenger and a gap where a drawer should be?"

"You don't have to be so negative. This is the best car ever."

Knowing that I could never respond to that statement, I climbed out of the PT Cruiser, jumped in my own car, and followed David home.

The topic of the PT Cruiser extended into our pillow talk.

"Honey," I asked, "if there was a fire, and your PT Cruiser and I were in a burning building, who would you rescue first?"

He didn't even pause for thought.

"Well, you're a person. You have legs. You could get out on your own."

David drove his new car all over town. Soon, it was time for his first fill-up.

"I got twenty miles to the gallon," he told me.

"Twenty? You were supposed to get twenty-five, at least."

"That's on the highway. You know how stop-and-go traffic is in Phoenix."

A few weeks later, David got an upper respiratory infection. He was miserable.

"I think I'd feel better if I went out and sat in my PT Cruiser," he wheezed.

That Valentine's Day, I saw a segment on television about keeping the spice in your marriage. The woman on the program suggested you leave a lipstick kiss on your husband's windshield so he'd know you still had passion in your relationship. I put on some bright red lipstick and planted a big one on the glass in front of the driver's side.

I got passion, all right, but it wasn't the romantic kind. David went out to the garage, and then burst back into the house.

"You've marked my car! You've marked my PT Cruiser."

I grabbed a Kleenex and wiped the lipstick off my rival.

"He's mine," I whispered.

Not long after that, my car was in the shop, so I had to drive the PT Cruiser. The narrow slit of a back window made it impossible to do anything safely except go forward.

"David," I asked, "how do you drive this thing? You can't see to back out."

"I expect people to get out of the way."

Who was this man?

Bad news came a short time later.

"Something terrible has happened," David told me.

"Oh, my gosh, has someone died?"

"No. My PT Cruiser has been recalled."

Such sorrow! Chrysler recalled every PT Cruiser built in the first two model years. More than 400,000 automobiles had to have their fuel tanks dropped six inches and foam spacers installed to keep the fuel pump from coming loose during a rollover.

David couldn't believe his beloved car had a flaw. He took it down to the dealer, still in a state of disbelief.

When he got home, I figured he'd finally have something bad to say about the PT Cruiser.

"Shelley, do you know what would be nice?"

"Trading in your car?"

He looked shocked. "Of course not. I think you should get a PT Cruiser, too."

~Shelley Mosley

Chapter 9

Family Matters

Not So Grave

Life was a funny thing that occurred on the way to the grave.

~Quentin Crisp

83

Trash Talk

*There is something deep in the human psyche that keeps people, myself
included, in sort of a hoarding mode. You have to overcome that.*
~Tim Winship

Y ou can learn a lot about someone from her trash, especially if she hasn't thrown anything away in decades. The
first thing you learn is that your relative is a hoarder, a fact
that is easy to hide when you are living alone in a large home with
multiple bedrooms and ample closet and cabinet space. When my
aunt died after a fourteen-year bout with cancer, I had no idea that
I would be embarking on a voyage of discovery, learning about my
aunt through taking out the trash.

My sister Grace and I had chosen a three-day weekend, starting
on a Friday, to begin preparing Aunt Margaret's home for listing with
a real estate broker. My daughter Lexie came home from college to
help, which was fun for me since Saturday was my birthday and her
presence would brighten an otherwise undesirable way to spend my
birthday weekend.

On Friday morning, with some trepidation, Grace, Lexie, and I
set out on our big adventure. I was so nervous that I missed the exit,
which I had taken hundreds of times before, and we had to go a few
miles out of our way, delaying the awkward moment that was coming. It was going to be weird opening that front door with our newly
issued set of keys, as if we were somehow breaking and entering.

When we crept inside that morning, we huddled together as we moved among the rooms, surveying the job ahead of us. The place was packed! Cabinet doors were half open, revealing shelves bulging with papers, closets were full from floor to ceiling, garbage and old papers were stuffed into corners, and into boxes and bags. There was so much furniture and so many lamps in one of the rooms that it looked like a consignment shop. All that was missing were the price tags on the dusty, worn items.

It was strange that none of us had ever noticed how overstuffed every room was while Margaret was alive. Her powerful personality must have filled up the rooms so that we didn't see anything else. We decided to start at the heart of the mess — Margaret's bedroom. After a few hours, I realized that the room was so full it had turned into a storage facility for her, and that must be why she had started sleeping in another bedroom.

As we cleaned, we kept noticing new things. After every few fifty-gallon trash bags were hauled out, filled with everything from decades-old half empty boxes of chocolates, to old cards and thank you notes, to hundreds of magazines, the layers of new stuff were revealed, as if we were peeling an onion. It took hours just to clean out one regular-size closet in her room, packed as it was floor to ceiling with mail, boxes and bags, decades of old bills, and souvenirs dating back to grade school years. Of course, we had to check everything we found, reading all the old correspondence. We found some real treasures this way — a letter my mother wrote from her honeymoon, fascinating photos of relatives who died before we were born, a family tree, and some real surprises, such as law school acceptance letters from the 1950s. We never knew that Margaret had considered becoming a lawyer.

We discovered that Margaret was quite superstitious. There were chicken wishbones everywhere — in boxes, between the pages of diaries, in drawers. We shrieked when Lexie, who was throwing out underwear and pantyhose, found a plate and carving knife at the bottom of an underwear drawer. Did Margaret carve out those wishbones in the privacy of her bedroom, away from the prying eyes of her live-in help? We knew she ate chicken almost every night. Perhaps this love of chicken had been motivated by a desire for more wishbones?

We also found hundreds of four-leaf clovers, carefully saved in envelopes and even mounted on pages in a binder. They were pretty, but so old that when we touched them, they disintegrated immediately.

Margaret had never lost a little girl's love for stuffed animals, and we threw away dozens of stuffed animals, many decades old. They, too, almost disintegrated as we lifted them from room corners and tables and beds to gently place them in garbage bags—they were so dusty and dry, and we could feel the stuffing inside them crackling. Margaret's favorite stuffed animal had always been her panda bear, and we had even found what appeared to be birthday greetings and notes that she had written to Panda Bear.

The panda bear had eluded our cleaning efforts so far, however. But as we threw out more stuff, and the layers of the onion were revealed, we suddenly realized that the panda bear and another bear were sitting in a chair in the corner of Margaret's bedroom, each acting as a mannequin for one of her wigs, carefully prepared with curlers, ready for their next use. Margaret had been wearing wigs for more than a decade as a result of the chemotherapy.

Finding the wigs was a poignant but somewhat disturbing moment. And finding them on top of the bears was funny, and a great reminder of our aunt's sense of humor, but still disconcerting. Here we were, sneaking around throwing away Margaret's most trea-sured possessions (at least that's what it felt like), and these two large stuffed animals, including Panda Bear, had witnessed the whole thing, watching us from a corner of the room, wearing Margaret's hair.

The bears had to go. Grace and I had to do it. We stood tall, took deep breaths, and prepared to do the deed. She held open the garbage bag while I gingerly lowered the perhaps seventy-year-old panda bear into it, still wearing the wig with its curlers. We were both squealing as if we were being forced to touch big ugly bugs. I felt a little guilty about Panda Bear, now at the bottom of his black plastic final resting place, but I soldiered on. I reached for the next bear, which looked like one of those large but cheap amusement park prizes. Still wearing its wig and curlers, I dropped it into the bag, it landed on Panda Bear, and we immediately heard a little digital voice coming from the bag, singing "Happy Birthday to You." We burst into loud laughter. Lexie came running in and started laughing too when she heard the bear singing from deep inside the garbage bag. There I stood, grimy, wearing rubber gloves, receiving my first birthday wishes of the weekend from a discarded bear wearing Margaret's wig singing inside a black garbage bag.

We kept finding wigs that day, screaming as we encountered each one. They were expensive, made from real human hair and probably worth selling, but we just couldn't face them. They were too much of a reminder of what our aunt had gone through, and way too personal to touch for more than a moment as we flung them into trash bags. It seemed that every time we turned around, we found another wig, inside drawers, in bags, behind cabinets. At the end of the day, we saw what we thought was a cat sunning itself on the windowsill in another room, but sure enough it was another wig!

Throwing out the trash took many visits, and as I discussed my findings with family members over the next couple of months, we felt closer to our dear departed Margaret and understood her better. Our seemingly powerful aunt, whose personality had filled her rooms, was really a vulnerable woman who had spent her life clinging to the past and looking backward not forward. And that had manifested itself in the hoarding.

We started throwing away more things in our own homes. One evening, returning from a day at Margaret's where I threw away two decades worth of Christmas and birthday cards that I found stashed in shopping bags, I was horrified to find the last two years of Christmas cards we received, in paper bags, in my own home office. What was I planning to do with them? Was hoarding in our blood? Out they went. My mother reported that my father started throwing away old books and papers, and my husband has finally agreed to throw away his old college textbooks and other "treasures" of that ilk, as he doesn't want the kids to have to do it for him. Thanks, Aunt Margaret!

~Constance Madison

84

Funerals by George

Beer is the cause and solution to all of life's problems.
~Homer Simpson

I spent a lot of time trying to decide whether to write this. On its face, it seems disrespectful. I mean, isn't telling a funny story about our stepfather's funeral in the poorest of taste? How could I find anything remotely humorous about what should be a solemn event?

The more I thought about it, though, the more I realized that our final respects to "Poppy" weren't contrived or phony. Rather, they were our loving goodbyes to one of the family. Indeed, it's the way I'd want to go.

Our mother, having grown tired of living with a man who resembled Ralph Kramden, acted like Archie Bunker, and possessed the social skills of Fred Flintstone, divorced our father and brought Walter—he only became known as "Poppy" once we had kids of our own—into our lives when we were children.

It still amazes me that she somehow managed to convince this relatively young man (in his mid-30s), that living with five kids was really not much worse than getting a prostate exam from Edward Scissorhands.

So it went through thick, thin, and adolescence until, even after the untimely death of our mother, it was Walter to whom we turned as head of the family.

Even though he remarried a few years later (what do you call a woman who marries your stepfather once your mother dies, a step-stepmother?), he was still the magnet that held us together.

He took us to ballgames, gave us advice, provided an anchor through tough times, and was a father to five kids when he didn't have to be. He may have thought onion dip with chips was high cuisine and Howard Stern was *Masterpiece Theater*, but he was our model for what it took to be a grown-up.

When he succumbed to cancer several years ago, we were overwhelmed with grief at the loss of someone who had guided us into adulthood. Our heartache was further increased by the knowledge that our own children wouldn't get to know him as we had.

As funeral preparations went into frenzied high gear, we didn't have a lot of time to dwell on the person we had lost. During the two-day viewing, my brothers, sister, and I took our proper places in the front row of the funeral home — the only place where being in the front row is not a good thing — and paid our respects to all who came to pay their respects.

We sat still, quiet as mummies, while mourners shuffled by the open casket. When they finished, they turned to us, murmuring "I'm sorry," "He looks so natural," (one of the stupidest sayings known to man), or some other such uncomfortable platitude.

Needless to say, it was rough. Enduring the parade of mourners while solemnly staring at someone who looked nowhere near natural took its toll.

The second night was a little different. Although prepared to be good soldiers throughout the duration, our solemn façades began to break down after the arrival of one of my brother's old girlfriends.

I've always admired her for showing up. She didn't come to see my brother; she came to say goodbye to a man she respected. This, of course, didn't stop the smirks from me and my other brothers and sister.

Through it all, though, we maintained a somewhat reverential demeanor.

Until another brother's old girlfriend walked through the door.

More smirks. Then, when one of my old girlfriends arrived—with a nose ring that looked downright painful—smirks became giggles.

Giggles became whispered jokes. And whispered jokes became throwing our voices at the casket when elderly relatives walked up to it. This—to us, anyway—was the very best in funeral home comedy.

As bad as our performances were at the "home," they were nothing compared to the actual funeral itself.

Starting off with a service at the Episcopalian church, we ended up at the biggest cemetery in town. Once there, I was reminded about that old joke about cemetery fences: nobody can break out and nobody wants to break in.

A military funeral, because he was in the Marines, the service was very dignified and steeped in an appropriate level of sadness. At the playing of "Taps," there was hardly a dry eye.

At its conclusion, everyone but the immediate family withdrew to a cold cuts, beer, and coffee fest at the Elks Lodge. I've always wondered what is about funerals that stokes a mad craving for doughnuts, pigs in a blanket, and boiled ham on little rolls.

My brothers, my sister, our spouses, and I stared silently at the casket as it sat suspended over the open vault. Festooned with an abundance of floral garlands, its mute presence reminded us of the loss we'd suffered.

It was then I felt guilty over our hi-jinks from the previous night.

As we began to move toward our cars, we heard an almost imperceptible "psst!" Quickly scanning the cemetery, I didn't see anything or anyone. Still looking, we heard it again and spotted a head peering around a tree.

We watched a friend we knew from high school, George, step into view, holding a 30-pack of Budweiser.

"Everybody gone?"

When we told him we were the only ones left, he came over to the site and placed the case of beer on the ground. "Well, here you are," he said.

Seeing we had no clue what he was talking about, he explained, "When Walter knew he was going to die, he told me to get a case of beer and go to his gravesite and hide. Then," he went on, "when everybody but the kids left, he told me to come on out and let you have a beer on him."

Stunned, we stared at George, the beer, and the grave. Nobody said a word for a few minutes. Then—I don't remember who—one of us stepped up and grabbed a can. The rest immediately followed.

Popping our tops, we raised our cans to Poppy in toast.

Before we drank, though, my brother said, "Wait!" Grabbing a can and opening it, he set it on top of the casket and said, "Well, here you go, cheaper than you can get at Yankee Stadium."

With that, we all had a beer to the memory of our father.

Needless to say, we finished that case and, despite the these-people-are-nuts looks from the cemetery workers, stayed until the casket was finally lowered into the ground.

It may have been a strange way to act at a funeral, but we knew that was the way Poppy would have preferred it.

Why else would he have had the presence of mind to contract the services of Funerals by George?

~Kenneth C. Lynch

Cops and Robbers

85

*The great gift of family life is to be intimately acquainted with
people you might never even introduce yourself to,
had life not done it for you.*
~Kendall Hailey

I was married at eighteen to my high school sweetheart. I came
from a very traditional but somewhat colorful family. My father
was a director for television and my mother had worked in pictures during my younger years.

The boy I married was from a somewhat different background.
His mother was attractive and fun. She had also been married five
times, twice to the same man. Three of my husband's uncles were
police officers and he had a cousin who was a firefighter.

My father-in-law's family was quite different. His father had been
a bootlegger as a young man and even did some time in prison. His
uncle was a well-connected fence for the mob. His uncle's son was an
enforcer for the head of the largest mob on the West Coast.

As a young sheltered bride I had no idea what any of this was
about. I just knew that both sides of the family were kind and lots
of fun.

We had a sudden death in the family. My husband's sister died
and the entire family was brought to their knees. I knew that I was
the only one who could handle the details of a funeral and reception
back at our home.

I made all the plans and telephoned every member of the

family... every member. I let my husband know that there was nothing to worry about. I had handled everything.

The funeral was a beautiful tribute to my special sister-in-law. We received hugs and condolences from both sides of our families and returned to our home for the reception. My friends had helped set everything up, as I knew we would be the last to arrive.

We walked into the house to a visual I had never anticipated. A house divided! The "Cops" were in the living room and the "Robbers" were in the den. They had never been together before! When I realized what I had done all I could do was laugh!

I later heard a wonderful story from the wife of one of our police officer uncles. She told me that after the funeral, the two sides of my husband's family became friendlier, and my bootlegger father-in-law would take his police officer brothers-in-law and their wives out to dinner and pick up the tab. My father-in-law was a very generous man, not only in his heyday, but in the lean years to come. As they all grew older and our uncle became more successful (he was a Captain with the Los Angeles Police department), he told his wife how wonderful his sister's husband had always been to the family. He vowed that never again would my father-in-law be allowed to pay a bill in his presence. The "cops" and "robbers" may have all had very separate careers, but they all had a very strong respect for each other and they were indeed family.

~Kristine Byron

Photo Op

Some family trees bear an enormous crop of nuts.
~Wayne H.

The funeral of my husband's grandfather definitely takes the prize for the weirdest funeral I have ever attended. As a matter of fact, as we left the funeral my husband looked over at me and said, "If I hadn't known you so long I would be mortified."

Throughout the fifteen years we had been together I had never known my husband's grandmother to be affectionate, or even care what any of her five grandchildren were doing, but when Grandpa Hank was sick I witnessed her true colors. As Grandpa Hank lay dying, she often was caught saying, "If he doesn't die soon I may drive him off the pier." I was horrified by her comment but chalked it up to a tired woman who had taken care of a very sick man for a long time. Not to mention that she was never nice to anyone — so why should she start now?

Once Grandpa Hank finally passed away, the funeral arrangements were made. The services were to take place at the Mormon Church they attended, and after the service we were to make the thirty-minute drive to the burial site and then back to the church for a potluck lunch put on by the members of the church.

Walking into the church we were handed a pamphlet outlining Grandpa Hank's life, only Grandma didn't want to spend the extra money on printing so Grandpa's photo was completely black on the cheap Xeroxed copy. The flower arrangement that my mother-in-law had ordered on behalf of her kids from a local florist included a cheesy banner that incorrectly said "We Love You Gandpa" in glitter-covered letters. At this point my husband and I just started to laugh, as things were going from bad to worse. Once seated in the pew we saw the coffin sitting at the front of the room with an American flag draped over it. I had no idea Grandpa Hank had served in the military and it would have been a nice addition had Grandma spent the money they requested to iron the flag. The flag was completely wrinkled.

Again, we tried to stifle our laughter when the speaker began the eulogy. As he started speaking it was clear he had no idea who Grandpa Hank was. He went on and on about some random things that must have been listed on a sheet of paper until he came across the note that said Grandpa Hank was from Utah. He stopped mid-sentence and said, "Wow, who knew? I am from Utah too." He then picked up with the rest of his reading, often stopping to comment on the fact that he was surprised at how much they had in common. As he finished, he picked up his guitar and began singing a song. None of us knew the song and it soon became clear neither did he! As he got to certain verses he just stopped mid-verse and hummed until he was able to pick back up with familiar words. We could not contain ourselves any longer. I made eye contact with my "normal" sister-in-law and within seconds there was not a dry eye in our row—we were working so hard to hold in the laughter that we were crying.

Finally, the indoor ceremony ended and the family was to cara-van to the burial where my husband, his father, and his two brothers would act as pallbearers. We were together on the freeway, but when we arrived at the cemetery my husband's older brother and his family were nowhere to be seen.

We waited and waited, worried that something had happened. We finally had to go on without them as Grandma had only budgeted a certain amount of time and money for this part of the ceremony. Because we were now missing one of the pallbearers, a random cem-etery worker had to step in as the fourth pallbearer. A few words about Grandpa Hank were said and then to our horror… Grandma broke out her camera. She wanted us to sit on the coffin and take pictures! Each family member was instructed how to pose and she kept snapping. I felt like at any moment we would be on a *Candid Camera* episode where you find out it was all a really bad joke… but that was not to be. This was very real and although I tried to hide, the next thing I knew, I too was draped across Grandpa Hank's coffin. I am not sure what her reasoning was for the photo shoot, whether it was to confirm that Grandpa Hank for sure was dead and wouldn't be a bother to her anymore or to fill a page in her photo album of family memories.

Once the photo session ended, up pulled my husband's brother… he had gotten hungry on the way and pulled off the freeway for some mini corndogs!

As the day ended and we were driving home recapping the events of the day, my husband asked that I never discuss this with anyone! It has been almost ten years now and I have finally been given permission to share it. As we arrived home to pay the babysitter she commented on how sad the services must have been due to how red our eyes were from crying… if she only knew.

~May D. Sonnenfeld

"DON'T WORRY DEAR, I CONTINUE TO BE UPBEAT & SUPPORTIVE."

Reprinted by permission of
Bruce Robinson ©2010

The Morgue Parade

In the business world, everyone is paid in two coins:
cash and experience.
~Harold Geneen

I was seven years old when I learned that the large house I lived in was also the local funeral home. It didn't take me long to discover that there was money to be gained from this arrangement.

It was the summer of 1953 in one of the smaller states of New England. My dad, Fred, was the local funeral director. I had just finished the second grade at the new elementary school. I had several close neighborhood friends, and we assembled daily as a tight-knit gang.

I remember this was the year that I became very fascinated by the fact that dead bodies appeared in one of the two front living rooms of my home every now and then. The dead body was the center of attention at my house as many of the townspeople came to visit, but they didn't come to visit with me. I remember thinking, "What's up with that? It's my house, so why don't they want to see me?"

Well, my curiosity started to get the best of me. I would venture into the parlor, as it was referred to by my father, and stare at the dead body in the casket, wondering where that person came from and how they got in that big box in this house. So, it was time to ask Dad. After hearing all the facts and procedures, I got to see places in our house that I never saw before.

This included the embalming room. One day, I ventured in, and there was a dead body under a sheet. I didn't know him, so I touched him. Wow, he was cold! Lifting the sheet, I saw that he had on underwear, but no socks. No wonder he was cold.

My dad said, "Don't ever come in this room alone."

Never tell that to an inquisitive kid!

Why? I wondered. I wasn't scared. To me, this place was really cool. I thought, "My friends have got to see this!" But this kind of activity had to be sworn to secrecy, so it had to have value. What could I get for the privilege of letting the gang see the special room and the person in it?

Well, I needed money to buy shooters and cat eyes, I thought. Five cents a peek should be doable. The gang agreed. So, the parading in and out, one by one, with me as tour director and escort, was sealed in the deal.

My trusted friend and best marble accomplice was the son of the local diner proprietor. Soon, he wanted half of the take so we could both buy marbles. Now the ante went up to a dime for a peek and a toe touch! The enticement was that I would lift the sheet, and anyone could touch the toes. Again, the parade was a big success.

By the middle of summer, the secret parade was almost a weekly event. It was then that I realized the value of my new business could go from a dime to a quarter, something I felt the market could bear. But maybe I would need to upgrade the peek show a little. Maybe I could remove the whole sheet. That should do it! So, I put the concept to the gang, and once again the response was, "Yes!"

I couldn't wait for the next star performer to arrive. Keep in mind that the gang consisted of girls as well as boys. We were all very mature and didn't scream at all. That was one of the requirements of parade gang membership.

I didn't anticipate, however, the difficulty my friends would have finding quarters lying around the house in the mid-1950s. One day, one of the girls couldn't find a quarter, and she went to her mother. "Mom, I need a quarter."

"Whatever for?"

"Well, Jimmy will let me look at a dead body and touch the toe, and..."

"Stop right there. Does his father know about this?"

It didn't take long for the secret of the morgue parade to come to light. My father got a call at suppertime that very day from the mother of my fallen gang member.

Immediately, the retribution procedure began.

Dad confronted me regarding my new business endeavors. "Jimmy, this little parade business of yours has to stop right now. Furthermore," Dad stated, "I hope you have collected enough money for all the marbles you'll need for the rest of the summer because, after washing all the cars, mowing the lawn, sweeping the driveway, weeding the flower gardens, and watering the lawns, you can start all over again every week. Maybe then you will have earned your marbles."

I grew up to be a funeral director with my dad. Thinking back on this endeavor, I realized that it was really a business crime I'd committed. I was very lucky I didn't get my hide sunburned and tanned with that strap Dad had.

In retrospect, I think Dad got a laugh out of the originality of my entrepreneurship, and I learned that creativity did pay off... even if it was short-lived.

~James T. Nelson

Where's Mama?

I wish to be cremated. One tenth of my ashes shall be given to my agent,
as written in our contract.
~Groucho Marx

You would have loved my sister, Audrey. I did. At least most of the time, even if she did have some very strange ideas about what was right. That's how Mama wound up sitting on the top shelf of Audrey's bookcase.

"I've decided to buy a fancy enameled vase," Audrey said.

Now I was totally confused. "What happened to the fireworks idea? I thought you were serious."

She rolled her eyes as if she thought I was dumber than dirt. "I was. Only Mikey couldn't get the explosives permit as easily as he thought he could and he won't shoot her out of the cannon without it."

"Smart Mikey. I told you I'd have paid up front to have her ashes scattered professionally. I promised you that long before Mama died."

"I know. I just thought she'd be happier to go out with a bang."

No, you just wanted to do this all your way, I thought, keeping my opinion to myself. Mama and my sister had spent the previous twenty-five years living together and I guess that entitled them to decide how these arrangements were to be handled.

"Fine," I said. "Do it your way. Just leave me out of it."

"You don't want part of…"

"No!" This was not the first time this subject had come up and I was more than ready to speak my mind in this instance. Besides, I wasn't sure what was going on in my sister's head. It had occurred to me, more than once, that her attachment to our mother was such that she was having trouble letting her go. Literally.

Audrey shrugged, said, "Okay. Have it your way," and I thought the discussion was closed. Boy, was I wrong. It wasn't over; it was just postponed for a few years. That didn't keep her from acting peculiar from time to time, though.

When Mom was alive, she'd loved holidays. A lot. That was the reason my sister gave for "decorating" the gaudy funeral urn with party hats, bunny ears and various "fun" things like tinsel and ornaments at Christmas. No, I'm not kidding. Who would make up something this bizarre?

Anyway, I had almost gotten to the point where I could visit my sister and overlook the big, blue-and-gold enameled urn, when I got the latest surprise.

"I found two smaller jars for Mom," Audrey said. "That way you can have one and I can keep one. Isn't that great?"

I nearly swallowed my teeth. "Great? Not hardly. I don't want anything to do with it," I said. "As far as I'm concerned, Mom's gone to heaven, just like she wanted to. She's not here anymore. And the stuff left over is just dust, like the Bible says."

I thought I'd made my point. My sister turned without a word, left the room and returned cradling the two new, sealed urns. They were prettier than the bigger one but I still wasn't about to sit the dust of my mother on my bookcase like a shrine, the way my sister did.

"You sure?" she asked, sounding as if she were resigned to my refusal.

"Positive. Those are very pretty. I just don't want one."

"Okay," Audrey said with a shrug. "But these weren't quite as big inside as I'd thought." She held up a plastic baggie. "And I had a little left over. You can take this, instead."

I gasped. Mama in a sandwich bag? How inappropriate was

that? I regained my lost voice and manage to croak out, "Only if I can scatter the ashes like Daddy's."

"Oh, no, you can't do that," Audrey insisted. "It wouldn't be right."

She replaced both urns—and the little bag—on the top shelf of her bookcase where they still reside. And, now, she sits beside them in a jar of her own. I like to think that she and Mom are somewhere in heaven, looking down and laughing at me as I write this.

That's the way I choose to remember both of them.

~Valerie Whisenand

89

Funeral Fun

A guest never knows how much to laugh at a family joke.
~Author Unknown

My family has always been, shall we say, a little different. Growing up, I assumed that everyone's uncle was still best friends with his childhood girlfriend, and by default, that made her an aunt to the rest of us, even if she already was married to someone else. I assumed that funerals were meant to be laughed during, and that pizza was supposed to be topped with mustard and catsup.

For me, this was normal. It was my family, and I loved them to death. But for those not born into this mess we refer to as family, it can take a while to get used to.

A while back, my cousin was dating a sweet, young girl from Alabama. She was a pre-med college student, had a great head on her shoulders, and was everything my cousin ever wanted. They had been dating for a while, and we had yet to see her at any family functions. But when our great-grandmother passed away, she decided to join him at the funeral to offer her support in our time of grief. Little did she know, she was walking into a Scott funeral, where the "usual" for us might come across as offensive to others not privy to our nature.

We were all quite excited to meet this girl, and I seem to remember that we set her up in something similar to a receiving line so we could all say our piece and welcome her. We took full advantage of this and swarmed her like bees to honey, asking questions about her family and her life. We picked on her for dating my cousin and asked if she was slumming that day simply because she hadn't found anything better to do on a Saturday afternoon.

If that wasn't awkward enough, shortly after her arrival, she was ushered in (sans my cousin) for a full viewing of our great-grandmother in her casket. She made the usual comments about how sorry she was and how beautiful my great-grandmother looked.

While she was making her comments, my family started being, well, my family. We told stories that would make the dead blush, laughing about my great-grandmother's kooky nature. We laughed about the pizza she wanted shortly before her passing, with mustard and catsup and pickles galore. We giggled, we joked, and we picked on everyone present. We were living, and we loved.

During the service, my family sat in the front and stifled giggles as the preacher recited memories of my great-grandmother. She was just as silly as the offspring she produced, and we couldn't help but burst out laughing as we remembered those times together.

My cousin's poor girlfriend just sat back and watched us with horror in her eyes. I was quite sure that we would never see her again when my father commented, as the hearse departed from the funeral home, "It's just like her to have to be at the front of the line." Our fit of giggles began once again as we made our way to the funeral procession line.

As the casket was lowered into the ground, we smiled and knew that my great-grandmother was looking down on us, smiling at our jokes. We experienced that day in the way she would have—with elation that she was finally going home. To those who observed us that day, we must have seemed like a bunch of wackos, but to the Scotts, this was the norm.

I am happy to report that my cousin's then-girlfriend has now become his wife. We told him that if she stuck with him after meeting us like that, she was a keeper. We have welcomed her into our little family of nuts with open arms and lots of jokes, and that will never cease. She apparently doesn't have anything better to do these days either, because you can still find her "slumming" with us at family get-togethers.

While some may look at my family and see them as "a little off," I see a group of people who brush off the norms of society and live for the moment at hand. This love of life is the greatest gift anyone could ever receive, even if it means eating pizza topped with mustard and catsup.

~Shannon Scott

Mayday

There is a fine line between comedy and tragedy.
~Unknown Author

W e were laughing uproariously, partly in relief that the ordeal was almost over, partly in shared solidarity after years of abuse. My aunt had died after a nine-year battle with cancer during which she had become increasingly estranged from the family and verbally abused most of us, berating us for imagined offenses and telling everyone how terrible we were.

No matter what we did, it was wrong. If we gave money to a charity, it was the wrong charity and she didn't approve. If we bought her a gift, she stashed it in a closet. If we made an investment in a stock, we were being "foolish." If we admired something in her home, she accused us of wanting to take it. She cancelled dates with us repeatedly and then told her friends that we never came to see her.

We kept trying. After all, family is family. Plus it was a surreal experience—a woman we had admired and loved had turned on us, and we were in shock. She was alone, never having married, and she still lived in her childhood home, surrounded by her late parents' possessions. Her life had been empty compared to ours, and she had to face cancer, alone. So we called and visited, enduring the verbal slings and arrows in recent years.

Now we were speculating as to whether my father would show up for the burial. Dad loved his sister deep down, but they had never gotten along very well. He also hated waiting for anything or anyone, and now we were being forced to wait in a line of cars at the cemetery while the workers scurried to prepare the gravesite.

It had been a tough winter and conditions were icy and treacherous. It was hard to dig a hole, difficult to navigate the hilly terrain of the cemetery, and impossible to pass on the narrow lanes, hemmed in by snow banks.

The lead car (after the hearse) was a stretch limo that contained only one party, a pseudo-cousin who May had turned into an honorary son. He did errands for her, held her health care proxy, and without meaning to, had contributed to edging her blood relatives out of her life. He was actually a nice guy who seemed to care for May, but no one wanted to ride with him, since May always talked about him while pointing out our perceived deficiencies. Although he was the step-grandnephew of a second cousin by marriage, May had decided that he was her cousin, but not a cousin of anyone else in the family. She called him "my cousin Dave" and during her final years we discovered that she had even prohibited her doctors from telling anyone but Dave about her condition, putting us in the awkward position of begging him for information about her status during her many hospitalizations.

We had all assumed that Dave would be her heir if she didn't leave her money to charity. She claimed to be a wealthy woman, but we didn't know if it was true. She was not known for her accuracy—this was the woman who told us, when Barack Obama announced Joe Biden as his running mate, that Biden was Jewish, had cancer, was on weekly chemo and would not live out Obama's term if elected. Obviously, she was describing herself, but such was the worldview of our aunt May.

Next after the stretch limo was our car, filled with me and my second wife (who May irrationally hated solely because she was not my first wife), my son and daughter, and my brother. For some reason, May loved my daughter, who could do no wrong, so she had been spared the constant criticism. Following us were my sister and her family, and behind them were my first wife and her husband.

My parents' car was missing. My line-hating father had refused to participate in the thirty-minute procession from the funeral home to the cemetery so he had sped off ahead of us. Where was he? It was definitely possible that he had gone home. We laughed some more about how messed up this whole family situation was.

Then my parents' car showed up, begrudgingly nosed into the back of our line, but still halfway onto the main road so that my father could make a quick getaway. I started circulating among the family members and discovered that the betting about whether my father would stay was going on in all three cars. Finally, my father strode up the hill and informed us that he had arrived twenty minutes before us, surveyed the incomplete preparations up the hill at the gravesite, and decided to leave. He had come back to tell us that, and then he returned to his car and backed onto the main road, leaving again. We were laughing hysterically over how crazy this was, hoping that Dave would not see us from the limo and witness our inappropriate hilarity.

Eventually, our procession of cars made its way up the hill but we were stopped and told that the gravesite was covered in snow and ice and we would have to conduct the burial service right where we were stopped. May's casket was perched awkwardly over the slush on a set of flimsy legs by the side of the road, an inelegant ending for a once-beautiful, formerly charming, possibly wealthy woman from the Jewish country club set.

We stood by our cars while the Rent-A-Rabbi intoned Jewish funeral phrases. Being very reform Jews, we had no idea what was going on, but we stood there trying to look respectful and solemn while May's casket teetered at the edge of the road. The Irish funeral home director was the only one who knew the words and could chant along with the rabbi.

My parents pulled up before it was over. My mother must have forced my father to turn around and come back. He reluctantly emerged from the car and stood there with us, still mad at his dead sister for not being ready for her burial on time. When the prayers were over, we picked up the slushy sand from under the tilting casket and dropped it on top, a poor substitute for the traditional ritual.

The service earlier that day at the funeral home had been interesting too. There were more medical professionals than family members, with at least a dozen doctors and "development" people from the two hospitals that May had favored. She had been a generous supporter of medical education and cancer research and they were obviously expecting more. We didn't know what she was worth, but we assumed whatever was left after all the years of full-time health-care aides and charitable giving was going to the hospitals... and cousin Dave.

The next day the lawyer e-mailed us the will. May had not left the hospitals another cent. I guess she figured that once she was dead she no longer needed to pay for VIP service. But she took very good care of cousin Dave, and she left one member of our family, my eighteen-year-old daughter, the bulk of her estate—which turned out to be millions of dollars, giving new meaning to Shakespeare's phrase, "the slings and arrows of outrageous fortune."

Months later, my father and I still find ourselves reaching for the phone almost every day to call May. We do miss her. And we wish Joe Biden a speedy recovery.

~M. Addison Weiss

Along for the Ride

It's been a pretty fun ride, to tell you the truth.
~R. Lee Ermey

Thursdays were always busy: classes, shopping, and laundry. One sunny Thursday in spring, I had to make a special stop before starting out on my errands. It was to our local mortuary to pick up Aunt Peg's ashes.

I was greeted by an "Igor-ian" looking gentleman who asked, "May I help you?" I could have sworn he said, "Would you like to see my crematorium?" Shaking my head to clear the voice, I looked around and didn't see another living soul in the place. Maybe it was because the lighting was so dim.

I explained to "Igor" that I was there to pick up ashes, and he eerily smiled and headed for the back of the facility. I stood glued to the spot for what seemed an hour, but was only a minute or so. Smiling and whistling, Igor handed me Aunt Peg, now reduced to a square box with her name neatly printed on top. Thanking him, I quickly made my getaway and safely stowed her under the driver's seat of the truck. Peg always loved going for car rides, so I thought it fitting to take her along on my errands.

Aunt Peg was my husband Doug's favorite aunt. She was a no-nonsense, articulate Stanford graduate of the 1920s. Her greatest passions were reading and listening to classical music. She became an accomplished bookbinder, rebinding many of her own two thousand volumes.

Stopping at each store, I told Peg where we were and what I was doing. Obviously, I wasn't going to take her with me into the stores, although I'm sure she'd have loved it. What fun to stroll the grocery aisles in the baby seat of the grocery cart!

Errands done, I brought Peg home and placed her on the dresser in our bedroom where she had a good view of the backyard, the bird feeders, and flowers.

"She'd love that," I said to myself.

By and by, Doug came home from work. As he was changing clothes in the bedroom and I was preparing dinner, I heard a weird gasp from the bedroom.

"Good God almighty, is that Peg?" he called out.

"Why, yes," I said. "She's been spending the day with me, and we've had a wonderful time."

Doug quickly grabbed his jeans and headed for the bathroom to change. "I don't think this is going to work, having Peg in our bedroom day and night," he said.

"She'll only be here until we take her out on the boat for burial," I replied. Since this was Thursday, it would only be a few days until we could go out to sea.

Preparing our boat, we set out Sunday morning with our children (who adored Peg) and headed out to sea. We decided on a nice, tranquil spot to put the boat in neutral and strew flowers. Bobbing up and down in the boat, I carefully and as dignified as possible opened the box containing a sturdy plastic bag filled with Peg's ashes. Among the ashes you could see various tiny bone fragments, fillings, even some gold flecks sparkling in the noonday sun.

Doug said he wanted to spread some of the ashes, so I handed him the box. The ever-practical engineer, he stuck his hand in the bag, grabbed a huge handful of Aunt Peg, and flung her over the side.

I thought perhaps a more dignified way would be to sprinkle the ashes from the bag, so I took the bag from him and began the sprinkling in earnest. Without warning, a gust of wind caught us off-guard. Aunt Peg came flying back to us: all over the boat, our clothes, our hair, really joining the family once again.

All we could do was laugh, and laugh we did. Peg would have loved this scene. She was one of the wittiest women I've ever known. As we doused ourselves with buckets of seawater, she finally made her way to her final resting place. I must say, dear Aunt Peg, the last laugh was literally ON us.

~Ann Michener Winter

The Joint Funeral of Pooky and Hermes

I love being married. It's so great to find that one special person you want to annoy for the rest of your life.

~Rita Rudner

The hurricane ripped through my house every Sunday morning before church. The front closet was torn apart every time my parents were going to a nice dinner, or she had an important business meeting. I thought she would stop looking for it when we moved houses, since she obviously didn't find it when she packed, but she didn't. And now, fifteen years later, my father still performs the obligatory search before every holiday and play opening.

The object of this search: a pale pink Hermes scarf.

She bought it on her first trip to New York City; it was her one extravagance. My mother has never had a particular flair for fashion. I don't think she even stepped into a Gap store until I was in high school. She bought the scarf without having anything to wear with it, and it literally changed her wardrobe.

It's been missing all these years. Since before I can remember, or… could remember. You see, a few weeks ago during a memory exercise in my advanced writing class, I solved the mystery of the missing scarf. It came to me as I shared a story about my first pet and first funeral: my hamster, Pooky. My classmates laughed, and I might have, too, if I had not been so terrified that my discovery would be relayed to her before I could get her on the phone to explain.

The scarf was a beautiful color of pink, light as a feather, and so soft to the touch that when I brought home Pooky for the first time, it was the only thing in which I could hold the poor thing to keep him from whimpering. Pooky became unusually attached to the scarf after that. So much so that when my mother went to the city for her weekly schedule of business meetings shortly thereafter, I arranged the scarf into a bed in Pooky's cage to keep him calm and warm. I congratulated myself on being such a good provider. I was a mother for the first time, and Pooky had fulfilled all my seven-year-old hopes and dreams from the moment he shuffled through the woodchips to curl up in my hand.

Pooky didn't last long. In fact, by the time Mom came home three days later, Pooky was dead and buried.

I was recalling this memory when it struck me. Suddenly, I had a vivid memory of my dad, feigning surprise at my lack of mothering capabilities and digging a shoebox out of the hall closet. He sat down next to me where I lay next to Pooky's cage, crying uncontrollably in my typical overly dramatic fashion. He gently tugged on the fabric and out rolled Pooky's stiff, egg-like body, still clinging to the scarf. I remembered Dad looking at me, with my eyes all red from crying, and then at the scarf, before he sighed and lifted Pooky and the scarf out of the cage and into the shoebox.

We buried Pooky in the plot of dirt outside my window. His cross would be joined by many others in the coming years, though none of the other victims would be lucky enough to be buried with such an heirloom.

I considered coming clean to my mom after that class and telling her that I knew exactly where she could finally find her long-lost luxury item. I rehearsed a long, tearful apology and researched the cost to replace it for her for Christmas. Eventually, I worked up the nerve to tell her.

I came home to find my parents arguing over what shirt my dad would wear to a play opening. My mom, with one shoe on and mascara wand in hand, was running around in her usual frenzied way, waving a striped shirt in his face and complaining that the one he had chosen an hour ago made him look like his mother. I sat down with the dog and watched the exchange in amusement as if it were a tennis match, our heads flipping back and forth, back and forth. Finally, she threw down the shirt and huffed away, mumbling something about how she had always hated that shirt until she disappeared in the bathroom.

I thought that maybe tonight wasn't the best time to give my confession. I looked back at my dad. He was grinning from ear to ear. "Are you going to change shirts?" I asked him. He looked at the shirt, then at me, then at the bathroom door, and said, "I'll let her stew about it for a bit longer." And he winked at me.

It was then I realized that, while I may have buried Hermes alive that day, I was still a kid. My seven-year-old self was obviously not aware of the significance of such an item. It took me fifteen years to remember my crime against fashion. But my father knew. All these years, he knew exactly where the scarf was, and he had never told. Instead, he diligently went through every closet and would consistently come up empty-handed.

I smiled. My dad emerged from his room, newly striped, just as my mother came raring out of the bathroom, this time with both shoes on, ready for round two. He kissed her on the head, and she sighed happily.

"Twenty-five years, kid," he said to me, smiling. "I do what I can."

I decided to let him have his fun. I kept my mouth shut. And ordered the most expensive pale pink scarf from Hermes.com.

~Alex Kingcott

Chapter
10

Family Matters

The Serious Side

Turn your wounds into wisdom.

~Oprah Winfrey

93

Breaking

Sisterhood is powerful.
~Robin Morgan

Unlike the rest of my world, the flight was perfect. I left New York City on the first plane of the morning, transferred in Chicago, and arrived in Houston before 11:30 a.m. I didn't want to land early. I didn't want to land at all. I wanted the Boeing 747 to continue south and stop somewhere in the British Islands or the Caribbean or even Cuba. It wasn't supposed to happen like this. It wasn't supposed to be her.

I didn't want to see my sister, Jill. I had never been so unsure of what I was walking into during my entire life. There was no way to prepare. Would she scream at me or even recognize me? I knew what she had been saying, seeing, claiming, but I had not witnessed it. My initial thought was that she had experienced a nervous breakdown. I hoped that she had been drugged, but I knew my sister. I knew exotic Asian teas and the bean sprouts she grew on her windowsill were the most outrageous things she consumed.

Earlier that day, my other sister, Angela, had tackled her to the ground when Jill realized she had been taken to a hospital.

"Whose side are you on?" she asked my mom.

Armed police officers stood in her room.

"We've seen LSD before," they reassured my parents. "This will wear off soon."

"It's so hot in here," Jill kept repeating as she tried to unlock the window latches. Everyone feared she might jump.

The two young cops left when the drug tests came back negative. I wished that they had been right.

Less than twenty-four hours after receiving the phone call, I saw Jill in the ER of some hospital in the Middle-of-Nowhere, Texas. She was wearing only a thin dress, with no undergarments or shoes. I went into the room where she was sleeping. Her head poked out of the white hospital sheets, and her mousy brown hair splashed across the pillow. It was her, but it wasn't. In that moment, I was scared of her and for her. My mom left the room so she could stretch her legs and asked me to stay. She wanted someone to be there if Jill woke up.

I looked at her sleeping face and remembered holding her for the first time when I was six years old. I wanted to hold her now. I wanted to know she was still in there somewhere.

That afternoon, when she woke up from her shot of Geodon, her first request was to see me.

"How was your flight?" she asked. "Thank you for coming."

She seemed okay, lethargic and dreamy, but okay. She noticed a peanut butter and jelly sandwich and a bag of chips on her bedside table and quickly devoured them. Later, we found out she hadn't eaten or slept in days.

• • •

My sister spent eleven days in the Behavioral Health Unit. My big-hearted, blue-eyed, college-educated sister was locked up. The first twenty-four hours, she was manic, her eyes beady and shifty. She looked fragile in her hospital-issued gown, but refused to put on clothes. She hesitated and then hugged us as we signed the guest book during visitation the first night. I took a deep breath and exhaled, trying desperately not to cry. She was somewhere we weren't. Saw things we didn't. I hated that for her. She fell to the floor, curling up in the fetal position.

"I'm so sorry. I'm so sorry," she repeated.

Standing, seconds later, she forcefully laughed, but it wasn't her laugh. She seemed tortured.

I watched an orderly in blue rubber gloves hold up her underwear and inspect the clothes I had given her. I'd brought in yoga pants and a long-sleeved T-shirt from my own suitcase. He told us he'd have to remove the drawstring.

I hated seeing her there, with those people. I feared someone would harm her. I longed to taker her home, but knew she wouldn't be safe there. Simply being home and in the presence of love wouldn't make anything better. Warm covers, homemade cookies and her favorite Earl Grey tea wouldn't make her feel anything. She was helpless.

For the one hour each day that I could see her, I had to be bold. I was strong. I did it for my sister, for the hell she had been through.

• • •

The next day before visiting hours, I wandered the self-help section of a bookstore. I skimmed books that sounded like they might offer any sort of help. Within two hours, I had researched bipolar, schizophrenia, schizophrenic disorders, nervous breakdowns, and psychosis. I wanted to learn all I could before she was released.

While sitting on the floor and reading, I noticed a dad in the children's section, baby-talking with his young daughter. He called his wife.

"She just said da-da! She just said da-da!" He beamed.

"Say it for Mom. Say da-da." He held out the phone to his daughter. "Oh, come on. Da-da. Da-da. Da-da." There was a long silence.

"I swear, honey, she just said da-da."

Although I found this terribly funny, I started to cry. That baby girl was so innocent and loved. Maybe one day she would grow up and be valedictorian and study in Sweden and be a great friend — and then break down. Her sisters would cry, and her parents wouldn't sleep. What would they do when their love wasn't enough to fix her problem? Would they remember this time, sitting on a yellow blanket in a bookstore, hearing da-da for the first time? I said a prayer for Jill and for that baby girl.

•••

A month prior, she was a Teaching Assistant, doing research for her master's degree in international relations. Suddenly, completing a jigsaw puzzle was worth celebrating. She could quote lengthy passages from the book of Ephesians, but couldn't tell me what day of the week it was when looking at a calendar. She had run a half marathon and traveled to Taiwan, but suddenly she believed that someone had tapped into her computer and changed her passwords.

I haven't given up hope for my little sister, Jill. I ache for her return to normalcy and to understand that she hasn't done anything wrong. I know that we, as a family, are going to be okay. But as each day passes, I taste a little more of the anguish of a broken heart.

~Stefani Chambers

White Walls and Flowered Curtains

There's no place like home except Grandma's.
~Author Unknown

I ran across the dark wood floor, sliding in my stockinged feet.

"Grampa! Grampa!" I said, throwing my arms around my grandfather's legs. He picked me up and hugged me.

"How's my Little Bertie?" he asked.

I buried my face in his shirt collar and held him tight, so tight it was hard for him to breathe.

That was the day my grandparents came to see me at the foster home where I was awaiting a stranger's decision: Who would raise me?

I've been blessed by my grandparents. They saved me from an uncertain life with a mother who, while well-meaning, was ill-equipped to raise a child. My mother suffered her own demons, and offered me only uncertainty and chaos. She was young and single. She had no way to support me, so we lived with her parents (my grandparents).

Now, I try to imagine my mother's life of dependence and anxiety. She had been "a little different" ever since she reached adolescence, but her behaviour grew more bizarre after my birth. My grandparents became protective. Instead of sleeping with my mother, I slept in a crib in their bedroom. This must have made my mother very unhappy, for she would come into the room while my grandparents slept and watch me.

Haunted by obsessive-compulsive disorder and postpartum depression, my mother was sad and restless. This was the sixties, a time when mental illness was misunderstood. My grandparents were alarmed by her outbursts of rage, as well as her odd habits and rituals, like checking the knife drawer and counting the knives. She would sleep long into the day, pacing the house at night and checking for locked doors. But while she endured a fractured life, she made plans.

We lived in a remote area with few neighbors. The closest town was an hour's drive. My mother wanted to get away, so she took me, her only child. We often went for walks: down to the lake or through the forest. But this day was special because my mother had prepared for it in advance. On this warm June day, she retrieved the clothes she had hidden in the forest.

"We're going on a big adventure, Bertie," she said, squeezing my hand.

We walked through the forest, down the road and across the bridge. We walked so far that my short legs grew tired, and my mother had to pick me up and carry me. In those days, well-meaning railroaders were happy to stop a freight train for passengers, especially if a person looked in need. Soon, a noisy, giant train went by. My mother stood on her tiptoes and waved her arm in the air. The train's brakes screamed. It slowed and finally stopped. Clutching me in her arms, my mother ran to catch up. She handed me up to a big, smelly man with a kind voice and scratchy face. I was frightened by the rumbling engine, but my mother was with me, so it was okay. Soon, we were half a province away.

I don't remember what happened during those weeks on the lam. My memory skips ahead to the bars of a crib that felt like the bars of a prison. Through the bars, the walls were winter white, and the sun shone through flowered curtains that made shadowy patterns on the wall. I was wrapped in a mauve waffle blanket, and

I rocked back and forth, sucking my thumb. There was no time. I had been there forever. Eventually, the bedroom door opened, and the Nice Lady walked in. She picked me up and brushed out the wrinkles in my little pink dress.

"You have visitors," she said.

She carried me downstairs, and Grandma and Grandpa were standing by the door. Grandpa held me for a long time, and then I was passed to Grandma. But it was Grandpa I wanted, so he held me a while longer, then said, "We have to go." He handed me to the Nice Lady and left quickly.

There are defining moments in our lives. I will always remember the relief I felt when my grandparents came to see me. And then I remember the betrayal when I learned they weren't taking me home.

After that day, I stopped speaking. I sucked my thumb. I rocked myself back and forth in the crib. I watched the other children play, and they watched back. But like ants under a magnifying glass, they remained separate. At mealtime, the Nice Lady sat next to me and coaxed me to eat. At night, she put me to bed, and I slept.

When I did go home, I had forgotten the words I once knew and again spoke the baby talk that I had long outgrown. I suffered from nightmares that woke me screaming in the night. I was left with an indelible fear of being abandoned.

After they were finally allowed to take me home, my grandparents showered me with unconditional love. They seemed intent on making up for all the sadness that had befallen my young life. My grandfather was my constant companion in those early years: telling me stories, reading me books, and taking me on long walks where he would talk about his own childhood. My grandmother accepted the role of mother: taking me to doctors' appointments, scrutinizing my report cards, and eventually helping me choose my wedding dress.

My mother never did receive the help she needed, and she has spent her life a lost soul, joining the community of mentally ill and terminally disenfranchised. I have not seen her in many years.

My grandparents were the best parents a kid could ask for. They saved me from a life I'm afraid to imagine, and they treated me like their own. Over the years, they endured much for my sake: a long custody battle and fears that I would be abducted in the dark of night. Over time, they mended my fears and replaced them with a sense of comfort and security that has lasted a lifetime. They are both gone now, but for their unconditional love and kindness, I will be forever grateful.

~Roberta Laurie

95

A Gift from Above

A baby is God's opinion that the world should go on.
~Carl Sandburg

On the day my daughter told me that she was pregnant, she also informed me, in the same breath, that she would not be keeping the child. Severe health issues forced her to face the fact that she could barely take care of herself, much less take on the challenge of caring for a demanding newborn. My heart sank as she debated her options—adoption and the other one that was too horrible to even consider.

My husband and I had been married for five years and thoroughly enjoyed our carefree lifestyle. Having already raised our own kids, we scoffed at friends with babysitting issues who cancelled plans at the last minute. We empathized with parents of teens who had become prisoners in their own home, unable to leave for fear that their home would be the next party venue. "Been there, done that, and happy to be done with that," was our mantra. At forty-three, I was in the process of selling a lucrative insurance business that I had built over eighteen years and was anxiously anticipating a life of writing, traveling and sipping margaritas from every cruise ship deck and Caribbean beach that we could find.

But the universe had other plans.

I convinced my daughter to hold off on making a final decision at least long enough for me to figure out what to do. I needed time to think. For days, I walked around like a zombie, unaware of where I'd been or whom I'd seen. Nights were no better. I would stay awake until dawn, cradled in my husband's arms. I would listen to his quiet breathing, the sounds of crickets, a train whistle in the distance, all while waiting and praying for answers that just wouldn't come. When sleep would finally overtake me, there was still no escape, for even in my dreams I was visited by a little girl who would hold her arms up to me, pleading, "Grandma, help me!" Mornings, I did my crying in the shower, reasoning that red swollen eyes could easily be blamed on irritating shower gels and shampoos.

Nevertheless, after a couple of days, my husband grew wary of my abnormal behavior and asked me what was wrong. The previous month, my doctor had found a grapefruit-sized tumor in my uterus that had to be removed, so I skirted the baby issue and tried my best to convince him that the upcoming surgery was to blame for my tangled nerves. But he just shook his head, put his arms around me, sat me down and told me to give him my troubles so he could fix them. He knew me so well that he could detect every mood change and nuance long before I knew myself there was anything wrong. His strength was one of the things that had attracted me to him. I knew he was someone I could lean on without him tipping over.

After I'd blubbered out the whole story, he simply said, "Get her on the phone." I quickly dialed my daughter's number. When she answered, I nervously handed the phone to my husband and waited for his response. He listened for a while, and then he told her to eat healthy. When the baby was born, we would take it and raise it. She must have agreed because when he hung up the phone, he asked, "Anything else?"

I dissolved into tears, this time without any reservations. I let it all come out, all the pain, all the angst, the fear and the guilt. Although I had been thinking of taking the baby myself, I just hadn't been able to ask the same of him. I couldn't believe that a man who was not my daughter's father would actually sacrifice his own future to raise someone else's child. He was definitely a keeper!

A few months later, we were holding a little bundle of joy in our arms. She was a colicky baby, but we soon found out that as long as she was lying on Papa's belly, she would stop fussing and crying, and immediately go to sleep. I had the hysterectomy two weeks after she was born, so I could only hold her with a stack of pillows on my lap and her on top. My mom was also a huge help, taking care of the baby and me while my husband worked.

As our new daughter grew and started school, we decided that I would homeschool her since her amazing thirst for knowledge was more than most teachers could handle. We found that she not only enjoyed studying French, Spanish, anthropology, geography, and religion from the texts that my professor husband brought home from the university, but she preferred them over the curriculum offered to children her age.

My daughter and the baby's father have stayed together and maintained contact with her. Even though our child calls us Mom and Papa, she has grown up knowing her biological parents as well. When she started walking and talking, however, she began to ask questions, so I would tell her the story of how she came to be.

"Papa and I," I would begin, "wanted a baby more than anything else in the world, so we asked God for a beautiful little girl. God then asked us, 'Will you love her and feed her and clothe her and educate her and make sure she gets a good HMO or a quality health plan?'

"'Oh, yes, yes, yes, and of course!' we answered.

"'Alright then,' God said, 'I have a smart, beautiful, and talented little girl you can have. I'll send her down to you right away so she can start growing in your belly. In nine months, you can give birth to her.'

"'But Lord,' I explained, 'I can't have babies anymore.'

"'Well, then, Nana will have to have the baby,' he said."

At this point, our little one would laugh hysterically at the thought of my seventy-seven-year-old mother having a baby, commenting on the fact that Nana couldn't possibly have babies.

"That's exactly what we said," I'd tell her. "So God thought about it for awhile and then said, 'Hey, why don't I place the baby in your daughter's belly? She's young and perfectly able to have children. Then after she's born, you can raise her.'

"What a great idea!" we'd all say, with her chiming in.

"And that's how I came to be!" she would say, ending the story with a big, contented smile on her face.

~Mary Amelia

My Hand or My Shoulder?

An older sister is a friend and defender—a listener, conspirator, a counsellor and a sharer of delights. And sorrows too.
~Pam Brown

"I need a shoulder to lean on."

My wedding was just a few months away, and my sister and I were sharing a quiet evening out. She spoke softly, head down, eyes averted. I was older by two years, and there was little we didn't know about each other—or so I thought. Yet, her tone and body language told me to be prepared for something new... and unpleasant. With a few words, she made me aware of a situation that shocked me, forcing me to face my own limitations and reassess how I approached all my relationships.

"I need a shoulder to lean on."

I've always found it easier to play the role of a hand in my relationships than to function as a shoulder. It's my nature to try to fix problems when someone shares a dilemma with me. My instinctive response is to evaluate the problem, then search for—and help implement—a solution. I view it as a challenge when I'm told I cannot make a difference. Offering a shoulder to lean on, without trying to fix the problem, is one of the most difficult roles I've ever had to learn and accept.

"I need a shoulder to lean on."

These words opened up the heartache of having my precious sister reveal that she was being sexually abused by a close family member. It had been going on for years, and even though she was now an adult, she labored under the misconception that she had to tolerate ongoing abuse out of respect for the family leadership role of her abuser. I begged her to seek professional help, but she refused. Her eyes widened in terror—not terror over being mistreated, but terror that she had exposed the dreadful secret she had carried for years. She made it clear she would deny everything she had shared if I discussed her circumstances with any third party on her behalf. Since she was of legal age, I could not force her to take action.

However, it made me angry that she was less frightened of being molested than of exposing her abuser. She had gone to considerable lengths to prevent family and friends—even me—from discovering that our apparent model family was not what it appeared to be. I found it impossible to understand the conditioning that made her think she had to continue tolerating mistreatment. How could one person feel so hopeless and helpless that she believed it better to remain a victim than to expose the abuse?

And how could I not have known? We lived in the same home; we had even shared a bedroom. But my school, work, and social commitments kept me out of the house from morning till evening. I hadn't been there when she needed me, and guilt consumed me.

Now she wanted and needed a friend to confide in. I reluctantly agreed to respect her wishes, hoping she would eventually change her mind. But how could I sit by and do nothing? At least I had access to a "third party" she couldn't object to: I could pray for her.

I married soon after that initial conversation. She rarely called me. If we spoke, it was because I reached out to her. Our conversations grew less frequent, most likely the combined result of her embarrassment and my increasing inability to hold my opinions in check. During the rare occasions when she would again share her heart, I became more and more frustrated. She was an adult, but she wasn't making adult choices. I was angry at her and angry at her abuser.

But I also had choices. I could allow anger to burrow deep into my soul, ending our relationship and disrupting my own emotional and spiritual health, or I could offer her what she had requested: a shoulder to lean on. I could also use my hands, but on her terms, not mine; to hug and to hold, but not to fix. It was a new role for me, one that I did not easily embrace. Nevertheless, it was all she wanted, and I could not force her to accept more.

She married a few years later and moved away. The abuse had finally stopped, but her healing had yet to begin. My concern crossed the miles, but our telephone conversations deteriorated into polite ritual.

"How are you?"

"I'm fine."

"Are you okay? Is there anything you want to talk about?"

"I'm really fine. How is the weather by you?"

We spoke of our jobs, recipes, headlines, music, fashion, politics, even sports. Everything except what we both knew was truly important. Words were exchanged, but little was said.

More than thirty years have passed since that first fateful conversation. While I am still here for her, our relationship bears little resemblance to what it once was. On those ever-so-rare occasions when I dare to broach the subject and suggest she receive counseling, she refuses and still defends her abuser. My heart aches to think of the lingering emotional damage she lives with. She still doesn't understand my frustration, and I still don't understand how a vibrant, intelligent woman could ever think she deserved to be treated in such a shameful manner.

In spite of, or maybe because of, the pain of watching someone I love suffer in this destructive situation, I've had to prayerfully accept the truth that there are many things I cannot fix, no matter how much I want to and no matter how hard I try. I've learned, and am still learning, that I can offer resources and suggestions, but I can't make choices for others. I can be there for support, but I can't live their life for them.

Most of all, I've learned a new and difficult lesson about forgiveness. Because my sister confused forgiveness with continued acceptance of abusive behavior, I thought that she was the one with the problem. I found to my chagrin, however, that by extension, I also had a problem. I was on a path to spending the rest of my life angry and resentful over the damage her abuser had caused. I was giving him power over me that he had no right to have.

But I had another option. I could choose to forgive, with the understanding that forgiveness does not signify tolerance of evil, but rather, frees me from a prison of my own making. Continued unforgiveness would only provide fertile soil for bitterness to take root in my heart, causing me to become an indirect victim of the wrong done to her. God forgives me for my sin. For my own good, I needed to extend forgiveness and release my anger.

This relationship caused me to reevaluate the strengths I thought I brought to all my relationships. Friendship does not mean that I have to fix every problem my friend experiences. Neither does it mean that I should sit back and do nothing. No matter how helpless I may feel to effect change, I can still pray for those who are hurting.

My head and my hands. There was so much I wanted to give her. But what she really wanted was my shoulder and my heart.

~Sue Jackson

97

The Lie, Redemption and Notre Dame

There are two kinds of people in the world, Notre Dame lovers and Notre
Dame haters. And, quite frankly, they're both a pain in the ass.
~Dan Devine, former Notre Dame football coach

Everyone has a dad story. Mine ends like this: outlined against the blue-gray November sky, a forty-year lie was laid to rest.

In dramatic lore, it is known as deceit. But, in this reality, the lie was retired on November 14, 2009, when I finally attended the Pitt-Notre Dame football game. Honest.

The story begins with a lie that I hatched at age eleven by telling my friends I was going to the Pitt-Notre Dame game. It was a desperate reach. I was the kid who felt he had nothing and needed to boost his stature. I surmised that game attendance was the answer. So, while others would live their pedestrian lives, I would watch the most nationally recognized team in college football play against the beloved, local university with a woeful team. I was convinced that because everyone had something that I didn't, I needed this. It was supposed to happen; too bad it didn't.

I was somewhat of a rarity in my small, western Pennsylvania community because my parents were separated. Beyond the pain and confusion of a broken family, I felt marked. There was a sense in the attitudes of others that ranged from pity to irrational loathing. I didn't ask for either. All I wanted was to go to a football game.

I dealt with my situation in the way that any child of that era may have — by lying. I lied to myself that someday things would go back to the way they were. I lied to my friends that my father was working out of town until further notice. I lied about a great father-son day we had. My relatively small world became even more condensed by my self-imposed restrictions. I had to build and live in an alternate reality in which this had happened. The lie was as intricate as Knute Rockne's famous backfield shift.

The lie subtly began when a neighbor and his father would play catch on a nightly basis. It festered when another friend's dad was also his coach, troop leader and even confidant. It caught full momentum when my dad did what many suddenly single parents do — he made a promise to impress and win the favor of his son. He said he could get tickets to any game, anytime, anywhere. Being a young football fan and having read of the many exploits of the most storied program in football, I thought it would be cool to tell everyone I knew that I went to see Notre Dame when they came to play at Pitt Stadium.

I asked if we could go and received a long pause. It was followed by a definitive, reassuring affirmative: "We'll see."

Having been a father for more than eighteen years, I now know what "we'll see" means. From this perspective, it means "No way in hell," or "You have a better chance of being on the next space shuttle" or, more appropriately, "You want to see a Pitt game? Become a better receiver." But back then, my perspective interpreted it to mean, "See you at 9:00 a.m. We'll get breakfast! And I hope you like stadium hot dogs, hot chocolate, a game program and a new Pitt tossle cap."

What I didn't realize was that he was lying, too. He had no connection to tickets of this magnitude, and I doubt he had an interest in seeing a game with me. He hadn't until then, so why would he now?

Game day came, and I waited on my front porch wearing a coat and gloves. No need for a tossle cap — I'd be getting a new one that day. I looked up and down the street. Minutes became an hour. Then two hours. It was an hour before kickoff when I went back inside and hoped that no one had seen me not getting into his car.

I spent the day hiding out. The radio in my room was my ticket to the game. I studied the Notre Dame football highlight show the next morning. I knew each play and became an expert on what it would have been like to see a Joe Theismann touchdown pass as it happened live and not on a thirteen-inch black-and-white TV about twenty hours later.

The weight of the lie increased. In the week that followed my alleged attendance, skeptics questioned the existence of my tickets or sought proof in the form of a game program. "I must've left them in my dad's car, of course. I just hope he didn't throw them away by accident." The doubters were brushed aside by a significant backer—a twelve-year-old acquaintance with clout. He was older and viewed in our circle as a man of the world because, well, he was older. He said he believed me, and so should they. And they did. Perhaps he didn't believe me either, but felt uncomfortable for me and backed me up. Or he was setting me up for a future return favor.

Eventually, I emerged from the state of lying to that of regular being. And, eventually, I got over why I lied in the first place, although I regret having fooled my friends for so long.

I realize that, in the long history of fatherhood, there have been worse dads. I also realize that my dad was just a guy who had problems and occasionally talked himself into a corner. I understand that his big talk got away from him, and he undoubtedly was embarrassed by not getting the tickets. I'm sure he wanted to come through like a Joe Montana Cotton Bowl comeback, but he didn't. Instead, it set up an even greater triumph.

On occasion, I'd come close to breaking the lie. I was once a sportswriter, but never had the opportunity to cover a Pitt-Notre Dame game. After a while, I just tucked it away as a lesson learned in how not to parent and definitely how not to react to a perceived wrong. Then I became luckier than anyone deserves to be as a husband and father. Last year, I noticed the Pitt football schedule and mentioned a condensed version of this story to my wife. This story's heroine listened and, upon hearing the story of the lie, surprised me with Pitt season tickets for the express purpose of being able to see the Panthers play against Notre Dame. And, like a Rocket Ismail punt return, boom — the lie was over.

In the week leading up to the game, I exhibited the zeal of a kid awaiting his first game. I read every pre-game story I could find and bored coworkers with pre-game analyses. On game day, we parked and began our trek toward Heinz Field. I had a skip in my walk and felt young again. When I caught sight of the stadium, which I'd seen numerous times, I stopped to savor the moment.

I didn't tap a "lie like a champion today" sign as we entered Heinz Field. I finally got my game program, but didn't need a tossle cap on that warm November evening. I scanned the seats and saw fathers and sons in attendance. I hoped they'd remember this great day. A few priests walked by, and I said a silent prayer that those who missed an important event would get their chance to recapture the day someday.

Late on the night of November 14, 2009, I could honestly say I went to the Pitt-Notre Dame game. But in the forty years between pseudo and actual attendance, a lot of growing up has taken place, including the acknowledgement and regret of a falsehood; the pardon of its contributing factor; and the realization that absolution can make one stand taller. No lie.

~Mike Morlacci

98

Forever Grateful

Simply having children does not make mothers.
~John A. Shedd

My mother-in-law, Nancy, has an around-the-clock caregiver. My husband and I jokingly refer to her as "St. Carolina" because she patiently caters, thanklessly, to Nancy's every demanding whim. The only problem is that Carolina speaks in broken English with a strong Polish accent. Occasionally, it is difficult to understand her. And her mispronunciation of one word in particular is especially amusing.

The most recent conversation I overheard went something like this: My mother-in-law said, "Carolina! Get in here, NOW! I want my fried chicken, and it better be crispy or I'm sending it back!"

Carolina bolted out of the kitchen, carefully balancing the chicken, fries, and soda on a platter, and placed it gently on the table beside Nancy's recliner.

"Here you go, crispy chicken, just right. I bring cupcake when finished. I adjust pillow—for more comfortable." Fluffing Nancy's pillow, Carolina innocently added, "Need anything else, Miss Nasty?"

I couldn't help it; I broke out laughing and immediately stifled my laugh with a fake cough. Fortunately, Nancy's hearing is poor, so she missed what Carolina had said. Nancy immediately started barking another order, "Go open that window another inch, no more, no less!" Then she rudely waved Carolina off, saying, "And get out of here when you're finished!"

As Carolina rushed to open the window, she glanced at me. Our eyes met, and I whispered, "Thank you!" for all she does for this woman. She nodded and gave me a little smile.

My mother-in-law is in fine health, though she has acted feeble and helpless during her entire life. She eats junk foods high in trans fats, never exercises, and lives in her recliner. She hates everyone—all nationalities, all "fat" people—and she even refers to her only daughter, Peg, as "Pig."

She never cooked for her two kids and never attended their school activities—plays, parent/teacher conferences, not even their high school graduations. Soon after we were married, her son and I were invited to her home for Christmas dinner. We accepted and graciously thanked her, but three weeks before the holiday, she called and canceled, stating she'd have a headache that day. After thirty-three years, my husband and I have still never eaten a meal at her home.

When my husband was diagnosed with cancer and needed ongoing topical chemotherapy treatments, we gently broke the news to his mother, thinking she'd be upset and worried about her only son. Instead, her reaction was, "Oh, phew! I thought you were going to tell me I had cancer."

She has some grandchildren who live nearby, but they don't know their grandmother. They were never welcome in her home. That is, until one day when she decided, "I want to fire my stupid caregiver, that Mexican. No, wait, I already fired her. I mean the Polish one, Carolina. I shouldn't have to pay her!" She added, "And I want that grandson of mine—what's-his-name, you know, the big fat one—to resign from his job and take care of me for free."

I rarely speak to my friends about my mother-in-law. If they knew what she was really like, how mean-spirited and abusive she was to my husband when he was growing up, they wouldn't believe it.

Still, I don't lose sight of the positives. Because of my husband's upbringing, he thinks I'm an ideal wife, and I'm not going to correct him. He's so appreciative of the smallest things I do that it naturally makes me want to do even more for him. Nothing's taken for granted. He certainly wasn't spoiled. He was never handed anything in life—no money, no emotional support, no guidance, and most of all, no love. So anything I do, the simplest things—a hug, a warm meal, a safe haven—mean everything to him. And that kind of mutual love and appreciation inevitably grows.

Miraculously, in spite of the cruel indifference of his mother, my husband was able to develop into a man filled with kindness, deep compassion, and a genuine appreciation of love. And for that, even in the midst of Miss Nasty's ugliest moments, I am forever grateful.

~Anna Michaelsan

99

PerspectiveS

The child supplies the power
but the parents have to do the steering.
~Benjamin Spock,
Dr. Spock's Baby and Child Care

"Y ou're so lucky. That means you can make as much noise as you want, and your parents can't tell you to be quiet!" raved the kids at recess.

"Well, no, actually, my parents can feel the vibrations when we run around," I would start to explain. But in elementary school, no one cares about the ways you are the same; they want to focus on how you are different.

"Say something in sign language," someone would interrupt. Alternatively, kids would wave their hands frantically in the air, fingers flailing. "Did I say anything? What did I say?" After dissolving into laughter, the next question was usually if I knew how to sign "asshole." My classmates were left disappointed when I didn't, due to the fact that my parents avoided using the word "asshole" when having a conversation with their daughter.

To my friends, I was lucky to have deaf parents because it meant more freedom. I apparently lived a life in which I regularly stampeded around the house, cursing a blue streak as I went. The reality was much more ordinary. If I jumped on my bed, I would soon hear heavy footsteps on the stairs, coming to catch me in the act. Any time

I whispered an obscenity under my breath at the dinner table, my father was the first to notice.

With adults, I was lucky for a different reason.

"It's such a blessing that you girls can hear," my Aunt Carol would say. "I don't know what your mom and dad would do if they didn't have you three to help out."

I knew what my parents would do. They'd go on tropical vacations and live in a bigger house. They'd spend less time driving us to basketball practice and sleepovers, and more time relaxing in their mansion. They wouldn't have to deal with bank tellers trying to conduct transactions through their eight-year-old daughter. They would point at the menu to order food, instead of being ignored as the waitress recited the daily specials to their children.

"I don't know why you don't become an interpreter," my grandmother would say every time we visited her Illinois farm. "You have such an advantage knowing the sign language, and you'll never be out of work. With your mother and dad being deaf, you know it better than anyone. I'm too old to learn it now."

Never mind that my dad had been deaf since his birth in 1955, when my grandmother had considerably nimbler fingers. Never mind that interpreting for a living would be suffocating, and I would feel an inescapable responsibility to my job because I had deaf parents. Parents who never thought I should be satisfied with convenience. Parents who always told me to dream big and make it happen.

One day, Dad drove me to pick up my car from a mechanic. As we stood in the lobby, signing and laughing about something insignificant, I felt the familiar sensation of being watched by a stranger. This time it was the desk clerk, a large, bald, imposing man in his forties. After I paid my bill and we turned to leave, the man stopped me.

"Is that your father?" he called, just as I pushed the door forward. Dad was already on his way toward the car, and I was anxious to catch up.

"Yes," I said.

"He's deaf?"

"Yes. Both of my parents are."

He paused for a moment. I waited for the sermon he was about to give me—the one where he told me how wonderful it was that I helped my parents, how lucky I was that I could hear—the speech I had heard on a continual loop for the past twenty-six years.

"That's beautiful, what you have," he said. "My daughter is sixteen years old, and I can't even get her to speak to me, let alone laugh with me. When I watch you and your father, it hurts, because I want that more than anything with my daughter. You're lucky to have that kind of a relationship."

I stammered something meaningless and thanked him, then went out to the parking lot. In less than five minutes, a complete stranger had managed to hit on one of the many genuine reasons that I did feel lucky to have my parents. In my entire lifetime, friends and family still couldn't see what this man saw instantly. I am lucky, not because I can take advantage of my parents or interpret for them. Not because I hear, and they do not.

I am lucky because my parents taught me to believe in my own power. I am lucky because my parents never told me that I couldn't (or shouldn't) do something because it would be too hard. I am lucky because my parents did not lead me to believe that my hearing privileged me in a way that their deafness had failed them. Instead, I had the opportunity to learn that the deaf culture is rich, varied, and full of abilities. I am lucky because now, as I become an adult, I see possibilities where other people see limitations.

When I caught up with my dad that day, he asked what had held me up.

"That man told me that we were lucky," I told him. My father put his arm around my shoulders and squeezed.

"He's right," he said. "I would never trade any one of my daughters for anything in the world."

It dawned on me later that I hadn't told my dad why we were lucky. I hadn't needed to.

~Lauren Fitzpatrick

Mr. Lucky's Magic Dust

Always look on the bright side of life.
~Monty Python

My father-in-law, Don, aka Mr. Lucky, was thankful for the simple things in life. His wife of fifty-plus years, Flora, allowed him to purchase one scratch-off ticket per week. Somehow, that ticket always ended up being the winning one.

"Send some of that magic dust our way, Lucky," his coworkers teased as they carried off fistfuls of worthless tickets.

"We're all lucky to be living in America," he'd reply.

As Mr. Lucky grew older, he developed two strikes against him.

Dad suffered from hearing loss and macular degeneration. Such a combination would have been devastating handicaps to a lesser man. Not Mr. Lucky, however.

He was seated in the break room one afternoon opening a sack lunch when a weather announcement came over the intercom.

"A tornado alert has been issued for the entire viewing area. Please be aware of these conditions!"

Dad looked up from his ham and cheese sandwich.

"A tomato alert! What's wrong with the tomatoes?" he shouted in alarm.

His coworkers simply shook their heads. "You really need to see about some hearing aids, Lucky! Take those tomatoes of yours and get yourself to a doctor!"

That afternoon as Dad drove home through the storm, he found it impossible to see. A mile up the road, he crashed into the back of a physician's Mercedes.

With his license revoked, there was no alternative but to move our parents to Virginia where we could chauffeur them around town.

The folks thrived in their cozy apartment. I found Dad a part-time job at a mall within walking distance. Before the mall opened each day, Dad would head for Dillard's department store. There, he'd vacuum the floors and empty all the trash cans.

"I'm the luckiest man on the face of the Earth," he'd comment on the rainy or cold days I'd drive him to work. "I have a wonderful wife, two terrific sons and their families, a job that I love, and a little spare change in my pocket. It doesn't get any better than that!"

I often wondered why the management at Dillard's continued to keep Dad on. His eyesight had gotten so bad that he couldn't possibly see well enough to vacuum properly. I was sure half the trash receptacles remained untouched as well.

One morning, I browsed the perfume counter waiting for Dad to get off work. I could hear him singing in the distance as he worked. Suddenly, one of the sales clerks chuckled.

"Come on, Mr. Lucky, tell me another joke to brighten my morning." As Dad happily obliged, I spotted the manager of the store quietly chuckling nearby.

Suddenly, the reason Dad still had a job became as clear as the sparkling perfume bottles in front of me. Mr. Lucky spread magic dust all over Dillard's department store.

The day finally arrived when Dad could no longer see well enough to perform his duties. My husband and I made a pact to take the folks out to lunch a couple times a week.

"I'm the luckiest man on the face of the Earth," Dad commented each time we'd meet.

One sunny afternoon, we arrived a little early. Mom joined us in the car while we waited for Dad to lock up the apartment.

Time passed. Still no sign of Dad.

"Where could he be?" Mom asked anxiously. "I spotted him coming out the door several minutes ago. Then we got to talking about where we'd like to eat today, and I lost track of him!"

That's when I happened to glance at the car parked next to us. An Indian couple wearing astonished expressions stared into their dashboard mirror. There in the back seat sat Dad, happily chattering like a magpie completely unaware of his blunder.

I hurried over to explain while Dad sheepishly climbed into the back seat of our car.

"I had no idea there were so many cars the same color as yours!" he chuckled. "Those were two of the most surprised people I've ever met in my life!"

Somehow, we managed to make it safely to the restaurant.

"Order me a margarita, will you? I'm going to the restroom." Before anyone could offer to accompany him, Dad was off and running, his cane swinging in the air.

We all ordered our beverages, glancing every once in a while in the direction Dad had taken. The waiter came and went several times.

Suddenly, we heard a familiar voice across the restaurant. There sat Dad with a family of strangers.

"That was a good one! But you can't leave until you tell us the punch line to that last joke," the man seated at the head of the table exclaimed.

"I guess we're going to be here a while," Mom sighed, reaching for another piece of bread from the basket.

We were sure Mr. Lucky's fortune had finally run out the sad day he was diagnosed with lung cancer and leukemia.

"I'm afraid there's nothing we can do for you, Don... I'm sorry," the doctor quietly murmured, placing a hand on Dad's thin shoulder. We gathered around his bed, silently asking God to send us the right words to comfort the dying man.

The clock ticked loudly on the wall.

Suddenly, Dad smacked his hand against his leg. "Well, listen now. It's not such bad news! I've had a great life! In fact, I've been the luckiest man on the face of the Earth. God blessed me with a wonderful wife of fifty-plus years and two terrific sons and their families. I've always had just enough change in my pocket. You can't beat that!"

"Time to take your blood pressure, Mr. Lucky," a smiling nurse exclaimed.

"Hey, Lana, here's a knock-knock joke for you… Aardvark."

"Aardvark who?"

"Aardvark a million miles for one of your smiles!"

The nurse chuckled gleefully.

Something floating in the air across the room caught my eye. I squinted, attempting to make it out as it danced in the sunlight before heading out the door.

There was only one thing it could be… Just as it had filled our hearts, Mr. Lucky's magic dust was filling the entire hospital.

~Mary Z. Smith

"X" Marked the Spot

Cleanliness is next to impossible.
~Author Unknown

My childhood home had more rules than modern-day air travel. Thanks to a mother who suffered from obsessive-compulsive disorder, I never developed a liking for rash decisions, impulsive acts, or the utterance of "because I felt like it." Every action in our home had purpose, and every item had its proper place. I learned early not to disrupt the illogical order of things.

As a teenager, I was the one tapping my friends on the shoulder and whispering, "Hey, guys, you really think we should be doing this?" As they giggled and plotted the next rule they'd break, I paced in the background, craned my neck in search of the authorities, and pictured us cuffed and hauled off to jail in the back of a squad car. I also feared that, while each of my friends' parents would come to bail them out shortly after our arrival, I'd become a lifer since my mom was a germaphobe and would never set foot in such a dirty place to reclaim me. My friends didn't know the complicated history behind my aversion to fun, and I believed proclaiming my mother a nut job during those tumultuous high school years would've been a detriment to my already damaged reputation as a "goody two-shoes" and a "brown-noser." Why add "crazy" to the arsenal of insults?

To be honest, I have nothing against routines and rules, per se, as long as they're logical and beneficial, making one's life easier and more manageable. At seven, my mother's insistence that I wash all of the packaged, jarred, and canned food from the grocery store prior to placing the items in the cupboard made sense to me. Since I had repeatedly been told, "I don't know where your hands have been," I was able to transfer this logic to her request. I pictured freakish shoppers with greasy hair and goo under their fingernails fondling our consumables, placing us in danger of contracting deadly diseases. So I'd sit on the kitchen floor and obediently scour the cans and plastic wrappers under my mother's supervision. By the age of twelve, however, new questions emerged.

"If the food is inside the can, why do I have to clean the outside?" I asked innocently.

"Because," my mother began, "you touch the can before you make the food." Satisfied, I continued to wash can after can.

Her logic became a stretch when I realized I could wash my hands after touching the can, prior to preparing the meal. I soon found that challenging the rituals and logic of someone with OCD was a waste of energy since a rule was countered with another rule that made less sense than the original.

For instance, I should've accepted the rule that I couldn't sit on the couch because it left the cushions crooked. But I couldn't help but question the logic since we had purchased the couch with the intention of sitting on it. I was enlightened that crooked cushions affected the symmetry of the entire room. Could it be that her way of thinking was a precursor to the feng shui movement? The simple act of my backside coming in contact with the couch set off the ritual that I coined "cushion counting." Standing in the middle of the living room, my mother licked her thumbs with precision, and made a beeline toward the cushions to put them back in their proper place. While she laboriously counted the number of times she nudged each cushion (a number she deemed to be lucky), my siblings and I stood wishing she'd crack open one of those sparkling jars of spaghetti sauce to feed us dinner. God help us if she became distracted and had to start counting from the beginning. The fact that we owned a sectional only prolonged our misery.

Unfortunately, the counting ritual bled over into the chore of counting sweeps while vacuuming and, with a wide expanse of carpet, the vacuuming continued on through the night. Both hungry and tired, her children found little benefit to a clean and orderly house. The person who claimed that "cleanliness is next to Godliness" had obviously never lived in the clutches of OCD.

As if we needed another obstacle while trying to get though the day, my mother insisted the family participate in her obsession to ward off germs. Initially, we removed our shoes in the garage since they had traveled outside the house. Coats soon followed, as well as backpacks tainted by those dirty classrooms. The unwelcomed items were lined up like soldiers positioned to storm the queen's fortress. Next, she requested we use Kleenex to turn doorknobs to enter the house since our hands had come in contact with filthy things throughout the day. I waited for the shower to be installed in the garage, but luckily that never happened.

Lines between dirty and clean became so blurred that I found it best not to touch anything. She deemed that we could, however, sit on the kitchen chairs since eating on the floor next to the couch would have made the carpet dirty, and who needed to prolong the whole vacuuming thing? But there was a rule: the chairs had to be returned to the "X" inscribed on the floor with a black marker. If a chair was off the "X" by the slightest degree, my mother stood in the middle of the kitchen, licked her thumbs, pressed in the chair, and counted her adjustments. It would have been easier to eat in the garage.

Thirty years later, I'd like to think I've acquired a healthy dose of OCD: enough to keep me organized and productive without appearing to be a loon. My pantry is stocked, but not alphabetized. My car is clean, but random objects roll around the floorboard. Socks are folded, but mismatched on occasion. Since OCD has a genetic link, I study my children for signs of the disease. "I thought you just washed your hands," I've been known to say. "What exactly is the reason that your corn cannot mix with your mashed potatoes?" And, "Why are you counting your spare change?" has slipped from my mouth.

I soon catch my hyper vigilance and relax, knowing that our house doesn't have "X's" on the floors, we don't wash cans, and my children not only bring their backpacks inside, but they spread their homework on the kitchen table. Not to mention, besides sitting on the couch, we stretch out and make ourselves comfortable. I rejoice that my children are typical adolescents and, if any doubts surface, I merely peek inside their bedrooms at the disarray they call home, or ask my teenage son when he showered last. When he says, "I don't know. Why?" I just smile, and all my fears subside.

~Elizabeth Philip

Family Matters

Meet Our Contributors

Meet Our Authors

About Bruce Jenner

Thank You

About Chicken Soup for the Soul

Meet Our Contributors

Mary Amelia was inspired by her life as a playwright, producer, director, actor, artist, photographer, businesswoman, motivator, reverend, author, and mom to write *Love Thyself: A Life Guide for Women*. She lives in California and re-energizes on the beach when she's not traveling. E-mail her at Mary@MaryAmelia.com.

Monica A. Andermann lives on Long Island where her family continues to inspire much of her writing. More of Monica's work can be found both online and in print, including several editions of the *Chicken Soup for the Soul* and *A Cup of Comfort* collections.

Annie (not her real name, of course) is a freelance writer whose work has appeared widely both online and in print. She is happy to report that her marriage has remained strong and loving for twenty years despite her mother-in-law's antics.

Linda Apple is the author of *Inspire! Writing from the Soul* and *Connect! A Simple Guide to Public Speaking for Writers*. Her stories have appeared in twelve *Chicken Soup for the Soul* books. She's a motivational speaker and serves as a speaker trainer for Stonecroft Ministries. Visit her website: www.lindacapple.com.

Eden Arneau is a freelance writer and speaker from the Heartland. Those long winter months are perfect for hours at the computer while her cubs are in school. Her husband is her biggest cheerleader and approved this story, as long as she remained anonymous. You can e-mail her at campfireministries@yahoo.com.

Gretchen Bauer is the pseudonym for someone who does not want her mother-in-law to know that she tattled on her.

Garrett Bauman, recently retired as a professor of English at Monroe Community College in Rochester, NY, has published several pieces about his father, who believed in fire extinguishers, insurance policies and emergency brakes. He never did crawl out on that roof.

Meghan Beeby has a B.A. in English Literature and is also a Registered Nurse with a strong interest in psychiatric-mental health nursing. She lives in rural upstate New York with her wonderful husband John, and large family of rescued companion animals, including special needs dogs.

Juliet Bell has had a varied career in theatre, teaching, and computer programming. She currently lives in New Hampshire where she enjoys life as a painter, maker of wooden jigsaw puzzles, and palmist. She has written several books and many stories for the young. She may be reached via e-mail at julietbell111@gmail.com.

Devyani Borade is a published writer of short humorous stories on topics drawn from everyday life. She likes chocolate cookies, *Calvin and Hobbes* comics and trying her husband's patience. Visit her blog at www.devyaniborade.blogspot.com to enjoy the adventures of Debora, her alter ego.

Marty Bucella is a full-time freelance cartoonist/humorous illustrator whose work has been published over 100,000 times in magazines, newspapers, greeting cards, books, the Web and so on. To see more of Marty's work, visit his website at: www.martybucella.com.

Kristine Byron worked as a trainer for Tupperware and in later years as an interior designer. She loves to cook and entertain. Kristine also loves to travel with her husband and spend quality time with her five grandchildren.

Martha Campbell is a graduate of Washington University, St. Louis School of Fine Arts and a former writer/designer for Hallmark Cards. She has been a freelance cartoonist and illustrator since leaving Hallmark. She lives in Harrison, AR.

Author **Talia Carner's** heart-wrenching suspense novels, *Puppet Child* and *China Doll*, were hailed for exposing society's ills. Her next novel, *Jerusalem Maiden*, will be published by HarperCollins in June 2011. Carner's award-winning short stories and essays have appeared in numerous anthologies and literary publications. Visit her website at www.TaliaCarner.com.

Dave Carpenter has been a fulltime cartoonist since 1981. Dave's cartoons have appeared in *Chicken Soup for the Soul* books, *Harvard Business Review*, *Reader's Digest*, *Barron's*, *The Wall Street Journal*, *Woman's World*, *Good Housekeeping*, *Better Homes & Gardens*, the *Saturday Evening Post*, and other publications. Contact Dave at davecarp@ncn.net.

Stefani Chambers, a native Texan, currently lives in New York City with her husband Chris. She received her Masters of Journalism from the University of North Texas. Answering phones from 9 to 5 pays the bills; writing creative nonfiction is what she was put on earth to do, as well as singing, running, and traveling with her husband.

Michele Christian lives in Abington, MA and is a published author in several short story books, including *Chicken Soup of the Soul: Twins and More*. Michele thanks her children and family for their continued support as well as providing her the best writing material! Please e-mail her at michelechristian819@yahoo.com.

J.M. Cornwell is a frequent contributor to *Chicken Soup for the Soul* and *A Cup of Comfort* anthologies. Her novel, *Past Imperfect*, is available online in paperback and e-book at Amazon, Powell's and Barnes & Noble. When not writing about family foibles, she contributes to www.redroom.com and may be e-mailed at fixnwrtr@gmail.com.

Cindy D'Ambroso-Argiento is originally from New York. She now lives in North Carolina with her family. Cindy is a freelance writer and receives a wealth of material from her family. To read more of Cindy's work check out her website at www.cindyargiento.com. Please e-mail her at cargiento@aol.com.

Rebecca Davis is a sophomore at Northeastern University. She is majoring in Media Communications with a minor in Spanish and Production. She has been writing since she learned how to speak and her ambition is to write a novel with her mother.

Gwen Daye has been a professional freelance writer since 1998, but began writing in 1979. Since then her family has inspired much of her work. She very much appreciates their love and support and, after this book is published, is hoping that they still speak to her.

Barbara Diggs is a freelance writer living in Paris, France, with her husband and two young sons. In addition to writing for various magazines, she is working on a book about intercultural weddings. She also blogs about freelance writing from abroad and child-friendly activities in Paris. Contact her at http://theexpatfreelancer.blogspot.com.

Moira Rose Donohue is the author of two picture books: *Alfie the Apostrophe*, 2006, which received "high marks" from Kirkus, and *Penny and the Punctuation Bee*, 2008, both published by Albert Whitman. Her other publishing credits include children's plays, magazine articles and an entry in *Chicken Soup for the Kid's Soul 2*.

Debbie Dufresne earned a master's degree in library and information science from Syracuse University. After many years working for a newspaper, she is now a freelance copy editor/proofreader/writer. She is an avid New York Yankees fan and also enjoys reading and searching for antiques and collectibles. E-mail her at debduf@localnet.com.

Irene Estrada received her Bachelor of Science, with honors, and Master of Arts from California State University, Dominguez Hills. She is a retired Director of Budgeting. Irene enjoys traveling, reading and writing. She is currently writing a combination autobiography and biography. The biography includes entries from her brother's journals.

Gail Eynon received her BA in psychology from the University of Hawaii at Hilo and is currently working on her Masters degree in Marriage and Family Therapy at Capella University preparing to graduate with honors. Gail enjoys writing in her spare time. She feels that you are never too old to enjoy life.

Susan Farr-Fahncke is the founder of www.2TheHeart.com, where you can find more of her writing and sign up for an online writing workshop! She also founded the amazing volunteer group, Angels2TheHeart, wrote *Angel's Legacy* and is co-author, editor, and contributor to over sixty books, including many *Chicken Soup for the Soul* books.

Lauren Fitzpatrick grew up in Indianapolis and has since lived and worked all over the world. She holds a BA in Communication and Culture from Indiana University, and an MA in Travel Writing from Kingston University. She is working on a novel about her travel experiences. Contact her via e-mail at lvfitzpatrick@hotmail.com.

Lori Giraulo-Secor is a single mom in western New York with two beautiful children, Adam and Leah. She writes nonfiction short stories and children's poems. She's inspired by her family and is working to compile their funniest moments for a novel. Read Lori's blog at http://loridreams.blogspot.com or e-mail her at Lsecor1@rochester.rr.com.

Chicken Soup for the Soul editor **Kristiana Glavin** earned a journalism degree from Syracuse University's S.I. Newhouse School of Public Communications in 2004. She previously worked as a reporter, and loves that she now reads, writes and edits for Chicken Soup for the Soul! Kristiana lives, runs and plays in Connecticut.

Judy Lee Green is an award-winning writer and speaker whose spirit and roots reach deep into the Appalachian Mountains. Tennessee-bred and cornbread-fed, she has been published hundreds of times and received dozens of awards for her work. Her family is the source for many of her stories. Reach her in Tennessee at JudyLeeGreen@bellsouth.net.

Stephanie Haefner is a wife, mother of two and novelist from Buffalo, NY. Her debut novel, *A Bitch Named Karma*, is available from Lyrical Press. This is her second *Chicken Soup for the Soul* publication. When not writing, Stephanie enjoys family activities, dance class, scrapbooking, and Walt Disney World.

Laurel Hausman lives in Northern Virginia with her husband and two Beagles, where she teaches high school mathematics. Her interests include biking, gardening, quilting, and reading. Her dream is to become a full-time writer of creative nonfiction.

Georgia A. Hubley retired after twenty years in financial management to write full-time. She's a frequent contributor to the *Chicken Soup for the Soul* series, *Christian Science Monitor* and various other magazines, newspapers and anthologies. She resides with her husband of thirty-two years in Henderson, NV. Contact her via e-mail at geohub@aol.com.

Carol Huff lives in Hartwell, GA, and enjoys freelance writing. She has had her work published in several national magazines, and has completed her third novel. She takes care of rescued animals on her farm, and enjoys horseback riding. E-mail her at herbiemakow@gmail.com.

Jody A. James prepares her waffles in a small Southwestern

Pennsylvania town where she is a dental hygienist. Her household consists of a thirty-something single mom, two active and life-loving boys, a pretentious hamster-loving cat, and a tortured cat-hating hamster. Please e-mail her at jodywilson3@gmail.com.

Marsha Jordan, zany grandmother and undiscovered shower singer, began her writing career on the restroom walls of St. Joseph's Catholic School. Her book, *Hugs, Hope, and Peanut Butter*, available at www.hugsandhope.org, earned honorable mention in the World's Funniest Humor Contest. She lives with her husband in Wisconsin. E-mail her at hugsandhope@gmail.com.

Ron Kaiser, Jr. has managed to finagle an astoundingly good-looking woman, far beyond him in every way, to marry him. They live together in New Hampshire, where he writes stories when he is not just dumbstruck looking at his radiant wife. He seeks to publish a book of short stories and a novel. E-mail him at kilgore.trout1922@gmail.com.

Paul Karrer has been published in the *San Francisco Chronicle*, *The Christian Science Monitor* and many *Chicken Soup for the Soul* books. He was North Monterey County's LULAC Educator of the year for 2009. He is a fifth-grade teacher and union negotiator in Castroville, CA. He frequently gives talks on education or writing matters.

Alex Kingcott grew up on the prairies of Alberta. Her parents exposed her to the arts early, and she quickly found her passion for theatre and storytelling. She studied Communications at Mount Royal University in Calgary, where she lives with her fabulous and endlessly amusing friends and family. Contact her via e-mail at alex.kingcott@gmail.com.

Mimi Greenwood Knight is a freelance writer and mama of four living in South Louisiana with her husband David and way too many pets. She enjoys Bible study, butterfly gardening, artisan breadmaking and the lost art of letter writing.

Jess Knox is the author of three *Chicken Soup for the Soul* stories. She graduated from the University of Southern California in 2007 with a degree in Screenwriting and is currently the publicity coordinator for OmniPop Talent Group in Los Angeles. Please e-mail her at knox.jess@gmail.com.

After thirty-plus years as a communications professional and corporate wordsmith for a Fortune 500 company, **Mitchell Kyd** has begun a new journey as a freelance writer and tale weaver. Her stories reflect the humorous and sometimes poignant moments of life in rural Pennsylvania. Please e-mail her at mitchellkyd@gmail.com.

Roberta Laurie received her degree in Communications from Grant MacEwan University in 2010. She is a freelance writer and editor. Roberta has seen her work published in several anthologies and numerous periodicals. You can learn more about Roberta's writing and other passions by going to her website: www.creativewhispers.ca.

Beth Levine is a freelance writer whose work has been published in many national magazines (*Woman's Day, More, Good Housekeeping*). She is the author of two nonfiction books, and she thinks Christmas cookies are a very good idea. To learn more about Beth visit her website at www.bethlevine.net.

Janeen Lewis is living the life she always dreamed of, writing from home while caring for her two children. When she isn't writing about her zany-but-lovable family, she enjoys spending time with them. Contact her via e-mail at jlewis0402@netzero.net.

Patricia Ljutic lives in California with a creative family that makes art with paper, paints and soapstone. Her work has appeared in *My Mom Is My Hero*, *A Cup of Comfort for Parents of Children with Special Needs*, *Contra Costa Times* and *Ciao! Travel with Attitude*. Her e-mail is PatriciaLjutic@comcast.net.

Barbara LoMonaco received her BS from the University of Southern California and has an elementary teaching credential. Barbara has worked for Chicken Soup for the Soul since 1998 as an editor and webmaster. She is a co-author of *Chicken Soup for the Mother and Son Soul* and *Chicken Soup for the Soul: My Resolution.*

Natalia K. Lusinski created her first newspaper, "Nat's Neat News Notes," at age ten, and has been writing ever since — from short stories and books to TV and film scripts. But "family matters" most, as is seen in this book, which includes her seventh published *Chicken Soup for the Soul* story. E-mail Natalia at writenataliainla@yahoo.com.

Kenneth C. Lynch is a retired U.S. Navy officer, having served twenty-seven years. Ken is currently a teacher's assistant for Pennsylvania's Pennridge School District. He has been published in *Chicken Soup for the Shopper's Soul* and in *The Storyteller* magazine.

John MacDonald is an English as a Second Language teacher in Albany, NY and enjoys poking fun at his family's quirky behavior through his writing. His stories have appeared in *Chicken Soup for the Soul: All in the Family* and *Conceive* magazine. Please e-mail him at jmcdon7@nycap.rr.com.

Judith Marks-White is a *Westport News* (CT) award-winning columnist of "The Light Touch," which has appeared every Wednesday for the past twenty-five years. She is the author of two novels published by Random House/Ballantine: *Seducing Harry* and *Bachelor Degree.* Judith teaches humor writing and lectures widely.

Dary Matera is the author of fourteen books, including the bestseller *Are You Lonesome Tonight?* He currently lives in Arizona.

Jeri McBryde lives in a small town outside Memphis, TN. She recently retired from the library system and spends her days reading and working on her dream of being published. Jeri loves crocheting and chocolate. Her family is the center of her life.

A freelance writer who loves to toy with words, **Dee McFoster** comes from a long line of quirky females. Consequently, she credits her own peculiarities and obsessions to deviant DNA. Although she considers herself a Daddy's Girl, it's the image of her mother that greets her in the mirror.

Lynn Maddalena Menna received her BA from Fairleigh Dickinson University, and her MA from Montclair State University. She is a frequent *Chicken Soup for the Soul* contributor and her new young adult novel is due to be published next year. Lynn lives in Hawthorne, NJ with her husband Prospero and cat Toonise. She can be reached via e-mail at prolynn@aol.com.

Anna Michaelsan is a freelance writer.

Mike Morlacci is a husband, father and communications specialist. He is also a freelance writer and a former sports writer and sports editor… really.

Retired library manager **Shelley Mosley** has co-authored several nonfiction books. She also writes romantic comedies with Deborah Mazoyer under the name Deborah Shelley. Shelley enjoys being with her family and friends, playing with her cats, reading, traveling, singing, playing the piano, and watching movies. Please e-mail her at deborahshelley@mindspring.com.

When **Lava Mueller** told her mother that "Cotton Balls" had been accepted for publication in *Chicken Soup for the Soul: Family Matters*, her mother said, "That's great, Sweetheart. I'm glad I could help you get rich. I think I just ate a bug." Lava lives in Vermont. E-mail her at lavamueller@yahoo.com.

JT Nelson graduated from the New England Academy of Funeral Service in 1965. He always wanted to write about growing up in a funeral home and the practice of small town funeral service. JT loves carpentry, fishing, boating, woodworking and living by the ocean and lakes. Please e-mail him at jtnelson45@comcast.com.

Sherylynn Niezen has an extended minor in English and is finishing up her Bachelor of Arts degree from UFV. She loves teaching and helping coach a synchronized skating team. She loves writing humorous poetry and hopes to one day write a full novel. Please e-mail her at s_niezen@hotmail.com.

Mark Parisi's "off the mark" comic, syndicated since 1987, is distributed by United Media. He won the National Cartoonists Society's award for Best Newspaper Panel in 2009. His humor also graces greeting cards, T-shirts, calendars, magazines, newsletters and books. See www.offthemark.com. Lynn is his wife/business partner. Daughter Jen contributes inspiration, as do three cats, one dog and an unknown number of koi.

Cynthia Patton, BS, JD, attended the University of California, Davis, and has worked as an environmental attorney, scientific editor, consultant, habitat restoration manager, and writer. The Northern California native has one daughter. Her nonfiction stories have appeared in magazines, newspapers, anthologies, and books. She's revising a memoir. E-mail Cynthia at cynthiapatton@att.net.

Ava Pennington is a writer, speaker, and Bible teacher. She has published numerous magazine articles and contributed to nineteen anthologies, including thirteen *Chicken Soup for the Soul* books. She has also authored *One Year Alone with God: 366 Devotions on the Names of God* (Revell, 2010). Learn more at www.AvaWrites.com.

Saralee Perel is an award-winning columnist/novelist and a multiple contributor to *Chicken Soup for the Soul*. Her newest book, *The Dog Who Walked Me*, is about her dog who became her caregiver after she suffered a major spinal cord injury and her cat who kept her sane. E-mail her at sperel@saraleeperel.com or visit her website at www.saraleeperel.com.

Elizabeth Philip received her Bachelor of Social Work and Master's of Arts in Teaching. She teaches high school English in Missouri. Elizabeth is currently at work on a novel. She shares her home with her husband, their two children, a Collie, an Australian Shepherd, and a Pembroke Welsh Corgi.

Lori Phillips lives with her omnivorous family in Southern California where she earned her Bachelor of Arts in communications, journalism and Master of Education. She is the Japanese Food and Living Simply editor for BellaOnline.com. Lori also enjoys writing about marriage, family, and spirituality. Please e-mail her at hope037@hotmail.com.

Helen Polaski (Szymanski) began writing professionally in 1984 and has thousands of articles and short stories in anthologies, newspapers, magazines. She has compiled and edited eight anthology books for Adams Media. The late Paul Harvey, of radio fame, read from her anthology books and endorsed them as his "preferred bedtime reading."

Felice Prager is a freelance writer and multisensory educational therapist from Scottsdale, AZ. Hundreds of her essays have been published locally, nationally, and internationally in print and on the Internet. She is the author of *Quiz It: Arizona*. To find out more about Felice's book or to find links to more of her work, please visit http://www.QuizItAZ.com.

T. Powell Pryce is a single mother of two who lives near Saint Louis, MO. She teaches and writes, and has contributed to several *Chicken Soup for the Soul* books.

Natalie June Reilly is a football mom of two extraordinary teenage boys and the author of the children's book, *My Stick Family: Helping Children Cope with Divorce*. Reilly is a freelance writer who loves her life and is looking forward to returning to college with her firstborn son in the fall. She can be reached via e-mail at Natalie@themeanmom.com.

Bruce Robinson is an award-winning internationally published cartoonist whose work has appeared in numerous consumer and trade periodicals including the *National Enquirer, The Saturday Evening Post, Woman's World, The Sun, First, Highlights for Children*, etc. He is also the author of the cartoon book *Good Medicine*. Contact him via e-mail at cartoonsbybrucerobinson@hotmail.com.

Gary Rubinstein is a teacher in New York City. He has two published books, *Reluctant Disciplinarian*, a memoir about his first year of teaching, and *Beyond Survival*, a textbook for new teachers. He was also published in *Chicken Soup for the Soul: Teacher Tales*, published in 2010. E-mail him at gary.m.rubinstein@gmail.com.

Jessie Miyeko Santala recently received her Master of Liberal Arts from the University of Denver. She is a photographer who is also currently working on her first book. Jessie enjoys Starbucks, the Denver Nuggets, her family and spending time with her husband, Mike. Please e-mail her at J.Santala@yahoo.com.

Shannon Scott works as a Public Information Officer in Atlanta for a sewer rehab contractor, and enjoys the challenges each day brings. In her free time she enjoys spending time with her family and children (ages four and six), reading, writing and being outdoors as much as possible.

Michael Jordan Segal, who defied all odds after being shot in the head, is a husband, father, social worker, freelance author (including a CD/Download of twelve stories, read with light background music, entitled *Possible*), and inspirational speaker. He's had many stories published in *Chicken Soup for the Soul* books. Please visit www.InspirationByMike.com.

Timothy A. Setterlund is an attorney practicing in Boca Raton, FL. He welcomes the relief of literature from the constipated legalese he works with daily. He intends to continue, and write fiction as well. Reach him via e-mail at taslaw1@aol.com.

Avery Shepard received her Bachelor's degree from San José State

University in 2002. She enjoys traveling, snowboarding and fast driving. Avery currently writes young adult fantasy, but plans to venture into both science and women's fiction. To learn more about Avery visit www.averyshepard.com.

When **Mary Z. Smith** isn't busy writing for *Chicken Soup for the Soul*, *Guideposts* or *Angels on Earth*, she can be found in her garden or walking her Rat Terrier Frankie. She and her husband Barry and her ninety-two-year-old mother-in-law Flora reside in Richmond, VA, where they enjoy visits from their grown children and grandchildren.

Jean Sorensen's cartoons have appeared in *Good Housekeeping*, *The Washington Post Magazine*, *The Lutheran*, and numerous textbooks. Her work has also been featured in greeting cards for Oatmeal Studios. Jean lives in the Washington, DC area with her high school sweetheart and three children, who always keep her laughing.

Cecil Swetland received his Bachelor of Arts from Simpson College and Master of Arts in Education from California State University. He is a frequent speaker to adults and teen groups on the topics of education and communication. He is a school administrator, enjoys traveling, and participates in international education projects.

From belly dancer, to fitness trainer, to speech pathologist, to memoir teacher, **Tsgoyna Tanzman** credits writing as the supreme "therapy" for raising an adolescent daughter. Published in four *Chicken Soup for the Soul* books and also on www.more.com, www.motheringmagazine.com, and in *The Orange County Register*. E-mail her at tnzmn@cox.net.

Marie Wells is a pseudonym for a daughter who desperately loves her mother and would not hurt her for anything in the world. But this daughter also recognizes that some stories are funny and they simply must be told, but only under a secret identity.

Lori Wescott is a freelance humorist living it up in the small town of Nolensville, TN, where she resides with her handsome husband and brilliant son. She enjoys most things mom-related and has been known to dominate a game of tee ball. Read more of her work at www.Loripalooza.com.

Valerie Whisenand, usually writing as Valerie Hansen, is the author of many Christian fiction paperback novels. When she moved to the Ozarks she found her calling, as well as a beautiful atmosphere filled with loving, caring people. She's been married to her high school sweetheart for a gazillion years! E-mail her at VAL@valeriehansen.com.

Arthur Wiknik, Jr. served in Vietnam with the 101st Airborne Division. His memoir *Nam Sense* is now in its second printing. This is the fifth *Chicken Soup for the Soul* book he has been published in. Arthur frequently shares his wartime experiences at schools and civic organizations. Visit his website at www.namsense.com.

Alan Williamson is a nationally published humor writer whose work explores the small dilemmas of everyday life. Shunning the complex issues and thorny global conundrums of the day, he chronicles the flaws, follies and convoluted capers that unite people in their humanity. Alan can be reached via e-mail at alwilly@bellsouth.net.

Ann Williamson received her Master of Arts in Creative Writing from Regis University in 2008. She was inducted into Alpha Sigma Nu, the Jesuit Honor Society and was published in *Apogee*, the Regis literary journal. She is a devoted grandmother and an avid reader. You may contact her via e-mail at anngracewilliamson@hotmail.com.

Ann Michener Winter has been writing poetry since age eleven and began writing nonfiction several years ago. Retired from twenty-three years of administrative work at UCSB, she loves family and friends, tap dancing, yoga, doo-wop singing, volunteering at the

South Coast Railroad Museum and traveling. Please e-mail her at amwinter@cox.net.

Helen Xenakis enjoys the retirement lifestyle since it provides plenty of time to pursue her love of writing. This is her fourth *Chicken Soup for the Soul* publication.

S. Nadja Zajdman is a writer and an actress. Her theater roles include the one-woman show, *Shirley Valentine*, and the title role in *Sheindele*. Her short stories, essays and memoirs have been featured in newspapers, magazines and literary journals. Nadja has performed her material on radio and in live readings.

Chicken Soup for the Soul

Meet Our Authors

Jack Canfield is the co-creator of the *Chicken Soup for the Soul* series, which *Time* magazine has called "the publishing phenomenon of the decade." Jack is also the co-author of many other bestselling books.

Jack is the CEO of the Canfield Training Group in Santa Barbara, California, and founder of the Foundation for Self-Esteem in Culver City, California. He has conducted intensive personal and professional development seminars on the principles of success for more than a million people in twenty-three countries, has spoken to hundreds of thousands of people at more than 1,000 corporations, universities, professional conferences and conventions, and has been seen by millions more on national television shows.

Jack has received many awards and honors, including three honorary doctorates and a Guinness World Records Certificate for having seven books from the *Chicken Soup for the Soul* series appearing on the New York Times bestseller list on May 24, 1998.

You can reach Jack at www.jackcanfield.com.

Mark Victor Hansen is the co-founder of Chicken Soup for the Soul, along with Jack Canfield. He is a sought-after keynote speaker, bestselling author, and marketing maven. Mark's powerful messages of possibility, opportunity, and action have created powerful change in thousands of organizations and millions of individuals worldwide.

Mark is a prolific writer with many bestselling books in addition to the *Chicken Soup for the Soul* series. Mark has had a profound influence in the field of human potential through his library of audios, videos, and articles in the areas of big thinking, sales achievement, wealth building, publishing success, and personal and professional development. He is also the founder of the MEGA Seminar Series.

Mark has received numerous awards that honor his entrepreneurial spirit, philanthropic heart, and business acumen. He is a lifetime member of the Horatio Alger Association of Distinguished Americans.

You can reach Mark at www.markvictorhansen.com.

Amy Newmark is the publisher and editor-in-chief of *Chicken Soup for the Soul*, after a thirty-year career as a writer, speaker, financial analyst, and business executive in the worlds of finance and telecommunications. Amy is a *magna cum laude* graduate of Harvard College, where she majored in Portuguese, minored in French, and traveled extensively. She and her husband have four grown children.

After a long career writing books on telecommunications, voluminous financial reports, business plans, and corporate press releases, Chicken Soup for the Soul is a breath of fresh air for Amy. She has fallen in love with Chicken Soup for the Soul and its life-changing books, and really enjoys putting these books together for Chicken Soup's inspiring readers. She has co-authored more than two dozen *Chicken Soup for the Soul* books and has edited another two dozen.

You can reach Amy through the webmaster@chickensoupforthesoul.com.

Susan M. Heim is a longstanding author and editor, specializing in parenting, women's and Christian issues. After the birth of twin boys in 2003, Susan left her job as a Senior Editor at a publishing company and is now a work-at-home mom.

Susan has published several books in the *Chicken Soup for the Soul* series, as well as *Boosting Your Baby's Brain Power*; *It's Twins!*; and, *Oh, Baby! 7 Ways a Baby Will Change Your Life the First Year*. Her articles and stories have appeared in many books, websites, and magazines. She shares parenting wisdom on her blog, Susan Heim on Parenting (http://susanheim.blogspot.com), and on TwinsTalk (www.twinstalk.com), a website for parents of multiples.

Susan and her husband are the parents of four sons. You can reach Susan at susan@susanheim.com. Visit her website at www.susanheim.com.

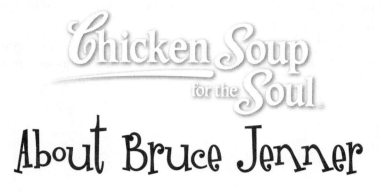

About Bruce Jenner

A devoted husband and father of ten, **Bruce Jenner** is called the glue that holds the family together on *Keeping Up with the Kardashians*, which is the #1-rated reality series on E! The television series documents the daily lives of the Kardashian/Jenner family.

Bruce first captivated the world during the 1976 Olympic Games when he broke the world record in the decathlon, netting the title of "World's Greatest Athlete." His accomplishments also earned him the coveted Wheaties cereal box, and he is one of seven Wheaties spokesmen.

Since then, he has been involved in a wide variety of projects and causes—from sportscasting and acting to supporting charitable organizations and serving on several advisory boards. Bruce has worked with nonprofits such as the Special Olympics, The National Dyslexia Research Foundation, and The Dream Foundation. Most recently, California's Governor Schwarzenegger appointed him the Athletic Boxing Commissioner for the state of California. Bruce also works to raise awareness for Chronic Obstructive Pulmonary Disease (COPD). He is currently involved in a Drive4COPD campaign.

A highly respected and sought-after motivational speaker, Bruce travels around the country speaking to corporate and community groups about "Finding the Champion Within." He focuses on the theme that any person who makes an effort can achieve something great—greatness is at the core of every man, woman and child who wants it. Also a successful author, Bruce has written several books including *Finding the Champion Within*.

In addition to his role on *Keeping Up with the Kardashians*, Bruce has appeared as a guest star on numerous primetime television programs, a commentator for NBC, ABC and Fox sports, and host of his own health show. He and his wife Kris have also produced multiple infomercials and videos on fitness products.

Bruce is also a sportscaster and commentator for a number of NBC sporting events, including the Olympic Games and received the title "Outstanding International Sportscaster of the Year."

Off screen and outside of work, Bruce finds time to enjoy his own hobbies including flying planes, racing cars in Grand Prix events and working on his golf game.

More information is available at his website, www.brucejenner.com.

Chicken Soup for the Soul

Thank You

We owe huge thanks to all of our contributors. We know that you poured your hearts and souls into the thousands of stories and poems that you shared with us, and ultimately with each other. We appreciate your willingness to open up your lives to other Chicken Soup for the Soul readers. Writing about your families was about as open as you could be! Many of you said that writing the stories made you feel better about a particular relative, or forced you to think through a situation and gain new insight.

We could only publish a small percentage of the stories that were submitted, but we read every single one and even the ones that do not appear in the book had an influence on us and on the final manuscript. They certainly were a great window into the human condition, and they made our own families seem "relatively" normal.

We owe special thanks to our webmaster and editor, Barbara LoMonaco, who worked with us to read the thousands of stories submitted for this book and helped narrow down the list to several hundred finalists. D'ette Corona, our assistant publisher, had a big job with this book. Her normal work with the contributors was a lot more complicated with this topic, due to the number of signed permission forms we needed to get from the subjects of the stories, and the number of contributors who ultimately felt it was more prudent to use their pen names for these particular stories. That is certainly understandable given the subject matter.

It was a huge undertaking, and everyone did a great job. This book could not have been made without their expertise, their input, and their innate knowledge of what makes a great Chicken Soup for the Soul story. We also want to thank Chicken Soup for the Soul editor Kristiana Glavin for her assistance with the final manuscript and proofreading, including finding all those great quotes before each story, and we also want to thank our editor Madeline Clapps for proofreading assistance.

We owe a very special thanks to our creative director and book producer, Brian Taylor at Pneuma Books, for his brilliant vision for our covers and interiors. We hope you went "nuts" over the fun cover and the clever artwork before each chapter. Finally, none of this would be possible without the business and creative leadership of our CEO, Bill Rouhana, and our president, Bob Jacobs.

Improving Your Life Every Day

Real people sharing real stories—for seventeen years. Now, Chicken Soup for the Soul has gone beyond the bookstore to become a world leader in life improvement. Through books, movies, DVDs, online resources and other partnerships, we bring hope, courage, inspiration and love to hundreds of millions of people around the world. Chicken Soup for the Soul's writers and readers belong to a one-of-a-kind global community, sharing advice, support, guidance, comfort, and knowledge.

Chicken Soup for the Soul stories have been translated into more than forty languages and can be found in more than one hundred countries. Every day, millions of people experience a Chicken Soup for the Soul story in a book, magazine, newspaper or online. As we share our life experiences through these stories, we offer hope, comfort and inspiration to one another. The stories travel from person to person, and from country to country, helping to improve lives everywhere.

Chicken Soup for the Soul

Share With Us

We all have had Chicken Soup for the Soul moments in our lives. If you would like to share your story or poem with millions of people around the world, go to chickensoup.com and click on "Submit Your Story." You may be able to help another reader, and become a published author at the same time. Some of our past contributors have launched writing and speaking careers from the publication of their stories in our books!

Our submission volume has been increasing steadily — the quality and quantity of your submissions has been fabulous. We only accept story submissions via our website. They are no longer accepted via mail or fax.

To contact us regarding other matters, please send us an e-mail through webmaster@chickensoupforthesoul.com, or fax or write us at:

Chicken Soup for the Soul
P.O. Box 700
Cos Cob, CT 06807-0700
Fax: 203-861-7194

One more note from your friends at Chicken Soup for the Soul: Occasionally, we receive an unsolicited book manuscript from one of our readers, and we would like to respectfully inform you that we do not accept unsolicited manuscripts and we must discard the ones that appear.

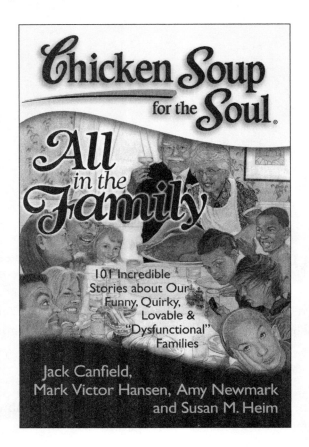

Full of stories about wacky yet lovable relatives, holiday meltdowns, and funny foibles, along with more serious stories of abuse and outbursts, this book is usually hilarious, and occasionally poignant. It is a quirky and fun holiday book, and a great bridal shower or wedding gift! Norman Rockwell's famous Thanksgiving family painting appears on the back cover and is lovingly parodied on the front, showing that all our families are just a little dysfunctional!

978-1-935096-39-9

More Great Storie.

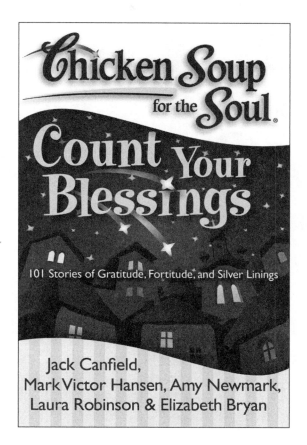

This uplifting book reminds readers of the blessings in their lives, despite financial stress, natural disasters, health scares and illnesses, housing challenges and family worries. This feel-good book is a great gift for New Year's or Easter, for someone going through a difficult time, or for Christmas. These stories of optimism, faith, and strength remind us of the simple pleasures of family, home, health, and inexpensive good times.

978-1-935096-42-9

about Real Life

Christmas is a magical time of year—a time of family, friends, and traditions. And all the joys, blessings, and excitement of the season are captured in this book of 101 new holiday stories. With stories about finding the perfect Christmas tree, being with family, and seeing the wonder in a child's eyes, this book will delight every reader, from the young to the young at heart, and bring back the magic of the holiday season. "Santa-safe" for kids!

978-1-935096-54-2

Holiday Cheer fo

Everyone loves Christmas and the holiday season. We reunite scattered family members, watch the wonder in a child's eyes, and feel the joy of giving gifts. The rituals of the holiday season give a rhythm to the years and create a foundation for our lives, as we gather with family, with our communities at church, at school, and even at the mall, to share the special spirit of the season, brightening those long winter days. "Santa-safe" for kids!

978-1-935096-15-3

he Whole Family

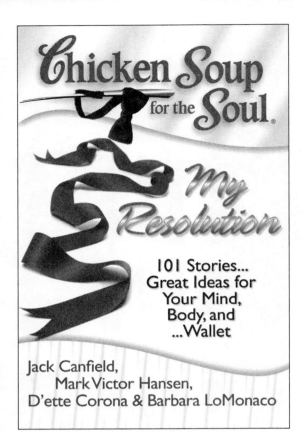

Chicken Soup for the Soul

My Resolution

101 Stories...
Great Ideas for
Your Mind,
Body, and
...Wallet

Jack Canfield,
Mark Victor Hansen,
D'ette Corona & Barbara LoMonaco

Everyone makes resolutions—for New Year's, for big birthdays, for new school years. In fact, most of us are so good at resolutions that we make the same ones year after year. This collection of great true stories covers topics such as losing weight, getting organized, stopping bad habits, restoring relationships, dealing with substance abuse, changing jobs, going green, and even today's hot topic—dealing with the economic crisis.

978-1-935096-28-3

Inspiration for

Chicken Soup for the Soul

Think Positive

101 Inspirational Stories about Counting Your Blessings and Having a Positive Attitude

Jack Canfield, Mark Victor Hansen & Amy Newmark
Foreword by Deborah Norville

Every cloud has a silver lining. Readers will be inspired by these 101 real-life stories from people just like them, taking a positive attitude to the ups and downs of life, and remembering to be grateful and count their blessings. This book continues Chicken Soup for the Soul's focus on inspiration and hope, and its stories of optimism and faith will encourage readers to stay positive during challenging times and in their everyday lives.

978-1-935096-56-6

Everyone, all Year

www.chickensoup.com